PELICAN BOOKS

The Pelican Economic History of Britain
Volume 3 · From 1750 to the Present Day

Industry and Empire

Eric J. Hobsbawm was born on 9 June 1917.
He was educated at Vienna, Berlin, London and
Cambridge, where he was a Fellow of King's
College from 1949 to 1955. At present he is
Reader in History at Birkbeck College, University
of London, having also taught at Stanford and
M.I.T. His main publications include: *Primitive
Rebels* (1959), *The Age of Revolution* (1962),
Labouring Men (1964), *Captain Swing* (1969; with
George Rudé), and *The Jazz Scene* (as Francis
Newton). Dr Hobsbawm, who lives in London,
is married, with two children.

The Pelican
Economic History of Britain

VOLUME 3

From 1750 to the Present Day

Industry and Empire

═══

E. J. HOBSBAWM

PENGUIN BOOKS
BALTIMORE · MARYLAND

Penguin Books Ltd, Harmondsworth, Middlesex, England
Penguin Books Inc., 7110 Ambassador Road, Baltimore, Maryland 21207, U.S.A.
Penguin Books Australia Ltd, Ringwood, Victoria, Australia

—

Commissioned by Penguin Books Ltd and first published by
Weidenfeld & Nicolson 1968
Published in Pelican Books 1969

—

Copyright © E. J. Hobsbawm, 1968, 1969

—

Made and printed in Great Britain
by Richard Clay (The Chaucer Press) Ltd,
Bungay, Suffolk
Set in Monotype Ehrhardt

For Marlene

CONTENTS

PREFACE

THIS book will certainly be read by some who wish to pass one or other of the numerous examinations in economic and social history which face students today, and I naturally hope that it will help them to do so. However, it is not designed simply as a textbook, nor can it be used very profitably as a book of reference. It attempts to describe and account for Britain's rise as the first industrial power, its decline from the temporary domination of the pioneer, its rather special relationship with the rest of the world, and some of the effects of all these on the life of the people in this country. All these matters should be of interest to any intelligent citizen, and I have therefore tried to write in as non-technical a way as possible and to assume no prior knowledge of any of the social sciences in the reader. This does not mean that the questions asked (and I hope answered) here in ordinary prose could not be reformulated in the more technical language of the various disciplines. However, I have assumed an elementary knowledge of the outlines of British history since 1750. It would be helpful if readers who happen not to know what the Napoleonic Wars were, or are ignorant of names such as Peel and Gladstone, were prepared to find out on their own.

Since neither the questions nor the answers about British economic and social history are universally agreed upon, I am unable to say that this book represents the consensus of scholars. If the study of the Industrial Revolution and its consequences had not been so strikingly neglected for a generation before the 1950s, it might be possible to speak with more confidence about it, but at present the discussions which have fortunately revived are far from concluded. They deal not only with highly general problems such as the nature of economic development and the social aspects of industrialization, but with particular problems such as the origins of the Industrial Revolution, what, if anything, went wrong with the British economy in the last third of the nineteenth century, the emergence of the working class, the effects of the inter-war depression, the character of 'imperialism', not to mention even more precisely defined questions. Specialists will probably recognize the interpretations I have adopted, but there are plenty of rival ones. There are also plenty of areas in which there has been very little recent work, and where the historian has no choice but to accept what his predecessors have written, or to leave a blank.

It is pleasant to observe that British economic and social history of the past 200 years is now a subject in which research is intense and discussion lively and sometimes passionate, but of course this makes the task of the historian who wishes to give a general interpretation of the entire period much more difficult, and his work much more provisional. Whether the answers given in this book will prove to be true is uncertain, though naturally I hope they will. Whether they make sense and a coherent whole is something which readers must judge for themselves.

Any book such as this is, of course, a product of a particular period in yet another way. It reflects not only the state of knowledge, but also the interests of the present, which are not always those of the past and may not be those of the future. For instance, twenty years ago economic historians would undoubtedly have paid a great deal of attention to the fluctuations of the British economy, since both they and economists still lived under the impact of the inter-war depressions. Today they are preoccupied rather by the problems of economic development and industrialization, and – under the impact of the great movements of political decolonization – by the sharp and growing cleavage between the 'developed' and the 'underdeveloped' or 'emerging' world. It will be obvious to readers that this book reflects such preoccupations of the 1950s and 1960s, and neglects some of the others, sometimes deliberately.

This is a work of synthesis, rather than of original research, and therefore rests on the labours of a great many other scholars. Even its judgements are sometimes those of others. To acknowledge all my debts fully would require an elaborate and bulky apparatus of references and, although an act of courtesy to my colleagues, would be of little value to ordinary readers. I have therefore confined references on the whole to sources of direct quotations and occasionally of facts taken from fairly recondite sources. Nor have I attempted to give full references where, as in some parts of the book, I have relied on primary sources and not secondary works. The guide to further reading and the bibliographical notes attached to each chapter mention some of the works on which I have drawn, those to which I am particularly indebted being marked with an asterisk. These guides do not constitute a proper bibliography. Works containing good bibliographies are marked (B).

One final word of warning. Economic history is essentially quantitative, and therefore uses statistics a good deal. However, figures have limitations which are not often understood by laymen and sometimes neglected by specialists who, since they need them, accept them with fewer questions than they might. So it is worth listing a few. There can be no statistics unless someone has first done the counting. In history often nobody has until relatively recently. (For instance, there are no figures for coal output before 1854, no adequate figures for unemployment before 1921.) In such cases we have no statistics but only informed estimates, or more or less wild guesses. The best we can expect is orders of magnitude. However much we may want to get more out of such figures, we may be unable to. Nobody can build a bridge carrying heavy trucks out of a few rotten planks. Statistics collected for any purpose have a margin of error, and the earlier they have been collected, the less reliable they are. All statistics are answers to specific and extremely narrow questions, and if they are used to answer other questions, whether in their crude form or after more or less sophisticated manipulation, they must be treated with extreme caution. In other words, readers must learn to beware of the apparent solidity and hardness of tables of historical statistics, especially when presented naked without the elaborate wrapping of description with which the skilled statistician surrounds them. They are essential. They allow us to express certain things with great conciseness and (for some of us) vividness. But they are not necessarily more reliable than the approximations of prose. The

Preface

ones I have used come largely from that admirable compendium, Mitchell and Deane's *Abstract of British Historical Statistics*.

I am indebted to Kenneth Berrill who read much of this book in manuscript, but is not responsible for its errors, though he has eliminated some. I am also grateful to those readers who have drawn my attention to several misprints and other errors, which have been corrected in the present edition. Apart from a few small changes, the text has not been modified. Though occasionally glancing beyond, it ends, for practical purposes, with the advent of the Labour government of 1964.

London, 1967 and 1968   E.J.H.

INTRODUCTION

THE Industrial Revolution marks the most fundamental transformation of human life in the history of the world recorded in written documents. For a brief period it coincided with the history of a single country, Great Britain. An entire world economy was thus built on, or rather around, Britain, and this country therefore temporarily rose to a position of global influence and power unparalleled by any state of its relative size before or since, and unlikely to be paralleled by any state in the foreseeable future. There was a moment in the world's history when Britain can be described, if we are not too pedantic, as its only workshop, its only massive importer and exporter, its only carrier, its only imperialist, almost its only foreign investor; and for that reason its only naval power and the only one which had a genuine world policy. Much of this monopoly was simply due to the loneliness of the pioneer, monarch of all he surveys because of the absence of any other surveyors. When other countries industrialized, it ended automatically, though the apparatus of world economic transfers constructed by, and in terms of, Britain remained indispensable to the rest of the world for a while longer. Nevertheless, for most of the world the 'British' era of industrialization was merely a phase – the initial, or an early phase – of contemporary history. For Britain it was obviously much more than this. We have been profoundly marked by the experience of our economic and social pioneering and remain marked by it to this day. This unique historical situation of Britain is the subject of this book.

Economists and economic historians have discussed the characteristics, advantages and disadvantages of being an industrial pioneer at great length and with different conclusions, depending mainly on whether they have tried to explain why undeveloped economies today fail to catch up with developed ones, or why early industrial starters – and most notably Britain – allow themselves to be outdistanced by later ones. The advantages of making an industrial revolution in the eighteenth and early nineteenth centuries were great, and we shall consider some of them in the chapters discussing this period. The disadvantages – for instance, a rather archaic technology and business structure which may become too deeply embedded to be readily abandoned, or even modified – are likely to emerge at a later stage; in Britain between the 1860s and the end of the nineteenth century. They will also be briefly considered in the chapters on that period. The view taken in this book is that the relative decline of Britain is, broadly speaking, due to its early and long-sustained start as an industrial power. Nevertheless this factor must not be analysed in isolation. What is at least equally important is the peculiar, indeed the unique, position of this country in the world economy, which was partly the cause of our early success and which was re-inforced by it. We were, or we increasingly became, the agency of economic interchange between the advanced and the back-ward, the industrial and the primary-producing, the metropoli-tan and the colonial or quasi-colonial regions of the world. Per-haps because it was so largely built round Britain, the world economy of nineteenth-century capitalism developed as a single system of free flows, in which the international transfers of capi-tal and commodities passed largely through British hands and institutions, in British ships between the continents, and were calculated in terms of the pound sterling. And because Britain began with the immense advantages of being indispensable to underdeveloped regions (either because they needed us or be-cause they were not allowed to do without us), and indispensable also to the systems of trade and payments of the developed world, Britain always had a line of retreat open when the challenge of other economies became too pressing. We could retreat further into both Empire and Free Trade – into our monopoly of as yet undeveloped regions, which in itself helped to keep them un-industrialized, and into our functions as the hub of the world's trading, shipping and financial transactions. We did not have to compete but could evade. And our ability to evade helped to per-petuate the archaic and increasingly obsolete industrial and social structure of the pioneer age.

The single liberal world economy, theoretically self-regulating, but in fact requiring the semi-automatic switchboard of Britain, collapsed between the wars. The political system which corresponded to it, and in which a limited number of Western capitalist states held the monopoly of industry, of military force and of political control in the undeveloped world, also began to collapse after the Russian Revolution of 1917, and very much more rapidly after the Second World War. Other industrial economies found it easier to adjust themselves to this collapse, for the nineteenth-century liberal economy had been merely an episode in their development. Indeed their emergence was one reason for its eventual breakdown. Britain found itself much more profoundly affected. It was no longer essential to the world. Indeed, in the nineteenth-century sense there was no longer a single world to be essential to. What new base for its economy could be found?

Unsystematically, often unintentionally, the country did indeed adjust itself, changing rapidly from an unusually small-scale and uncontrolled into an unusually monopolist and state-controlled economy, from relying on export-based basic industries to home-market-based ones, and, rather more slowly, from older technologies and forms of industrial organization to newer ones. Yet the great question remained unanswered: could such adjustments provide a basis sufficiently large for the relatively gigantic economy of what still remained in 1960 the third economic power in the world to maintain itself on its accustomed scale? And if not, what were the alternatives?

Social historians have discussed the peculiarities due to Britain's pioneer start less often than economists. Yet they are very marked. For Britain combines, as everyone knows, two at first sight incompatible phenomena. Its social and political institutions and practices maintain a remarkable, if superficial, continuity with the pre-industrial past, symbolized by all those things which, by their very rarity in the modern world, attract the foreign sightseer and a fortunately increasing amount of foreign tourist currency: Queen and Lords, the ceremonials of long-obsolete or archaic institutions and the rest. At the same time this is in many respects the country which has broken most radically with all previous ages of human history: the peasantry most completely eliminated, the proportion of men and woman earning their living purely by wage (or salaried) labour higher than anywhere else, urbanization earlier and probably greater than elsewhere. Consequently this is also the country in which class divisions were, at least until recently, more simplified than elsewhere (as indeed were regional divisions). For in spite of the usual existence of a fairly large number of levels of income, status and snobbery, most people in fact tend to work on the assumption that there are only two classes which count, namely the 'working class' and the 'middle class', and the British two-party system has reflected this duality to a considerable extent. That it has not produced the political consequences which the early socialists anticipated is quite another matter.

Both phenomena are evidently connected with Britain's early economic start, though their roots go back, at least in part, to a period before the one dealt with in this book. How drastically the formal political and social institutions of a country are transformed in the process of turning it into an industrial and capitalist state depends on three factors: on the flexibility, adaptability, or the resistance of its old institutions, on the urgency of the actual need for transformation, and on the risks inherent in the great revolutions, which are the normal ways in which they come about. In Britain the resistance to capitalist development had ceased to be effective by the end of the seventeenth century. The very aristocracy was, by continental standards, almost a form of 'bourgeoisie', and two revolutions had taught the monarchy to be adaptable. As we shall see, the technical problems of industrialization were unusually easy, and the extra costs and inefficiencies of handling them with obsolete institutional equipment (and especially a grossly obsolete legal system) were easily tolerable. And when the mechanism of peaceful adjustment worked worst, and the need for radical change seemed most urgent – as in the first half of the nineteenth century – the risks of revolution were also unusually great, just because if it got out of control it looked like turning into a revolution of the new working class. No British government could rely, like all nineteenth-century French, German or American governments, on mobilizing the political forces of country against city, of vast masses of peasants and small shopkeepers or other petits-bourgeois against a minority – often a scattered and localized minority – of proletarians. The first industrial power of the world was also the one in which the manual working class was numerically dominant. To keep social tensions low, to prevent the dissensions among sectors of the ruling classes from getting out of hand, was not merely advisable, but seemed essential. It also happened, with brief exceptions, to be quite practicable.

Britain thus developed the characteristic combination of a revolutionary social base and, at least at one moment – the period of militant economic liberalism – a sweeping triumph of doctrinaire ideology, with an apparently traditionalist and slow-changing institutional superstructure. The immense barrier of power and profit built up in the nineteenth century protected the country against those political and economic catastrophes which might have forced radical changes upon it. We were never defeated in war, still less destroyed. Even the impact of the greatest non-political cataclysm of the twentieth century, the Great Slump of 1929–33, was not as sudden, acute and general as in other countries, including the USA. The *status quo* was sometimes shaken, but never utterly disrupted. We have so far suffered erosion, but not collapse. And whenever crises threatened to become unmanageable, the penalties of allowing them to get out of hand were always present in the minds of the country's rulers. There has been hardly a moment when the politically decisive section of them forgot the fundamental political fact of modern Britain, namely that this country could not and cannot be run in flat defiance of its working-class majority, and that it could always afford the modest cost of conciliating a crucial section of this majority. By the standards of other leading industrial countries hardly any blood has been shed *in Britain* (as distinct from colonies or dependencies) in defence of the political and economic system for more than a century.* Between British employers and workers, British rulers and ruled, there is no chasm labelled 'Paris Commune', or 'Homestead Strike', or 'Free Corps' and 'SS'.

* The few exceptions – Trafalgar Square 1887, Featherstone 1893, Tonypandy 1911 – stand out in the history of British labour dramatically.

This evasion of drastic confrontations, this preference for sticking old labels on new bottles, should not be confused with the absence of change. In terms both of social structure and of political institutions the changes since 1750 have been profound, and at certain moments both rapid and spectacular. They have been concealed both by the taste of moderate reformers for advertising negligible modifications of the past as 'peaceful' or 'silent' revolutions,* of all respectable opinion for disguising major changes as additions to precedent, and by the very striking traditionalism and conservatism of so many British institutions. This traditionalism is real, but the word itself covers two quite distinct phenomena.

The first of these is the preference for maintaining the *form* of old institutions with a profoundly changed content; indeed in many cases the creation of a pseudo-tradition and a pseudo-customary legitimacy for quite new institutions. The functions of the monarchy today have very little in common with those of the monarchy in 1750, while the 'public schools' as we now know them barely existed before the middle of the nineteenth century, and their incrustation of tradition is almost entirely Victorian. The second, however, is the marked tendency for once-revolutionary innovations to acquire the patina of their own tradition by the length of their existence. Since Britain was the first industrial capitalist country, and was for long one in which changes were comparatively sluggish, it has provided ample opportunities for such industrialized traditionalism. What passes for British Conservatism is, ideologically, the *laissez-faire* liberalism which triumphed between 1820 and 1850, and, except formally, this is also the content of the age-old and customary Common Law, at all events in the field of property and contract. So far as the content of their decisions is concerned, most British judges should be wearing top hats and mutton-chop whiskers rather than full-bottomed wigs. So far as

---

*Thus the achievements of the Labour governments of 1945–51, which marked, if anything, a retreat from the effectively socialist wartime economy of Britain, were at one time advertised as such a 'revolution', and so was the educational progress of Britain in the first half of the twentieth century, which strikes the observer as unusually hesitant.

the way of life of the British middle classes is concerned, its most characteristic aspect, the suburban house and garden, merely goes back to the first phase of industrialization, when their ancestors began to move out from the smoke and fog of the polluted town centres to the hills and commons beyond. So far as the working class is concerned, as we shall see what is called its 'traditional' way of life is if anything more recent still. It is hardly found complete anywhere before the 1880s. And the 'traditional' mode of life of the professional intellectual, garden suburb, country cottage, intellectual weekly and all, is more recent still, since that class itself hardly existed as a self-conscious group before the Edwardian period. 'Tradition' in this sense is not a serious obstacle to change. Often it is merely a British way of giving a label to any moderately enduring facts, especially at the moment when these facts are themselves beginning to change. After they have been changed for a generation, they will in turn be called 'traditional'.

I do not wish to deny the autonomous power of accumulated and fossilized institutions and habits to act as a brake upon change. Up to a point they have this power, though it is counteracted, at least potentially, by that other ingrained British 'tradition', which is never to resist irresistible changes, but to absorb them as quickly and quietly as possible. What passes for the power of 'conservatism' or 'traditionalism' is often something quite different: vested interest and the absence of sufficient pressure. Britain is in itself no more traditionalist than other countries; less so in, say, social habits than the French, much less so in the official inflexibility of obsolete institutions (such as an eighteenth-century Constitution) than the USA. It has so far merely been more conservative, because the vested interest in the past has been unusually strong, more complacent, because more protected; and perhaps also more unwilling to try new paths for its economy, because no new paths seem to lead to half so inviting a prospect as the old ones. These may now be impassable, but other roads do not appear very passable either.

This book is about the history of Britain. However, as even the past few pages will have made clear, an insular history of Britain (and there have been too many such) is quite inadequate.

In the first place Britain developed as an essential part of a global economy, and more particularly as the centre of that vast formal or informal 'empire' on which its fortunes have so largely rested. To write about this country without also saying something about the West Indies and India, about Argentina and Australia, is unreal. Nevertheless, since I am not here writing the history of the world economy or of its British imperial sector, my references to the outside world must be marginal. We shall see in later chapters what Britain's relations to it were, how Britain was affected by changes in it, and occasionally, in a brief phrase or two, how dependence on Britain affected those parts of it which belonged directly to the British satellite or colonial system: for instance, how the industrialization of Lancashire prolonged and developed slavery in America, or how some of the burdens of British economic crisis could be passed on to the primary-producing countries for whose exports we (or for that matter other industrialized countries) were the only outlet. But the purpose of such remarks is simply to remind the reader constantly of the inter-relations between Britain and the rest of the world, without which our history cannot be understood. It is no more.

However, another kind of international reference cannot be avoided either. The history of British industrial society is a particular case – the first and at times the most important – of the general phenomenon of industrialization under capitalism, and if we take an even broader view, of the general phenomenon of any industrialization. Inevitably we must ask how typical of this phenomenon the British example is; or in more practical terms – for the world today consists of countries trying to industrialize rapidly – what other countries can learn from the British experience. The answer is that they can learn much in principle, but rather little in actual practice. The very priority of British development makes this country's case in most respects unique and unparalleled. No other country had to make its industrial revolution virtually alone, unable to benefit from the existence of an already established industrial sector of the world economy, to draw on its resources of experience, skill, or capital. Both the extremes to which, for instance, British social development was pushed (for example the virtual elimination of the peasantry and the small-scale artisan producers) and the highly peculiar pattern of British economic relations with the under-developed world may well be largely due to this situation. Conversely, the fact that Britain made its industrial revolution in the eighteenth century, and was reasonably well prepared for making it, minimized certain problems which have been acute in later industrializers, or in those which faced a greater initial leap from backwardness to economic advance. The technology with which developing countries must operate today is more complex and expensive than that with which Britain made its industrial revolution. The forms of economic organization are different: countries today are not confined to a private enterprise or capitalist model but can also choose a socialist one. The political context is different. Industrializing countries today develop in the context of strong labour movements and socialist world powers, which make the idea of industrializing without any provisions for social security or trade unionism politically almost unthinkable.

The history of Britain is therefore not a model for the economic development of the world today. If we seek any reasons for studying and analysing it, other than the automatic interest which the past, and especially past greatness, holds for many people, we shall find only two very convincing ones. Britain's past since the Industrial Revolution still lies heavily on the present, and the practical solution of the actual problems of our economy and society therefore require us to understand something about it. More generally, the record of the earliest, the longest-lived industrial and capitalist power cannot but throw light on the development of industrialization as a phenomenon in the history of the world. For the planner, the social engineer, the applied economist (in so far as he does not concentrate his attention on British problems), this country is merely one 'case-study', and for twentieth-century purposes not the most interesting or relevant. For the historian of human progress from the cave-man to the wielders of atomic power and the cosmic travellers, it is of unique interest. No change in human life since the invention of agriculture, metallurgy and towns in the

New Stone Age has been so profound as the coming of industrialization. It came, inevitably and temporarily, in the form of a capitalist economy and society, and it was probably also inevitable that it should come in the form of a single 'liberal' world economy depending for a time on a single leading pioneer country. That country was Britain, and as such it stands alone in history.

I

BRITAIN IN 1750[1]

WHAT the contemporary observer sees is not necessarily the truth, but the historian neglects it at his peril. Britain – or rather England – in the eighteenth century was a much-observed country, and if we are to grasp what has happened to it since the Industrial Revolution, we may as well begin by trying to see it through the eyes of its numerous and studious foreign visitors, always anxious to learn, generally to admire, and with ample leisure to pay attention to their surroundings. By modern standards they needed it. The traveller who landed around 1750 at Dover or Harwich after an unpredictable and often lengthy crossing (say thirty-odd hours from Holland) would be well advised to rest the night in one of the expensive, but remarkably comfortable, English inns which invariably impressed him very favourably. He would travel perhaps fifty miles by coach the next day, and, after another night's rest at Rochester or Chelmsford, would enter London in the middle of the next day. Travel at this rate required leisure. The alternative for the poor man – walking or coastal shipping – was cheaper and slower, or cheaper but unpredictable. Within a few years the new rapid mail coaches might get him from London to Portsmouth between morning and nightfall, from London to Edinburgh in sixty-two hours, but in 1750 he would still have to reckon on ten to twelve days for the latter journey.

He would immediately be struck by the greenness, tidiness, the apparent prosperity of the countryside, and by the apparent comfort of 'the peasantry'. 'The whole of this country', wrote the Hanoverian Count Kielmansegge in 1761 of Essex, 'is not unlike a well-kept garden,'[2] and he spoke for most other tourists. Since the usual English tour confined itself to the south and middle parts of England, this impression was not quite accurate, but the contrast with most parts of the continent was real enough. The tourist would then, equally invariably, be deeply impressed by the immense size of London, and quite rightly, for with something like three quarters of a million inhabitants it was by far the largest city in Christendom, perhaps twice the size of its nearest rival, Paris. It was certainly not beautiful. It might even strike the foreigner as gloomy. 'After having seen Italy,' observed the Abbé Le Blanc in 1747, 'you will see nothing in the buildings of London that will give you much pleasure. The city is really wonderful only for its bigness.' (But he, like all others, was 'struck with the beauties of the country, the care taken to improve lands, the richness of the pastures, the numerous flocks that cover them and the air of plenty and cleanliness that reigns in the smallest villages'.)[3] Nor was it a clean or well-lit city, though rather better in this respect than centres of industry like Birmingham, where 'the people seem so entirely engrossed by their business within doors that they care very little what sort of an appearance is made without. The streets are neither paved nor lighted.'[4]

There were no other English cities which could even faintly compare with London, though the ports and commercial or manufacturing centres of the provinces were, unlike in the seventeenth century, expanding rapidly and visibly prospering. No other English town had 50,000 inhabitants. Few of them would be worth the non-commercial visitor's attention, though if in 1750 he had gone to Liverpool (which the London stage coach had not yet reached) he would doubtless have been impressed with the bustle of that fast-rising port, based, like Bristol and Glasgow, largely on the trade in slaves and colonial products – sugar, tea, tobacco, and increasingly cotton. Eighteenth-century port cities prided themselves on their solid and new harbour installations, and on the provincial elegance of their public buildings, forming as the visitor would approvingly note 'a pleasing epitome of the metropolis'.[5] Their less elegant inhabitants might see more of the tough brutality of the waterside, filled with taverns and prostitutes for the seamen flush off the ships, or about to be shanghaied by labour contractors or by His Majesty's press-gang for the Navy. Ships and overseas trade were, as everyone knew, the lifeblood of Britain, the Navy its most powerful weapon. Around the middle of the eighteenth century the country owned perhaps six thousand mercantile ships of perhaps half a million tons, several times the size of the French mercantile marine, its main rival. They formed perhaps one tenth of all capital fixed investments (other than real estate) in 1700, while their 100,000 seamen were almost the largest group of non-agricultural workers.

In the middle of the eighteenth century the foreign tourist would probably pay rather less attention to manufactures and mines, though already impressed with the quality (though not the taste) of British workmanship, and aware of the ingenuity which so strikingly supplemented its hard work and industry. The British were already famous for machines 'which', as the Abbé Le Blanc noted, 'really multiply men by lessening their work. . . . Thus in the coal pits of NEWCASTLE, a single person can, by means of an engine equally surprising and simple, raise five hundred tons of water to the height of a hundred and eighty feet.'[6] The steam engine, in its primitive form, was already present. Whether the British gift for using inventions was due to their own inventiveness, or to their capacity to use other people's innovations, was a matter of argument. Probably the latter, thought the sagacious Wendeborn of Berlin, who travelled the country in the 1780s, when industry was already the object of very much more interest. Still, as with most tourists, the word 'manufactured' brought into his mind chiefly such cities as Birmingham, with its variety of small metal goods, Sheffield, with its admirable cutlery, the potteries of Staffordshire, and the woollen industry, widely distributed throughout the country-side of East Anglia, the west country and Yorkshire, but not associated with towns of any large size except the decaying Norwich. This was, after all, the basic and traditional manu-facture of Britain. He barely mentioned Lancashire, and that only in passing.

For if the farming and manufactures were prosperous and expanding, they were clearly, in the eyes of foreigners, much less important than trade. England was, after all, 'the nation of shopkeepers', and the merchant rather than the industrialist was its most characteristic citizen. 'It must be owned', said the Abbé Le Blanc, 'that the natural productions of the country do not, at most, amount to a fourth part of her riches: the rest she owes to her colonies, and the industry of her inhabitants who, by the transportation and exchange of the riches of other countries continually augment their own.'[7] The commerce of the British was, by the standards of the eighteenth-century world, a very remarkable phenomenon. It was both businesslike and warlike, as Voltaire observed, in the 1720s, when his *Letters from England* set the fashion for admiring foreign reportage of these islands. More than this: it was closely linked with the unique political system of Britain, in which kings were subordinate to Parliament. British historians rightly remind us that that Parliament was controlled by an oligarchy of landowning aristocrats rather than by what was not yet called the middle classes. Yet, by continental standards, what unaristocratic nobles! How strangely – how ridiculously, thought the Abbé Le Blanc – inclined to ape their inferiors: 'At London masters dress like their valets, and duchesses copy after chambermaids.' How remote in spirit from the aristocratic ostentation of really noble societies:

One does not find the English set up for making a figure, either in their clothes or equipages; one sees their household furniture as plain as sumptuary laws could prescribe it . . . and if the tables of the English are not remarkable for their frugality, they are at least so for their plainness.[8]

The whole British system was based, unlike that of less-go-ahead and certainly less prosperous countries, on a government concerned for the needs of what the Abbé Coyer called 'the honest middle class, that precious portion of nations'.[9] 'Commerce', wrote Voltaire, 'which has enriched the citizens of England has helped to make them free, and that liberty in turn has expanded commerce. This is the foundation of the greatness of the state.'[10]

Britain then struck the foreign visitor chiefly as a rich country, and one rich primarily because of its trade and enterprise; as a powerful and formidable state, but one whose power rested chiefly on that most commercially-based and trade-minded weapon, a Navy; as a state of unusual liberty and tolerance – both of which were yet again closely linked with trade and the middle class. Though perhaps deficient in the aristocratic graces of life, in wit, and in *joie de vivre*, and given to religious and other eccentricities, it was unquestionably the most flourishing and progressive of economies, and one which more than held its own in science and literature, not to mention technology. Its common people, insular, conceited, competent, brutal and given to riot, appeared to be well-fed and prosperous, by the modest standards which were then applied to the poor. Its institutions were stable, in spite of the remarkable weakness of the apparatus for maintaining public order, or for planning and administering the country's economic affairs. For those who wished to put their own countries on the road to economic progress there was clearly a lesson in this visible success of a nation based essentially on private enterprise. 'Meditate on this,' cried the Abbé Coyer in 1779, 'oh you, who still support a system of regulations and exclusive privilege', [11] as he observed that even roads and canals were constructed and maintained by the profit motive.*

Economic and technical progress, private enterprise, and what we would now call liberalism: all these were evident. Yet nobody expected the imminent transformation of the country by an industrial revolution – not even travellers who visited Britain in the early 1780s, when we know that it had already started. Few expected its imminent population explosion, which was about to raise the English and Welsh population from perhaps six and a half millions in 1750 to over nine millions in 1801, and to sixteen millions by 1841. In the middle of the eighteenth century, and even some decades later, men were still arguing whether the British population was rising or stagnant; by the end of the century Malthus was already assuming as a matter of course that it was growing much too fast.

If we look back on 1750 we shall no doubt see many things which were overlooked by contemporaries, not obvious to them (or on the contrary too obvious for remark), but we shall not find ourselves in fundamental disagreement. We shall note,

---

*Not everyone agreed, especially when, like the 'celebrated Madam Du Bocage', they were told that the reason for the filth of London was 'that in a free nation citizens pave as they think proper, each before his own door'. 'Liberty,' said the Abbé Le Blanc, 'it seems, is the blessing that hinders them from having either a good pavement or a good policy in London.'

above all, that England (Wales and large parts of Scotland were still somewhat different – compare Chapter 15) was already a monetary and market economy on a national scale. A 'nation of shopkeepers' implies a nation of producers for sale on the market, not to mention a nation of customers. In the cities this was natural enough, for a close and self-sufficient economy is impossible in towns above a certain size, and Britain was – economically – lucky enough to possess the greatest of all Western cities (and consequently the largest of all concentrated markets for goods) in London, which by the middle of the century contained perhaps fifteen per cent of the English population and whose insatiable demand for food and fuel transformed agriculture all over the south and east, drew regular supplies by land and river from even the remoter parts of Wales and the north, and stimulated the coalmines of Newcastle. Regional price variations in non-perishable and easily transportable foodstuffs like cheese were already small. What is more important, England no longer paid the heaviest penalty of self-sufficient local and regional economies, famine. 'Dearth', common enough on the continent, hardly forgotten in Lowland Scotland, was no longer a serious problem, though bad harvests still brought sharp rises in the cost of living and consequent rioting over large parts of the country, as in 1740-1, 1757 and 1767.

What was already so startling about the British countryside was the absence of a peasantry in the continental sense. It was not merely that the growth of a market economy had already seriously undermined local and regional self-sufficiency, and enmeshed even the village in a web of cash sales and purchases, though this was, by contemporary standards, obvious enough. The growing use of such entirely imported commodities as tea, sugar and tobacco measures not only the expansion of overseas trade, but the commercialization of rural life. By the middle of the century about 0·6 lb. of tea was legally imported per head of the population, plus a considerable amount smuggled in, and already there was evidence that the drink was not uncommon in the countryside, even among labourers (or more precisely, their wives and daughters). The British, thought Wendeborn, consumed three times as much tea as the rest of Europe put together.

It was also that the owner-occupying small cultivator, living substantially on the produce of his family-worked holding, was becoming notably less common than in other countries (except in the backward Celtic fringe and a few other areas, mainly of the north and west). The century since the Restoration of 1660 had seen a major concentration of landownership in the hands of a limited class of very large landlords, at the expense both of the lesser gentry and the peasants. We have no reliable figures, but it is clear that by 1750 the characteristic structure of English landownership was already discernible: a few thousand landowners, leasing out their land to some tens of thousands of tenant farmers, who in turn operated it with the labour of some hundreds of thousands of farm-labourers, servants or dwarf holders who hired themselves out for much of their time. This fact in itself implied a very substantial system of cash-incomes and cash sales.

What is more, a good deal – perhaps most – of the industries and manufactures of Britain were rural, the typical worker being some kind of village artisan or smallholder in his cottage, increasingly specializing in the manufacture of some product – mainly cloth, hosiery, and a variety of metal goods – and thus by degrees turning from small peasant or craftsman into wage-labourer. Increasingly, villages in which men spent their spare time or seasons weaving, knitting or mining, tended to become industrial villages of fulltime weavers, knitters or miners, and eventually some – but by no means all – developed into industrial towns. Or more likely, the little market centres whence merchants issued to buy up the village products, or to distribute ('put out') the raw material and rent out the looms or frames to the cottage workers, became towns, filled with workshops or primitive manufactories to prepare and perhaps finish the material and goods distributed to and collected from the scattered out-workers. The nature of such a system of rural 'domestic' or 'putting-out' industry spread it widely throughout the countryside, and tightened the meshes of the web of cash transactions which spread over it. For every village which specialized in manufactures, every rural area which became an industrial village area (like the Black Country, the mining regions, and most of the textile regions), implied some other zone which specialized in selling it the food it no longer produced.

This wide scattering of industry throughout the countryside had two linked and important consequences. It gave the politically decisive classes of landlords a direct interest in the mines which happened to lie under their lands (and from which, unlike on the continent, they rather than the king drew 'royalties') and the manufactures in their villages. The very marked interest of the local nobility and gentry in such investments as canals and turnpike roads was due not merely to the hope of opening wider markets to local agricultural produce, but to the anticipated advantages of better and cheaper transport for local mines and manufactures.* But in 1750 these improvements in inland transport had hardly begun: 'turnpike trusts' were still being set up at the rate of less than ten a year (between 1750 and 1770 they appeared at the rate of over forty a year) and canals hardly began at all until 1760.

The second consequence was that manufacturing interests could already *determine government policy*, unlike in the other great commercial country, the Netherlands, where the interests of the merchant were supreme. And this in spite of the modest wealth and influence of the budding industrialists. Thus it was estimated that in 1760 the poorest class of 'merchants' earned as much as the richest class of 'master manufacturers' (the wealthiest earned on average three times as much), and that even the top stratum of the much more modest 'tradesmen' earned twice the income of the equivalent stratum of 'master manufacturers'. The figures are guesswork, but they indicate the relative standing of commerce and industry in contemporary opinion.† In every respect trade seemed to be more lucrative, more important, more prestigious than manufactures, especially overseas trade. Yet when it came to choosing between the interests of commerce (which lay in freedom to import, export and re-export) and those of industry (which at this stage lay, as usual, in protecting the British home market against the foreigner

* Canals and turnpike trusts were rarely expected to do more than pay for themselves with perhaps a modest return on capital.

† The figures (in £ per year) were around 1760 (see table opposite):

and capturing the export market for British products), the domestic producer prevailed, for the merchant could mobilize only London and a few ports in his interest, the manufacturer the political interests of large stretches of the country and of government. The matter was decided at the end of the seventeenth century, when the textile-makers, relying on the traditional importance of woollen cloth to British government finance, secured the prohibition of foreign 'calicoes'. British industry could grow up, by and large, in a protected home market until strong enough to demand free entry into other people's markets, that is 'Free Trade'.

Yet neither industry nor commerce could have flourished but for the unusual political circumstances which so rightly impressed the foreigners. Nominally, England was not a 'bourgeois' state. It was an oligarchy of landed aristocrats, headed by a tight, self-perpetuating peerage of some two hundred persons, a system of powerful rich cousinages under the aegis of the ducal heads of the great Whig families – Russells, Cavendishes, Fitzwilliams, Pelhams and the rest. Who could compare to them in wealth? (Joseph Massie in 1760 estimated the incomes of ten noble families at £20,000 a year, of twenty at £10,000, and another 120 at £6–8,000, or more than ten times what the richest

Occupation	Number of families	Income
Merchants	1,000	600
	2,000	400
	10,000	200
Tradesmen	2,500	400
	5,000	200
	10,000	100
	20,000	70
	125,000	40
Master manufacturers	2,500	200
	5,000	100
	10,000	70
	62,500	40

For comparison, the average income of lawyers and innkeepers was estimated at £100, of the wealthiest farmers at £150, of 'husbandmen' and provincial labourers at 5 or 6 shillings a week.

class of merchants was supposed to earn.) Who could compare with them in influence in a political system which gave any duke or earl who chose to exercise it almost automatic high office, and an automatic bloc of relatives, clients and supporters in both houses of parliament, and which made the exercise of the least political rights dependent on the ownership of landed property, which was increasingly hard to come by for those who did not already own estates? Yet, as the foreigners saw much more clearly than we may do, the grandees of Britain were not a nobility comparable to the feudal and absolutist hierarchies of the continent. They were a post-revolutionary élite, the heirs of the Roundheads. Honour, bravery, elegance and largesse, the virtues of a feudal or court aristocracy, no longer dominated their lives. A medium-sized German *Junker* might have a larger train of servants and domestic dependants than the Duke of Bedford himself. Their parliaments and governments made war and peace for profit, colonies and markets and in order to stamp on commercial competitors. When a genuine relic of an older era irrupted into England, like Charles Edward Stuart, the 'Young Pretender' in 1745, with his army of loyal, but strictly uncommercial Highlanders, the distance between Whig England, however aristocratic, and more archaic societies became obvious. The Whig grandees (though not so much the lesser Tory country squires) knew quite well that the power of the country, and their own, rested on a readiness to make money militantly and commercially. It so happened that in 1750 not a great deal of money was yet to be made in industry. When it was, they would have no great difficulty in adjusting themselves to the situation.

Yet, if we placed ourselves in the Britain of 1750 without the wisdom of hindsight, would we have predicted the imminent Industrial Revolution? Almost certainly not. We should, like the foreign visitors, have been struck by the essentially 'bourgeois', commercial, nature of the country. We should have admired its economic dynamism and progress, perhaps its aggressive expansionism, and we might have been impressed with the remarkable results of its multifarious and hardly controlled private entrepreneurs. We would have predicted an increasingly prosperous and powerful future for it. But would we have expected its transformation – still less the ensuing transformation of the world? Would we have expected that in less than a century the son of a 'master-manufacturer' – and one who in 1750 was only just abandoning the countryside of his yeomen ancestors to settle in a smallish Lancashire town – would be Prime Minister of Britain? We would not. Would we have expected the quiescent England of 1750 to be rent by Radicalism, Jacobinism, Chartism, Socialism? Looking back, we can see that no other country was as well-prepared for the Industrial Revolution. But we must still see why in fact it burst out in the last decades of the eighteenth century, with results which, for good or ill, have become irreversible.

NOTES

1. See the works of Cole and Postage, Ashton, Wilson, Deane and Cole, listed in Further Reading, 2 and 3, p. 365. See also Figures 1, 3, 10, 14, 16, 26, 28, 37.
2. Count Friedrich Kielmansegge, *Diary of a Journey to England 1761–2* (London, 1902), p. 18.
3. Mons. L'Abbé Le Blanc, *Letters on the English and French Nations* (London, 1747), Vol. I, p. 177.
4. *A Tour through England, Wales and part of Ireland made during the summer of 1791* (London, 1793), p. 373.
5. ibid., p. 354.
6. Le Blanc, op. cit., I, p. 48.
7. ibid., II, p. 345.
8. ibid., I, p. 18; II, p. 90.
9. Abbé Coyer, *Nouvelles observations sur l'Angleterre* (1779), p. 15.
10. Voltaire, *Lettres philosophiques*, Letter X.
11. Abbé Coyer, op. cit., p. 27.

2

ORIGIN OF THE INDUSTRIAL
REVOLUTION[1]

THE problem of the origin of the Industrial Revolution is not an easy one, but it is made even more difficult if we fail to clarify it. So it is as well to begin with a little clarification.

First, the Industrial Revolution is not merely an acceleration of economic growth, but an acceleration of growth because of, and through, economic and social transformation. The early observers, who concentrated their attention on the qualitatively new ways of producing – the machines, the factory system and the rest – had the right instinct, though they sometimes followed it too uncritically. It was not Birmingham, a city which produced a great deal more in 1850 than in 1750, but essentially in the old way, which made contemporaries speak of an industrial revolution, but Manchester, a city which produced more in a more obviously revolutionary manner. In the late eighteenth century this economic and social transformation took place in and through a capitalist economy. As we know from the twentieth century, this is not the only form industrial revolution can take, though it was the earliest and probably, in the eighteenth century, the only practicable one. Capitalist industrialization requires in some ways a rather different analysis from non-capitalist, because we must explain why the pursuit of private profit led to technological transformation, and it is by no means obvious that it automatically does so. In other ways, doubtless, capitalist industrialization can be treated as a special case of a more general phenomenon, but it is not clear to what extent this is helpful to the historian of the British Industrial Revolution.

Second, the British revolution was the first in history. This does not mean that it started from zero, or that earlier phases of rapid industrial and technological development cannot be found. Nevertheless, none of these initiated the characteristic modern phase of history, self-sustained economic growth by

34

means of perpetual technological revolution and social transformation. Being the first, it is therefore also in crucial respects unlike all subsequent industrial revolutions. It cannot be explained primarily, or to any extent, in terms of outside factors such as – for instance – the imitation of more advanced techniques, the import of capital, the impact of an already industrialized world economy. Subsequent revolutions could use the British experience, example and resources. Britain could use those of other countries only to a very limited and minor extent. At the same time, as we have seen, the British revolution was preceded by at least two hundred years of fairly continuous economic development, which laid its foundations. Unlike, say, nineteenth- or twentieth-century Russia, Britain entered industrialization prepared and not virtually unprepared.

However, the Industrial Revolution cannot be explained in purely British terms, for this country formed part of a wider economy, which we may call the 'European economy' or the 'world economy of the European maritime states'. It was part of a larger network of economic relationships, which included several 'advanced' areas, some of which were also areas of potential or aspiring industrialization, and areas of 'dependent economy', as well as the margins of foreign economies not yet substantially involved with Europe. These dependent economies consisted partly of formal colonies (as in the Americas) or points of trade and domination (as in the Orient), partly of regions which were to some extent economically specialized in response to the demands of the 'advanced' areas (as in some parts of eastern Europe). The 'advanced' world was linked to the dependent world by a certain division of economic activity: a relatively urbanized area on one hand, zones producing and largely exporting agricultural products or raw materials on the other. These relations may be described as a system of economic flows – of trade, of international payments, of capital transfers, of migration, and so on. The 'European economy' had shown marked signs of expansion and dynamic development for several centuries, though it had also experienced major economic setbacks or shifts, notably in the fourteenth to fifteenth and seventeenth centuries.

Nevertheless it is important to observe that it also tended to be divided, at least from the sixteenth century, into independent and competing politico-economic units (territorial 'states') like Britain and France, each with its own economic and social structure, and containing within itself advanced and backward or dependent sectors and regions. By the sixteenth century it was fairly obvious that, if industrial revolution occurred anywhere in the world, it would be somewhere within the European economy. Why this was so cannot be discussed here, for the question belongs to an earlier era of history than the one with which this book is concerned. However, it was not clear which of the competing units would turn out to be the first to industrialize. The problem of the origins of the Industrial Revolution which concerns us here is, essentially, why it was Britain which became the first 'workshop of the world'. A second and connected question is why this breakthrough occurred towards the end of the eighteenth century and not before or after.

Before setting about the answer (which remains a matter of debate and uncertainty), it may be useful to eliminate a number of explanations or pseudo-explanations which have long been current, and are still sometimes maintained. Most of them leave more unexplained than they elucidate.

This is true of theories which attempt to account for the Industrial Revolution in terms of climate, geography, biological change in the population or other exogenous factors. If (as has been held) the stimulus for the revolution came from, say, the unusually long period of good harvests in the earlier eighteenth century, then we have to explain why similar periods before this date (and they have occurred from time to time throughout history) had not similar consequences. If Britain's ample reserves of coal explain her priority, then we may well wonder why her comparatively scant natural supplies of most other industrial raw materials (for example iron ore) did not hamper her just as much, or alternatively why the great Silesian coalfields did not produce an equally early industrial start. If the moist climate of Lancashire is to explain the concentration of the cotton industry there, then we ought to ask why the many other equally damp regions of the British isles did not also attract or hold it. And so on. Climatic factors, geography, the distribution of natural resources operate not on their own, but only within a given economic, social and institutional framework. This is true even of the strongest of such factors, ease of access to the sea or to good rivers, that is to the cheapest and most practicable – indeed for bulk goods the only economic form of transport in the pre-industrial age. It is almost inconceivable that a totally landlocked region should have pioneered the modern Industrial Revolution; though such regions are rarer than one thinks. Nevertheless, even here non-geographic factors must not be neglected: the Hebrides have more access to the sea than most of Yorkshire.

The problem of population is somewhat different, for its movements may be explained by exogenous factors, by the changes in human society, or by a combination of both. We shall consider it further below. At present we need note merely that purely exogenous explanations are not at present widely held by historians, and are not accepted in this book.

Explanations of the Industrial Revolution by 'historic accidents' ought also to be rejected. The mere fact of overseas discovery in the fifteenth and sixteenth centuries does not account for industrialization, and neither does the 'scientific revolution' of the seventeenth.* Neither can explain why the Industrial Revolution occurred at the end of the eighteenth century and not, let us say, at the end of the seventeenth, when both the European knowledge of the outer world and scientific technology were potentially quite adequate for the sort of industrialization which developed eventually. Nor can the Protestant Reformation be made responsible for it, either directly or via some special 'capitalist spirit' or other change of economic attitude induced by Protestantism; not even for why it occurred in Britain and not in France. The Reformation occurred more than two centuries before the Industrial Revolution. By no means all areas which converted to Protestantism became pioneers of industrial revolution, and – to take an obvious example – the parts of the Netherlands which remained Catholic (Belgium)

* It is irrelevant for our purposes whether these things were purely fortuitous or (as is much more likely) the outcome of earlier European economic and social developments.

industrialized before the part which became Protestant (Holland).*

Lastly, purely political factors must also be rejected. In the second half of the eighteenth century practically all governments in Europe wanted to industrialize, but only the British succeeded. Conversely, British governments from 1660 on were firmly committed to policies favouring the pursuit of profit above other aims, but the Industrial Revolution did not occur until more than a century later.

To reject such factors as simple, exclusive, or even primary explanations is not, of course, to deny them *any* importance. That would be foolish. It is merely to establish relative scales of importance, and incidentally to clarify some of the problems of countries setting about their industrialization today, in so far as they are comparable.

*

The main preconditions for industrialization were already present in eighteenth-century Britain, or could be easily brought into being. By the standards generally applied to 'underdeveloped' countries today, England was not underdeveloped, though parts of Scotland and Wales were, and Ireland certainly was. The economic, social and ideological links which immobilize most pre-industrial people in traditional situations and occupations were already weak, and could be easily severed. To take the most obvious example, by 1750 it is as we have seen already doubtful whether we can any longer speak of a landholding peasantry in large parts of England, and it is certain that we can no longer speak of subsistence agriculture.† Hence there were no major obstacles to the transfer of men from non-industrial to industrial pursuits. The country had accumulated and was of sufficient size to permit investment in the necessary, but before

*Moreover, the theory that French economic development in the eighteenth century was crippled by the expulsion of the Protestants at the end of the seventeenth is not now widely accepted, or is, at the very least, highly debatable.

†When early-nineteenth-century writers talked of 'the peasantry', they tended to mean 'the farm-labourers'.

the railways not very costly, equipment for economic transformation. Enough of it was concentrated in the hands of men willing to invest in economic progress, while relatively little was in the hands of men likely to divert resources to alternative (and economically less desirable) uses, such as mere display. There was neither a relative nor an absolute shortage of capital. The country was not merely a market economy – one in which the bulk of goods and services outside the family are bought and sold – but in many respects it formed a single national market. And it possessed an extensive and fairly highly developed manufacturing sector and an even more highly developed commercial apparatus.

What is more, problems which are acute in modern underdeveloped countries setting about their industrialization were mild in eighteenth-century Britain. As we have seen, transport and communications were comparatively easy and cheap, since no part of Britain is further than seventy miles from the sea, and even less from some navigable waterway. The technological problems of the early Industrial Revolution were fairly simple. They required no class of men with specialized scientific qualifications, but merely a sufficiency of men with ordinary literacy, familiarity with simple mechanical devices and the working of metals, practical experience and initiative. The centuries since 1500 had certainly provided such a supply. Most of the new technical inventions and productive establishments could be started economically on a small scale, and expanded piecemeal by successive addition. That is to say, they required little initial investment, and their expansion could be financed out of accumulated profits. Industrial development was within the capacities of a multiplicity of small entrepreneurs and skilled traditional artisans. No twentieth-century country setting about industrialization has, or can have, anything like these advantages.

This does not mean that there were no obstacles in the path of British industrialization, but only that they were easy to overcome because the fundamental social and economic conditions for it already existed, because the eighteenth-century type of industrialization was comparatively cheap and simple, and because the country was sufficiently wealthy and flourishing to be untroubled by inefficiencies which might have crippled less fortunate economies. Perhaps only so lucky an industrial power as this could have ever afforded that distrust of logic and planning (even private planning), that faith in the capacity to muddle through, which became so characteristic of Britain in the nineteenth century. We shall see below how some of the difficulties of growth were overcome. The important thing to note at the outset is that they were never crucial.

The question about the origin of the Industrial Revolution which concerns us here is not, therefore, how the material for the economic explosion was accumulated, but how it was ignited; and we may add, what stopped the first explosion from fizzling out after an impressive initial bang. But was a special mechanism necessary at all? Was it not inevitable that a sufficiently long period of accumulating explosive material would, sooner or later, somehow, somewhere, produce spontaneous combustion? Perhaps so. Nevertheless it is the 'somehow' and 'somewhere' which must be explained; all the more so as the way in which an economy of private enterprise brings about industrial revolution raises a number of puzzles. We know that in fact it did so in some parts of the world; but we also know that it failed to do so in other parts, and took a rather long time doing so even in western Europe.

The puzzle lies in the relationship between making profit and technological innovation. It is often assumed that an economy of private enterprise has an automatic bias towards innovation, but this is not so. It has a bias only towards profit. It will revolutionize manufactures only if greater profits are to be made in this way than otherwise. But in pre-industrial societies this is hardly ever the case. The available and prospective market – and it is the market which determines what a businessman produces – consists of the rich, who require luxury goods in small quantities, but with a high profit-margin per sale, and the poor, who – if they are in the market economy at all, and do not produce their own consumer goods domestically or locally – have little money, are unaccustomed to novelties and suspicious of them, unwilling to consume standardized products and may not even be concentrated in cities or accessible to national manufacturers. What is more, the mass market is not likely to grow very much more rapidly than the relatively slow rate of population increase. It will make more sense to dress princesses in *haute couture* models than to speculate on the chances of capturing peasants' daughters for artificial silk stockings. The sound businessman, if he has any choice, will produce very expensive jewelled timepieces for aristocrats rather than cheap wrist-watches, and the more expensive the process of launching revolutionary cheap goods, the more he will hesitate to risk his money in it. A French millionaire in the mid nineteenth century, operating in a country in which the conditions for modern industrialism were relatively poor, expressed this admirably. 'There are three ways of losing your money,' said the great Rothschild, 'women, gambling and engineers. The first two are pleasanter, but the last is much the most certain.'[2] Nobody could accuse a Rothschild of not knowing the best way to the biggest profits. In a non-industrialized country it was not through industry.

Industrialization changes all this, by enabling production – within certain limits – to expand its own markets, if not actually to create them. When Henry Ford produced his model-T, he also produced what had not existed before, namely a vast number of customers for a cheap, standardized and simple automobile. Of course his enterprise was no longer as wildly speculative as it seemed. A century of industrialization had already demonstrated that mass-production of cheap goods can multiply their markets, accustomed men to buy better goods than their fathers had bought and to discover needs which their fathers had not dreamed of. The point is that *before* the Industrial Revolution, or in countries not yet transformed by it, Henry Ford would not have been an economic pioneer, but a crank, inviting bankruptcy.

How then did conditions come about in eighteenth-century Britain which led businessmen nevertheless to revolutionize production? How did entrepreneurs come to see before them, not the modest if solid expansion of demand which could be filled in the traditional manner, or by a little extension and improvement of the old ways, but the rapid and limitless expansion which required revolution? A small, simple and cheap revolution by our standards, but nevertheless a revolution, a leap into the dark. There are two schools of thought about this question. One emphasizes chiefly the *domestic* market, which was clearly by far the largest outlet for the country's products; the other stresses the foreign or *export* market, which was, equally clearly, far more dynamic and expandable. The right answer is probably that both were essential in different ways, as was a third, and often neglected factor: *government*.

The domestic market, large and expanding as it was, could grow in only four important ways, three of which were not likely to be exceptionally rapid. There could be growth of population, which creates more consumers (and, of course, producers); a transfer of people from non-monetary to monetary incomes, which creates more customers; an increase of income per head, which creates better customers; and a substitution of industrially produced goods for older forms of manufacture or imports.

The question of *population* is so important, and has in recent years been the subject of so large and flourishing a concentration of research, that it must be briefly discussed here. It raises three questions of which only the third is directly relevant to the problem of market expansion, but all of which are important for the more general problem of British economic and social development. They are: (1) What happened to British population and why? (2) What effect did these population changes have on the economy? (3) What effect did they have on the structure of the British people?

Reliable measures of the British population hardly exist before about 1840, when the public registration of births and deaths was introduced, but its general movement is not in much dispute. Between the end of the seventeenth century when there were perhaps five and a quarter million inhabitants of England and Wales, and the middle of the eighteenth century, it rose only very slightly, and may at times have been static or even falling. After the 1740s it rose substantially and from the 1770s very rapidly indeed by contemporary, though not by our standards.*

---

* In 1965 the population of the fastest-growing continent, Latin America, was increasing at not far short of double this rate.

It doubled in fifty to sixty years after 1780, and again in the sixty years from 1841 to 1901, though in fact both birth and death rates began to drop rapidly from the 1870s. However, these global figures conceal very substantial variations, both chronological and regional. Thus for instance, while in the first half of the eighteenth century, and even up to 1780, the London area would have been depopulated but for massive immigration from the countryside, the future centre of industrialization, the northwest, and the east Midlands were already increasing quite rapidly. After the real start of the Industrial Revolution, rates of natural increase of the major regions (though not of migration) tended to become similar, except for the murderous environment of London. *Deane & Cole*

These movements were clearly not much affected, before the nineteenth century, by international migration, not even of the Irish. Were they due to variations in the rate of births or in mortality, and what were the causes of these? Quite apart from the deficiency of our information, these questions, though of great interest, are immensely complicated.* They concern us here only in so far as they throw light on the question of how far the rise in population was a cause, how far a consequence of economic factors, for example how far people married or conceived children earlier because of better chances of getting a piece of land to cultivate or a job or – as has been argued – because of the demand for child labour, how far their mortality declined because they were fed better or more regularly or because of environmental improvements. (Since one of the few facts we know with any certainty is that most of the fall in death rates was due to fewer infants, children and perhaps young adults dying, rather than to any real prolongation of life beyond the biblical span of three score years and ten,† such falls might entail a rise in the birth rate. For instance, if fewer women die before, say, thirty, more of them are likely to have the children

---

* For a guide to these problems, see D. V. Glass and E. Grebenik, 'World Population 1800–1950', in *Cambridge Economic History of Europe* VI, i, pp. 60–138.

† This is still so. More people survive to live out their span, but old people do not on the whole die at a greater age than in the past.

they might be expected to have between thirty and the meno-
pause.)

As usual, we cannot answer such questions with any certainty.
It seems clear that people were much more responsive to
economic factors in marrying and/or having children than has
sometimes been supposed, and that some social changes (for
instance, the decline in the practice of workers 'living in' with
their employers) must have encouraged, or even required
earlier and perhaps larger families. It is also clear that a family
economy which can be balanced only by the labour of all its
members, and forms of production which used child labour,
would also encourage population. Contemporaries certainly
thought of population as something which responded to changes
in the demand for labour, and the birth rate probably went up
between the 1740s and the 1780s, though it may not have risen
significantly after that. As for mortality, medical improvements
almost certainly played no important part in its reduction
(except maybe for smallpox inoculation) until after the middle of
the nineteenth century, so its changes must have been largely
due to economic, social or other environmental changes. But
until quite late in the nineteenth century it does not seem to
have declined dramatically. At present we cannot go much
beyond such generalities without entering a scholarly battlefield
which remains obscured by the fog of learned dispute.

What were the economic effects of these changes? More
people means more labour and cheaper labour, and it has often
been supposed that this is in itself a stimulus to economic
growth, at any rate under capitalism. As we can see in many
underdeveloped countries today, it is not. It may produce merely
distress and stagnation, perhaps catastrophe, as in Ireland and
the Scottish Highlands in the early nineteenth century (see p.
300 below). Cheap labour may actually retard industrialization.
If in eighteenth-century England a growing labour force assisted
development, as it undoubtedly did, it was because the economy
was already dynamic, not because some extraneous demographic
injection made it so. In any case population grew rapidly all over
northern Europe, but industrialization did not occur everywhere. On the other hand more people certainly means more

consumers, and it has been argued with more force that this certainly provides a stimulus both for agriculture (for they must be fed) and for manufactures.

But as we have seen, the national population grew only very gradually in the century before 1750, and its rapid rise coincided with the Industrial Revolution but did not (except here and there) precede it. If Britain had been a less developed economy, there might have been more room for sudden and large transfers of people from, say, a subsistence to a cash economy, or from domestic and artisan manufacture to industry. But, as we have seen, England was already a market economy with a large and growing manufacturing sector. The average English income probably increased substantially in the first half of the eighteenth century, thanks if anything to a stagnant population and labour shortage, so that this period is rightly described in the Vicar of Bray's song as 'pudding time'. People were better off and could buy more; what is more, they probably at this time included a smaller percentage of children (who divert the expenditure of poor parents sharply towards the purchase of necessities) and a larger proportion of young small-family adults (who have income to spare). It is quite likely that in this period many Englishmen learned to 'cultivate new wants and establish new levels of expectation',[3] and there is some evidence that around 1750 they began to prefer to take out their extra productivity in more consumer goods rather than in more leisure. Still, this increase also resembled the movement of a respectable river rather than the exhilarating leaps of a waterfall. It explains why so many English towns were rebuilt (without any technological revolution) in the rural elegance of classical architecture, but not in itself why there was an industrial revolution.

Except perhaps in three special cases: transport, food and capital goods, particularly coal.

Very substantial and expensive improvements in inland transport – by river, canal and even road – were undertaken from the early eighteenth century, in order to diminish the prohibitive cost of moving goods overland: in the middle of the century twenty miles land transport might double the cost of a ton of goods. How important these were for the development of industrialism is uncertain, but there is no doubt that the impetus for them came from the home market, and more especially from the growing demand of the cities for food and fuel. The landlocked manufacturers of household goods in the west Midlands (potters in Staffordshire, makers of various metal goods in the Birmingham region) also pressed for cheaper transport. The difference in transport costs was so dramatic that major investments were patently worth while. Canals cut the cost per ton between Liverpool and Manchester or Birmingham by eighty per cent.

Food industries compete with textiles as the pace-setters of private-enterprise industrialization, because a vast market for both exists visibly and (at least in the cities) at all times, merely awaiting exploitation. The least imaginative businessman can realize that everybody, however poor eats, drinks and wears clothes. The demand for manufactured food and drink is admittedly more limited than that for textiles, except for such products as flour and alcoholic drinks, which are domestically manufactured only in rather primitive economies, but on the other hand food products are much more immune to foreign competition than textiles. Their industrialization therefore tends to play a rather more important part in undeveloped than in advanced countries. Still, flour-milling and beer-brewing were important pioneers of technological revolution even in Britain, though they attract less attention than textiles, because they do not so much transform the surrounding economy as appear, like giant monuments of modernity, within it, as the Guinness brewery did in Dublin and the celebrated Albion steam mills (which so impressed the poet William Blake) in London. The larger the city (and London was by far the greatest in Western Europe), and the more rapid the urbanization, the greater the scope for such developments. Was not the invention of the beer-handle, known to every drinker in Britain, one of the first triumphs of Henry Maudslay, one of the great pioneers of engineering?

The home market also provided a major outlet for what later became capital goods. *Coal* grew almost entirely with the number of urban – and especially metropolitan – fire-places; iron – to a much smaller extent – reflected the demand for domestic pots, pans, nails, stoves and the like. Since the quantities of coal burned in British homes were very much greater than their needs of iron (thanks in part to the unusual inefficiency of the British fireplace compared to the continental stove), the pre-industrial base of the coal industry was much sounder than that of the iron industry. Even before the Industrial Revolution its output could already be measured in millions of tons, the first commodity to which such astronomic criteria were applicable. And steam-engines were the product of the mines: in 1769 a hundred 'atmospheric engines' had already been erected round Newcastle-on-Tyne, and fifty-seven were actually at work. (However, the more modern engines of James Watt's type, which were really the foundation of industrial technology, made their way only slowly in the mines.)

On the other hand the total British consumption of iron in 1720 was less than 50,000 tons, and even in 1788, after the Industrial Revolution was well under way, it cannot have been much more than 100,000 tons. The demand for steel was negligible at the then price of this metal. The greatest civilian market for iron was probably still agricultural – ploughs and other implements, horse-shoes, wheel-rims, and so on – which increased substantially, but was hardly large enough yet to start an industrial transformation. In fact, as we shall see, the real Industrial Revolution in iron and coal had to wait until the era of the railway provided a mass market not only for consumer goods but for capital goods. The pre-industrial domestic market, and even the first phase of industrialization, did not yet do so on a sufficient scale.

The main advantage of the pre-industrial home market was therefore its great size and steadiness. It may not have promoted much in the way of industrial revolution, but it undoubtedly promoted economic growth, and what is more, it was always available to cushion the more dynamic export industries against the sudden fluctuations and collapses which were the price they paid for their superior dynamism. It came to their rescue in the 1780s, when war and the American Revolution disrupted them, and probably again after the Napoleonic Wars. But more than this, it provided the broad foundations for a *generalized* industrial economy. If England thought tomorrow what Manchester thought today, it was because the rest of the country was prepared to take its lead from Lancashire. Unlike Shanghai in pre-communist China, or Ahmedabad in colonial India, Manchester did not remain a modern enclave in the general backwardness, but became the model for the rest of the country. The domestic market may not have provided the spark, but it provided fuel and sufficient draught to keep it burning.

Export industries worked in very different, and potentially much more revolutionary conditions. They fluctuated wildly – up to fifty per cent in a single year – so that the manufacturer who could leap in fast enough to catch the expansions could make a killing. In the long run they also expanded much more, and more rapidly, than home markets. Between 1700 and 1750 home industries increased their output by seven per cent, export industries by seventy-six per cent; between 1750 and 1770 (which we may regard as the runway for the industrial 'take-off') by another seven per cent and eighty per cent respectively. Home demand increased – but foreign demand multiplied. If a spark was needed, this is where it came from. Cotton manufacture, the first to be industrialized, was essentially tied to overseas trade. Every ounce of its raw material had to be imported from the sub-tropics or tropics, and, as we shall see, its products were to be overwhelmingly sold abroad. From the end of the eighteenth century it was already an industry which exported the greater part of its total output – perhaps two thirds by 1805.

The reason for this extraordinary potential of expansion was that export industries did not depend on the modest 'natural' rate of growth of any country's internal demand. They could create the illusion of rapid growth by two major means: capturing a series of other countries' export markets, and destroying domestic competition within particular countries, that is by the political or semi-political means of war and colonization. The country which succeeded in concentrating other people's export markets, or even in monopolizing the export markets of a large part of the world in a sufficiently brief period of time, could expand its export industries at a rate which made industrial revolution not only practicable for its entrepreneurs, but some-

MARX

times virtually compulsory. And this is what Britain succeeded 米
in doing in the eighteenth century.*

Yet conquering markets by war and colonization required not
merely an economy capable of exploiting those markets, but also
a government willing to wage war and colonize for the benefit of
British manufacturers. This brings us to the third factor in the
genesis of the Industrial Revolution, *government*. Here the
advantage of Britain over her potential competitors is quite
evident. Unlike some of them (such as France) she was prepared
to subordinate *all* foreign policy to economic ends. Her war aims
were commercial and (what amounted to much the same thing)
naval. The great Chatham gave five reasons in his memorandum
advocating the conquest of Canada: the first four were purely
economic. Unlike others (such as the Dutch), her economic
aims were not completely dominated by commercial and
financial interests, but shaped also, and increasingly, by the
pressure group of manufacturers; originally the fiscally important
woollen industry, later the rest. This tussle between industry
and commerce (represented most dramatically by the East India
Company) was decided in the home market by 1700, when
British producers won protection against Indian textile imports;
it was not won in the foreign market until 1813, when the East
India Company was deprived of its monopoly in India, and that
sub-continent opened to deindustrialization and the massive
import of Lancashire cottons. Lastly, unlike all its other rivals,
British policy in the eighteenth century was one of systematic
aggressiveness – most obviously against the chief rival, France.
Of the five great wars of the period, Britain was clearly on the
defensive in only one.† The result of this century of intermittent warfare was the greatest triumph ever achieved by any

*It follows that if one country did this others would be unlikely to
develop the basis for industrial revolution. In other words, under pre-
industrial conditions there was probably room for only one pioneer national
industrialization (as it turned out the British), but not the simultaneous
industrialization of several 'advanced economies', consequently also – at
least for some time – for only one 'workshop of the world'.

†The Spanish Succession (1702–13), the Austrian Succession (1739–48),
the Seven Years' War (1756–63), the War of American Independence
(1776–83) and the Revolutionary and Napoleonic Wars (1793–1815).

state: the virtual monopoly among European powers of overseas colonies, and the virtual monopoly of world-wide naval power. Moreover, war itself – by crippling Britain's major competitors in Europe – tended to boost exports; peace, if anything, tended to slow them up.

Furthermore, war – and especially that very commercially-minded and middle-class organization, the British Navy – contributed even more directly to technological innovation and industrialization. Its demands were not negligible: the tonnage of the Navy multiplied from about 100,000 in 1685 to about 325,000 in 1760, and its demand for guns grew substantially, though in a less dramatic manner. War was pretty certainly the greatest consumer of iron, and firms like Wilkinson, the Walkers, and the Carron Works owed the size of their undertakings partly to government contracts for cannon, while the South Wales iron industry depended on battle. More generally, government contracts, or those of vast quasi-government bodies like the East India Company, came in large blocks and had to be filled on time. It was worth a businessman's while to introduce revolutionary methods to supply them. Time and again we find some inventor or entrepreneur stimulated by so lucrative a prospect. Henry Cort, who revolutionized iron manufacture, began in the 1760s as a Navy agent, anxious to improve the quality of the British product 'in connexion with the supply of iron to the navy'.[4] Henry Maudslay, the pioneer of machine-tools, began his career in the Woolwich Arsenal and his fortunes (like those of the great engineer Mark Isambard Brunel, formerly of the French navy) remained closely bound up with naval contracts.*

If we are to sum up the role of the three main sectors of demand in the genesis of industrialism, we can therefore do so as follows. Exports, backed by the systematic and aggressive help of government, provided the spark, and – with cotton textiles – the 'leading sector' of industry. They also provided major improvements in sea transport. The home market provided the broad base for a generalized industrial economy and

---

*The pioneering role of the government's own establishments must not be forgotten. During the Napoleonic Wars they anticipated, among other things, conveyor belts and the canning industry.

(through the process of urbanization) the incentive for major improvements in inland transport, a powerful base for the coal industry and for certain important technological innovations. Government provided systematic support for merchant and manufacturer, and some by no means negligible incentives for technical innovation and the development of capital goods industries.

If we finally return to our original questions – why Britain and not another country? why at the end of the eighteenth century and not before or after? – the answer cannot be so simple. By 1750, indeed, there was not much doubt that if any state was to win the race to be the first industrial power it would be Britain. The Dutch had retired to that comfortable role of old-established business, the exploitation of their vast commercial and financial apparatus, and their colonies. The French, though expanding about as fast as the British (when the British did not prevent them by war), could not regain the ground they had lost in the great era of economic depression, the seventeenth century. In absolute figures they might look – until the Industrial Revolution – like a power of equivalent size, but *per capita* their trade and manufactures were even then far behind the British.

On the other hand this does not explain why the industrial breakthrough came when it actually did – in the last third or quarter of the eighteenth century. The precise answer to this question is still uncertain, but it is clear that we can find it only by turning back to the general European or 'world' economy of which Britain was a part,* that is to the 'advanced' areas of (mainly) western Europe and their relations with the colonial and semi-colonial dependent economies, the marginal trading partners, and the regions not as yet substantially involved in the European system of economic flows.

The traditional pattern of European expansion – Mediterranean, and based on Italian merchants and their associates, Spanish and Portuguese conquerors, or Baltic, and based on

* The word must be understood to mean only that the European economy was the centre of a world-wide network, but *not* that all parts of the world were involved in this network.

German city states – had perished in the great economic depression of the seventeenth century. The new centres of expansion were the maritime states bordering the North Sea and North Atlantic. The shift was not merely geographical, but structural. The new kind of relationship between the 'advanced' areas and the rest of the world, unlike the old, tended constantly to intensify and widen the flows of commerce. The powerful, growing and accelerating current of overseas trade which swept the infant industries of Europe with it – which, in fact, sometimes actually *created* them – was hardly conceivable without this change. It rested on three things: in Europe, the rise of a market for overseas products for everyday use, whose market could be expanded as they became available in larger quantities and more cheaply; and overseas the creation of economic systems for producing such goods (such as, for instance, slave-operated plantations) and the conquest of colonies designed to serve the economic advantage of their European owners.

To illustrate the first fact: around 1650 one third of the value of East India goods sold in Amsterdam consisted of pepper – the typical commodity in which profits are made by 'cornering' a small supply and selling it at monopoly prices – by 1780 this proportion had fallen to eleven per cent. Conversely, by 1780 56 per cent of such sales consisted of textiles, tea and coffee, whereas in 1650 they had only amounted to 17·5 per cent. Sugar, tea, coffee, tobacco and similar products rather than gold and spices were now the characteristic imports from the tropics, as wheat, linen, iron, hemp and timber were those from the east of Europe, and not furs. The second fact can be illustrated by the expansion of that most inhuman traffic, the slave trade. In the sixteenth century fewer than a million Negroes were transferred from Africa to the Americas; in the seventeenth perhaps three millions – mainly in the second half, or if earlier, to the Brazilian plantations which anticipated the later colonial pattern; in the eighteenth century perhaps seven millions.* The third fact hardly requires illustration. In 1650 neither Britain nor France had much in the way of empires, and much of the old

---

*Even if, as is almost certain, these figures are exaggerated, the relative orders of magnitude are realistic.

Spanish and Portuguese empires lay in ruins, or consisted of mere outlines on a world map. The eighteenth century saw not merely a revival of the older empires (for example in Brazil and Mexico), but the expansion and exploitation of new ones – British, French, not to mention now forgotten essays by Danes, Swedes and others. What is more, the sheer size of these empires as economies increased vastly. In 1701 the future USA had fewer than 300,000 inhabitants, in 1790 almost four millions; and even Canada grew from 14,000 in 1695 to almost half a million in 1800.

And as the network of international trade grew tighter, so did the role of such overseas trade in the commerce of Europe. In 1680 the East India trade amounted to perhaps eight per cent of the total foreign commerce of the Dutch, but in the second half of the eighteenth century to something like one quarter, and the evolution of French trade was similar. The British relied on colonial trade earlier. Around 1700 it amounted already to fifteen per cent of our commerce – but by 1775 to as much as a third. The general expansion of trading in the eighteenth century was impressive enough, in almost all countries, but the expansion of trade connected with the colonial system was stupendous. To take a single example: after the war of the Spanish Succession between two and three thousand tons of British ships cleared from England every year for Africa, mainly as slavers; after the Seven Years' War between fifteen and nineteen thousand; after the American War of Independence (1787) twenty-two thousand.

This vast and growing circulation of goods did not merely bring to Europe new needs, and the stimulus to manufacture foreign imports at home. 'If Saxony and other countries of Europe make up fine China', wrote the Abbé Raynal in 1777,[5] 'if Valencia manufactures Pekins superior to those of China; if Switzerland imitates the muslins and worked calicoes of Bengal; if England and France print linens with great elegance; if so many stuffs, formerly unknown in our climates, now employ our best artists, are we not indebted to India for all these advantages?'* More than this, it provided a limitless horizon of

*Within a few years he would not have failed to mention the most successful imitator of the Indians, Manchester.

sales and profit for merchant and manufacturer. And it was the British who – by their policy and force as much as by their enterprise and inventive skill – captured these markets.

Behind our Industrial Revolution there lies this concentration on the colonial and 'underdeveloped' markets overseas, the successful battle to deny them to anyone else. We defeated them in the East: in 1766 we already outsold even the Dutch in the China trade. We defeated them in the West: by the early 1780s more than half of all slaves exported from Africa (and almost twice as many as those carried by the French) made profits for British slavers. And we did so for the benefit of *British* goods. For some three decades after the war of the Spanish Succession British ships bound for Africa still carried mainly foreign (including Indian) goods; from shortly after the War of the Austrian Succession they carried overwhelmingly British ones. Our industrial economy grew out of our commerce, and especially our commerce with the underdeveloped world. And throughout the nineteenth century it was to retain this peculiar historical pattern: commerce and shipping maintained our balance of payments, and the exchange of overseas primary products for British manufactures was to be the foundation of our international economy.

While the stream of international exchanges swelled, sometime in the second third of the eighteenth century a general quickening of the domestic economies became noticeable. This was not a specifically British phenomenon, but one which occurred very generally, and is registered in the movements of prices (which began a long period of slow inflation, after a century of fluctuating and indeterminate movement), in what little we know about population, production and in other ways. The Industrial Revolution was generated in these decades – after the 1740s, when this massive but slow growth in the domestic economies combined with the rapid – after 1750 extremely rapid – expansion of the international economy; and it occurred in the country which seized its international opportunities to corner a major share of the overseas markets.

NOTES

1. Modern discussion of industrial revolution and economic development starts with Karl Marx, *Capital*, Vol. I, Parts 3, 4, Chapters 23–4. For more recent marxist views, see M. H. Dobb, *Studies in Economic Development* (1946) and *Some Aspects of Economic Development* (Delhi, 1951), and the immensely stimulating *K. Polanyi, *Origins of Our Time* (1945). *D. S. Landes, *The Unbound Prometheus* (1969), is a fine introduction to modern academic treatment of the subject; see also Phyllis Deane, *The First Industrial Revolution* (1965) (B). For Anglo-American and Anglo-French comparisons, *H. J. Habbakuk, *American and British Technology in the 19th Century* (1962), P. Bairoch, *Révolution industrielle et sous-développement* (1963).

   For a survey of academic theories on economic development in general, several textbooks among which B. Higgins, *Economic Development* (1959). For more sociological approaches, Bert Hoselitz, *Sociological Aspects of Economic Growth* (1960), Wilbert Moore, *Industrialization and Labour* (1951), Everett Hagen, *On the Theory of Social Change* (1964) (B). See also Figures 1–3, 14, 23, 26, 28, 37.

   On Britain in the eighteenth-century world economy, F. Mauro, *L'expansion européenne 1600–1870* (La Nouvelle Clio, 1964), Ralph Davis, 'English Foreign Trade 1700–1774' (*Economic History Review*, 1962).

2. C. P. Kindleberger, *Economic Growth in France and Britain* (1964), p. 158.

3. From an unpublished paper, 'Population and Labour Supply', by H. C. Pentland.

4. Samuel Smiles, *Industrial Biography*, p. 114.

5. Abbé Raynal, *The Philosophical and Political History of the Settlements and Trade of the Europeans in the East and West Indies* (1776), Vol. II, p. 288.

3

THE INDUSTRIAL REVOLUTION
1780–1840[1]

NOT BY LANDES

WHOEVER says Industrial Revolution says cotton. When we think of it we see, like the contemporary foreign visitors to England, the new and revolutionary city of Manchester, which multiplied tenfold in size between 1760 and 1830 (from 17,000 to 180,000 inhabitants), where 'we observe hundreds of five- and six-storied factories, each with a towering chimney by its side, which exhales black coal vapour'; which proverbially thought today what England would think tomorrow, and gave its name to the school of liberal economics that dominated the world. And there can be no doubt that this perspective is right. The British Industrial Revolution was by no means *only* cotton, or Lancashire or even textiles, and cotton lost its primacy within it after a couple of generations. Yet cotton was the pace-maker of industrial change, and the basis of the first regions which could not have existed but for industrialization, and which expressed a new form of society, industrial capitalism, based on a new form of production, the 'factory'. Other towns were smoky and filled with steam-engines in 1830, though not to anything like the same extent as the cotton towns – in 1838 Manchester and Salford possessed almost three times as much steampower as Birmingham* – but they were not towns dominated by *factories* until the second half of the century, if then. Other industrial regions possessed large-scale enterprises operated by proletarian masses, and surrounded by impressive machinery, like coal-mines and iron-works, but their often isolated or rural location, the traditional background of their labour force and its different social environment made them somehow less typical of the new era, except in their capacity to transform buildings and landscapes into an unprecedented scene

---

* The respective populations of the two urban areas in 1841 were about 280 and 180 thousand.

of fire, slag and iron structures. The miners were – and have largely remained – villagers, and their ways of life and struggle were strange to the non-miners with whom they had little contact. The iron-masters might, like the Crawshays of Cyfartha, demand – and often receive – political loyalty from 'their' men which recalls the relation between squires and the farming population rather than between industrial employers and their operatives. The new world of industrialism in its most obvious form was not to be seen there, but in and around Manchester.

The cotton manufacture was a typical by-product of that accelerating current of international and especially colonial commerce without which, as we have seen, the Industrial Revolution cannot be explained. Its raw material, first used in Europe mixed with linen to produce a cheaper version of that textile ('fustian'), was almost entirely colonial. The only pure cotton industry known to Europe in the early eighteenth century was that of India, whose products ('calicoes') the Eastern trading companies sold abroad and at home, where they were bitterly opposed by the domestic manufacturers of wool, linen and silk. The English woollen industry succeeded in 1700 in banning their import altogether, thus accidentally succeeding in giving the domestic cotton manufacturers of the future something like a free run of the home market. They were as yet too backward to supply it, though the first form of the modern cotton industry, calico-printing, established itself as a partial import substitution in several European countries. Modest local manufacturers established themselves in the hinterland of the great colonial and slave-trading ports, Bristol, and even more Glasgow and Liverpool, though the new industry was finally localized near the last of these. For the home market it produced a substitute for linen or wool and silk hosiery; for the foreign market, so far as it could, a substitute for the superior Indian goods, particularly when wars or other crises temporarily disrupted the Indian supply to export markets. Until 1770 over ninety per cent of British cotton exports went to colonial markets in this way, mainly to Africa. The vast expansion of exports after 1750 gave the industry its impetus: between then and 1770 cotton exports multiplied ten times over.

Cotton thus acquired its characteristic link with the under-developed world, which it retained and strengthened through all the various fluctuations of fortune. The slave plantations of the West Indies provided its raw material until in the 1790s it acquired a new and virtually unlimited source in the slave plantations of the southern USA, which therefore became in the main a dependent economy of Lancashire. The most modern centre of production thus preserved and extended the most primitive form of exploitation. From time to time the industry had to fall back on the British domestic market, where it increasingly substituted for linen, but from the 1790s on it always exported the greater part of its output; towards the end of the nineteenth century something like ninety per cent of it. Cotton was and remained essentially an export industry. From time to time it broke into the rewarding markets of Europe and the USA, but wars and the rise of native competition put a brake on such expansion and the industry returned, time and again, to some old or new region of the undeveloped world. After the middle of the nineteenth century it found its staple outlet in India and the Far East. The British cotton industry was certainly in its time the best in the world, but it ended as it had begun by relying not on its competitive superiority but on a monopoly of the colonial and underdeveloped markets which the British Empire, the British Navy and British commercial supremacy gave it. Its days were numbered after the First World War, when the Indians, Chinese and Japanese manufactured or even exported their own cotton goods and could no longer be prevented from doing so by British political interference.

As every schoolchild knows, the technical problem which determined the nature of mechanization in the cotton industry was the imbalance between the efficiency of spinning and weaving. The spinning wheel, a much less productive device than the hand-loom (especially as speeded up by the 'flying shuttle' which was invented in the 1730s and spread in the 1760s), could not supply the weavers fast enough. Three familiar inventions tipped the balance: the 'spinning jenny' of the 1760s, which enabled one cottage spinner to spin several threads at once; the 'water frame' of 1768, which used the original idea of spinning by a combination of rollers and spindles; and the fusion of the two, the 'mule' of the 1780s,* to which steam power was soon applied. The last two innovations implied factory production. The cotton factories of the Industrial Revolution were essentially spinning-mills (and establishments for carding the cotton preparatory to spinning it).

Weaving kept pace with these innovations by a multiplication of hand-looms and manual weavers. Though a power-loom had also been invented in the 1780s, this branch of manufacture was not mechanized on any scale until after the Napoleonic Wars. Thereafter the weavers who had been attracted into the industry before were eliminated from it by the simple device of starvation, and replaced by women and children in factories. In the meantime their starvation wages delayed the mechanization of weaving. The years from 1815 to the 1840s therefore saw the spread of factory production throughout the industry, and its perfection by the introduction of 'self-acting' devices in the 1820s and other improvements. However, there was no further technical revolution. The 'mule' remained the basis of British spinning, and 'ring-spinning' (invented in the 1840s and general today) was left to the foreigners. The power-loom dominated weaving. The overwhelming world predominance which Lancashire had established by this time had begun to make it technically conservative, though not stagnant.

The technology of cotton manufacture was thus fairly simple, and so, as we shall see, was that of most of the rest of the changes which collectively made up the 'Industrial Revolution'. It required little scientific knowledge or technical skill beyond the scope of a practical mechanic of the early eighteenth century. It hardly even required steam power, for though cotton adopted the new steam engine rapidly, and to a greater extent than other industries (except mining and metallurgy), as late as 1838 one quarter of its power was still provided by water. This does not reflect either a shortage of scientific innovation or a lack of

---

* It was not the original idea of its patentee, Richard Arkwright (1732–92), an unscrupulous operator who – unlike most real inventors of the period – became very rich.

interest by the new industrialists in technical revolution. On the contrary, scientific innovation abounded, and was readily applied to practical matters by scientists who still refused to make the subsequent distinction between 'pure' and 'applied' thought. And industrialists absorbed these innovations with great speed, where necessary or advantageous, and above all, applied a rigorous rationalism to their methods of production such as is highly characteristic of a scientific age. Cotton-masters soon learned to build in a purely functional way ('often' as a foreign observer out of tune with modernity said 'at the cost of external beauty'),[2] and from 1805 lengthened the working day by illuminating their factories with gas. Yet the first experiments in gaslighting went no farther back than 1792. They immediately bleached and dyed textiles by the most recent inventions of chemistry, a science which can be said to have come of age in the 1770s and 1780s, with the Industrial Revolution. Yet the chemical industry which flourished in Scotland by 1800 on this basis went back to the suggestion, made as recently as 1786 by Berthollet to James Watt, that chlorine could be used for bleaching.

The early Industrial Revolution was technically rather primitive not because no better science and technology was available, or because men took no interest in it or could not be persuaded to use it. It was simple because, by and large, the application of simple ideas and devices, often of ideas available for centuries, often by no means expensive, could produce striking results. The novelty lay not in the innovations, but in the readiness of practical men to put their minds to using the science and technology which had long been available and within reach; and in the wide market which lay open to goods as prices and costs fell rapidly. It lay not in the flowering of individual inventive genius, but in the practical situation which turned men's thought to soluble problems.

This situation was very fortunate, for it gave the pioneer Industrial Revolution an immense, perhaps an essential, push forward. It put it within the reach of an enterprising, not particularly well-educated or subtle, not particularly wealthy body of businessmen and skilled artisans, operating in a flourishing and expanding economy whose opportunities they could easily seize. In other words, it minimized the basic requirements of skills, of capital, of large-scale business or government organization and planning, without which no industrialization can succeed. Let us consider, by way of contrast, the situation in the 'emerging' nation of today which sets about its own industrial revolution. The most elementary steps forward – say, the construction of an adequate transport system – assume a command of science and technology which is centuries removed from the skills familiar to more than a tiny fraction of the population until yesterday. The most characteristic kinds of modern production – say, the manufacture of motor-vehicles – are of a size and complexity which put them beyond the experience of most of the small class of local businessmen who may have hitherto emerged, and require a quantity of initial capital investment far beyond their independent powers of capital accumulation. Even the minor skills and habits whose existence we take for granted in developed societies, but whose absence would totally disrupt them, are scarce as rubies: literacy, a sense of punctuality and regularity, the conduct of routines. To take a simple example: it was still possible in the eighteenth century to develop a coal-mining industry by digging relatively shallow shafts and lateral galleries, putting men at the end with picks and transporting the coal back to the surface by hauling small carts manually or by ponies and raising the mineral in baskets.* It would be utterly impossible to develop oilwells in any comparable way today, at all events in competition with the giant and sophisticated international petroleum industry.

Similarly, the crucial problem of the backward country's economic development today is, more often than not, the one expressed in the phrase of the late J. V. Stalin, who had plenty of experience of it: 'Cadres decide everything.' It is a great deal easier to find the capital for the construction of a modern industry than to run it; much easier to staff a central planning

* I am not implying that this did not require a great deal of accumulated know-how, and some quite elaborate techniques, or that the British coal industry did not possess or develop more sophisticated and powerful equipment, such as the steam engine.

commission with the handful of Ph.D.s which most countries can supply, than to acquire the mass of persons with intermediate skills, technical and administrative competence and so on without whom any modern economy risks grinding into inefficiency. Successfully industrializing backward economies have also been the ones which have found ways of rapidly multiplying such cadres, and of using them in the context of a general population still lacking the skills and habits of modern industry. They have found the history of British industrialization irrelevant to their needs in this respect, simply because Britain hardly faced this problem. At no stage, for instance, did this country visibly suffer from a shortage of men competent to work metals, and as the British usage of the word 'engineer' indicates, the higher grades of technology could be readily recruited from among the men with practical workshop experience.* Britain could even manage to do without a system of state elementary education until 1870, of state secondary education until after 1902.

The British way can best be illustrated by an example. The greatest of the early cotton industrialists was Sir Robert Peel (1750–1830), a man who at his death left almost one and a half million pounds – a vast sum for those days – and a son just about to become Prime Minister of Britain. The Peels were a family of yeoman peasants of middling status who, like others in the Lancashire hills, combined farming and domestic textile production, at any rate from the mid seventeenth century. Sir Robert's father (1723–95) still hawked his goods about the countryside, moved into the town of Blackburn only in 1750, and even then had not yet quite abandoned farming. He had some – non-technical – education, some gift for simple design and invention (or at least the sense to appreciate the inventions of such men as his fellow-townsman James Hargreaves, weaver, carpenter and inventor of the 'spinning-jenny'), and perhaps £2,000–£4,000's worth in land, which he mortgaged in the early 1760s when he formed a calico-printing firm with his brother-in-law Haworth and one Yates, who brought into it the

* It stands both for the skilled metal-worker and the specialized higher technologist, such as the 'civil' or 'electrical' engineer.

accumulated savings of his family's innkeeping business at the Black Bull. The family had experience: several members of it were in textiles, and the prospects for calico-printing, hitherto mainly a London speciality, seemed excellent. They were. Three years later – in the middle 1760s – its demand for cotton to print was such that the firm went into the manufacture of cloth itself; a fact which, as a local historian was to observe, 'affords proof of the facility with which money was then made'.[3] The business prospered and divided: Peel remained in Blackburn, while his two partners moved to Bury, where they were joined in partnership in 1772 by the future Sir Robert with some initial but little subsequent backing from his father.

There was little need for it. Young Peel, an entrepreneur of remarkable energy, had no difficulty in raising additional capital by taking in partners from among local men anxious to invest in the growing industry, or merely useful in establishing the firm in new towns and branches of activity. Since the printing side of the firm alone was to make steady profits of £70,000 a year for long periods, there was no capital shortage. By the middle 1780s it was a very substantial business indeed, easily capable of adopting any useful and profitable new devices that were available, such as steam engines. By 1790 – at the age of forty and a mere eighteen years after entering business himself – Robert Peel was a baronet, a member of Parliament and the acknowledged representative of a new class, the industrialists.[*] He differed from other hard-headed Lancashire entrepreneurs of his kind, including several of his partners, chiefly in not retiring into a comfortable affluence – which he might easily have done by the middle 1780s – but rising to even dizzier heights as a captain of industry. Given a modest base of business acumen and energy, any member of the Lancashire rural

[*] 'He was a favourable specimen of a class of men, who, availing themselves in Lancashire of the discoveries of other heads and of their own, and profiting by the peculiar local facilities for making and printing cotton goods as well as the wants and demands, which, half a century and more ago, manifested themselves for the articles manufactured, succeeded in realizing great opulence, without possessing either refinement of manners, culture of intellect, or more than commonplace knowledge.' P. A. Whittle, *Blackburn As It Is* (Preston, 1852), p. 262.

middle class going into the cotton business when Peel did could hardly have helped making a very great deal of money very quickly. It is perhaps characteristic of the essentially simple approach to the business that for many years after the firm began printing calicoes it contained no 'drawing shop', that is it made only the most primitive provision for designing the patterns on which its fortunes were based. The truth was that at this stage practically anything sold, especially to the unsophisticated customer at home and abroad.

A new industrial system based on a new technology thus emerged with remarkable speed and ease among the rainy farms and villages of Lancashire. But it emerged, as we have seen, by a combination of the novel and the old-established. The new prevailed over the old. Capital accumulated within industry replaced the mortgages of farms and the savings of innkeepers, engineers the inventive weavers-cum-carpenters, power-looms the hand-weavers, and a factory proletariat the combination of a few mechanized establishments with a mass of dependent domestic workers. In the decades which followed the Napoleonic Wars the old elements in the new industrialism gradually receded, and modern industry, from being the achievement of a pioneering minority, became the norm of Lancashire life. The number of power-looms in England rose from 2,400 in 1813 to 55,000 in 1829, 85,000 in 1833 and 224,000 in 1850, while the number of hand-loom weavers, still rising to a maximum of about a quarter of a million in the 1820s, fell to just over 100,000 by the early 1840s, to little more than 50,000 starving wretches by the middle 1850s. Yet it is unwise to neglect the relative primitiveness of even this second phase of the transformation and the heritage of archaism it left behind.

Two consequences of it may be mentioned. The first is the extremely decentralized and disintegrated business structure of the cotton industry, as indeed of most other British nineteenth-century industries, the product of its emergence from the unplanned activities of small men. It emerged as, and it largely remained, a complex of highly specialized firms of medium size (often highly localized) – merchants of various kinds, spinners, weavers, dyers, finishers, bleachers, printers, and so on, often specialized even within their branches, linked with each other by a complex web of individual business transactions in 'the market'. Such a form of business structure has the advantage of flexibility and lends itself readily to rapid initial expansion, but at later stages of industrial development, when the technical and economic advantages of planning and integration are far greater, develops considerable rigidities and inefficiencies. The second consequence was the development of a strong trade-union movement in an industry normally characterized by extremely weak or unstable labour organization, because it was working with a labour force consisting largely of women and children, unskilled immigrants, and so on. The Lancashire cotton industry's unions were based on a minority of skilled male mule spinners, who were not, or could not be, dislodged from their strong bargaining position by more advanced stages of mechanization – attempts to do so in the 1830s failed – and who eventually succeeded in organizing the unskilled majority which surrounded them in subordinate unions largely because it was composed of their wives and children. Cotton thus developed as a factory industry organized by something like the methods of craft unionism, and these methods succeeded because in its crucial phase of development it was a very archaic kind of factory industry.

Nevertheless it was, by the standards of the eighteenth century, revolutionary. When all allowances for its transitional characteristics and continued archaism have been made, that fact must never be forgotten. It represented a new economic relationship between men, a new system of production, a new rhythm of life, a new society, a new historical era, and contemporaries were aware of it almost from the start:

As in a sudden flood, medieval constitutions and limitations upon industry disappeared, and statesmen marvelled at the grandiose phenomenon which they could neither grasp nor follow. The machine obediently served the spirit of man. Yet as machinery dwarfed human strength, capital triumphed over labour and created a new form of serfdom. . . . Mechanization and the incredibly elaborate division of labour diminish the strength and intelligence which is required among the masses, and competition depresses their wages to the minimum of a bare subsistence. In times of those crises of glutted markets, which occur at periods of diminishing length, wages fall below this subsistence minimum. Often work ceases altogether for some time . . . and a mass of miserable humanity is exposed to hunger and all the tortures of want.[4]

The words – curiously similar to those of social revolutionaries like Frederick Engels – are those of a German liberal businessman writing in the early 1840s. But even a generation earlier another industrialist – Robert Owen, himself a cotton-master – had underlined the revolutionary character of the change in his *Observations on the Effect of the Manufacturing System* (1815):

The general diffusion of manufactures throughout a country generates a new character in its inhabitants; and as this character is formed upon a principle quite unfavourable to the individual or general happiness, it will produce the most lamentable and permanent evils, unless its tendency is counteracted by legislative interference and direction. The manufacturing system has already so far extended its influence over the British Empire as to effect an essential change in the general character of the mass of the people.

The new system which contemporaries saw exemplified above all in Lancashire, consisted, so it seemed to them, of three elements. The first was the division of the industrial population into capitalist employers and workers who owned nothing but their power to labour, which they sold for wages. The second was production in the 'factory', a combination of specialized machines with specialized human labour, or, as its early theorist Dr Andrew Ure called it, 'a vast automaton composed of various mechanical and intellectual organs, acting in uninterrupted concert . . . all of them being subordinate to a self-regulating moving force'.[5] The third was the domination of the entire economy – indeed of all life – by the capitalists' pursuit and accumulation of profit. Some of them – those who saw nothing fundamentally wrong with the new system – did not care to distinguish between its social and its technical aspects. Others – those who were pressed into the new system against their will and got nothing from it but pauperization, like that third of the population of Blackburn in 1833 which lived on a *family* income of 9s. 2d. a week (or an average sum of about

1s. 8d. per person)* – were tempted to reject both altogether. A third group – Robert Owen was its first major spokesman – separated industrialism from capitalism. It accepted the
Industrial Revolution and technical progress as the bringers of
potential knowledge and plenty for all. It rejected its capitalist
form as the bringer of actual exploitation and pauperism.

It is, as usual, easy to criticize the contemporary view in
detail, because the structure of industrialism was by no means
as 'modern' as it suggests even on the eve of the railway era,
let alone in the year of Waterloo. Neither the 'capitalist employer' nor the 'proletarian' were at all common in the pure
state. There were plenty in 'the middle rank of society' (it
only came to call itself a middle class in the course of the first
third of the nineteenth century) ready to make profits, but only
a minority ready to apply to profit-making the full, ruthless
logic of technical progress and the commandment to 'buy in the
cheapest market and sell in the dearest'. There were plenty of
men and women who lived only by wage-work, though a great
many who were still degenerate versions of formerly independent craftsmen, smallholders seeking spare-time employment,
part-time petty entrepreneurs and so on. But there were few
genuine factory operatives. Between 1778 and 1830, time and
again there were revolts against the extension of machinery.
That these revolts were often supported and sometimes actually
instigated by local businessmen and farmers shows how limited
the 'modern' sector of the economy still was, for those within it
tended to accept, if not to welcome, the machine. It was those not
yet within it who tried to hold it up. That, on the whole, they
failed shows on the other hand that the 'modern' sector had
become dominant in the economy.

Again, we have had to wait for the technology of the mid
twentieth century to make possible the semi-automation or
automation in factory production which the 'steam intellect'

---

* 'A singular estimate was taken in 1833, respecting the income of
families, which is as follows: the total income of 1,778 families (all working
people) in Blackburn, comprising 9,779 individuals, amounted to only
£828 19s. 7d.' P. A. Whittle, *Blackburn As It Is* (Preston, 1852), p. 223.
See also Chapter 4 below.

philosophers of the first half of the nineteenth century anticipated with so much satisfaction, and which they discerned in the very imperfect and archaic cotton-mills of their time. Before the coming of the railways there was probably no enterprise except perhaps the occasional gasworks or chemical plant which a modern production engineer would regard as having anything but archaeological interest. Yet the fact that the cotton-mills inspired such visions of working men narrowed and dehumanized into 'operatives' or 'hands' before being dispensed with altogether by completely 'self-acting' (automated) machinery is equally significant. The 'factory' with its logical flow of processes, each a specialized machine tended by a specialized 'hand', all linked together by the inhuman and constant pace of the 'engine' and the discipline of mechanization, gas-lit, iron-ribbed and smoking, *was* a revolutionary form of work. Though factory wages tended to be higher than those in domestic industries (other than those of highly skilled and versatile manual workers), workers were reluctant to enter them, because in doing so men lost their birthright, independence. Indeed this is one reason why they were filled, where possible with the more tractable women and children: in 1838 only twenty-three per cent of textile factory workers were adult men.

*

No other industry could compare in importance with cotton in this first phase of British industrialization. Its share of the national income was perhaps not impressive in quantity – perhaps seven or eight per cent towards the end of the Napoleonic Wars – though it was larger than that of other industries. But it began to expand earlier and continued to grow faster than the rest, and in a sense its pace measured that of the economy.*

*Rate of growth of UK industrial production (percentage increase per decade)

1800s to 1810s	22·9	1850s to 1860s	27·8
1810s to 1820s	38·6	1860s to 1870s	33·2
1820s to 1830s	47·2	1870s to 1880s	20·8
1830s to 1840s	37·4	1880s to 1890s	17·4
1840s to 1850s	39·3	1890s to 1900s	17·9

The drop in the 1850s–60s is due in large part to the 'Cotton Famine' which resulted from the American Civil War.

When cotton expanded at the remarkable rate of six to seven per cent per annum, in the twenty-five years following Waterloo, British industrial expansion was at its height. When cotton ceased to expand – as in the last quarter of the nineteenth century, when its rate of growth sank to 0·7 per cent per annum – all British industry sagged. Even more unique was its contribution to Britain's international economy. Broadly speaking, in the post-Napoleonic decades something like *one half* of the value of *all* British exports consisted of cotton products, and at their peak (in the middle of the 1830s) raw cotton made up twenty per cent of total net imports. In a real sense the British balance of payments depended on the fortunes of this single industry, and so did much of Britain's shipping and overseas trade in general. Thirdly, it almost certainly contributed more to the accumulation of capital than other industries, if only because rapid mechanization and the massive use of cheap (women's and juveniles') labour permitted a very successful diversion of incomes from labour to capital. In the twenty-five years following 1820 the net output of the industry grew by about forty per cent (in current values), its wage bill by only about five per cent.

That it stimulated industrialization and technical revolution in general need hardly be pointed out. Both the chemical industry and the engineering industry owed much to it: by 1830 only the Londoners contested the superiority of the Lancashire machine-makers. Yet in this respect, it was not unique, and it lacked the *direct* capacity to stimulate what, as analysts of industrialization, we know needed stimulation most, namely the heavy capital goods industries of coal, iron and steel, for which it provided no outstandingly great market. Fortunately the general process of urbanization provided a substantial stimulus for *coal* in the early nineteenth century as in the eighteenth. As late as 1842 the smoky fireplaces of British homes still consumed two thirds of Britain's domestic coal supplies, which then stood at about thirty million tons, or perhaps two thirds of the entire output of the Western world. The actual production of coal remained primitive. A squatting man hacking with a pick in an underground passage was its foundation. But the sheer bulk of coal output forced mining to pioneer technical change – to pump the increasingly deeper mines and above all to transport the mineral from the coal face to pithead and thence to ports and markets. Mining thus pioneered the steam engine long before James Watt, employed its improved versions for winding gear from the 1790s, and above all invented and developed the *railway*. It was no accident that the constructors, engineers and drivers of the early railways so often came from Tyneside: beginning with George Stephenson. The steam ship, however, whose development pre-dated the railway, though its general use came later, owed nothing to the mines.

Iron faced greater difficulties. Before the Industrial Revolution Britain produced it neither in large quantity nor in outstanding quality, and even in the 1780s the total demand for it would hardly have exceeded 100,000 tons.* War in general and the Navy in particular gave the iron industry constant encouragement and an intermittent market; fuel economy gave it a permanent incentive to technical improvement. For these reasons – until the railway age – the industry's iron capacity tended to run ahead of the market, and its rapid spurts were followed by dragging depressions which the iron-masters sought to solve by a desperate search for new uses for their metal, and to palliate by price-cartels and cuts in output (steel remained virtually unaffected by the Industrial Revolution). Three major innovations raised its capacity: the smelting of iron with coke (instead of charcoal), the inventions of puddling and rolling, both of which came into wider use in the 1780s, and James Neilson's 'hot blast' after 1829. They also shifted the location of the industry firmly to the coalfields. After the Napoleonic Wars, when industrialization began to develop in other countries, iron acquired an important export market: between fifteen and twenty per cent of output could already be sold abroad. British industrialization produced a miscellaneous domestic demand for the metal, not only for machines and tools, but also for bridges, pipes, building material and domestic utensils, but even so total output

*But British per capita consumption was far higher than that of other comparable countries; for example it was about three and a half times as large as French consumption in 1720–40.

remained much below what we would today consider necessary for an industrial economy, especially if we bear in mind that non-ferrous metals were then of rather small importance. It probably never reached half a million tons before the 1820s, and barely 700,000 tons at its pre-railway peak in 1828.

Iron stimulated not only all iron-consuming industries but also coal (of which it consumed about one quarter in 1842), the steam engine, and – for the same reasons as coal – transport. Nevertheless, like coal, it did not undergo its real industrial revolution until the middle decades of the nineteenth century, or about fifty years later than cotton; for while consumer goods industries possess a mass market even in pre-industrial economies, capital goods industries acquire such a market only in already industrializing or industrialized ones. It was the age of the railway which trebled the production of coal and iron in twenty years and virtually created a steel industry.*

There was obvious and striking economic growth and some industrial transformation elsewhere, but hardly as yet an industrial *revolution*. A large number of industries – such as those producing clothing (except hosiery), footwear, building and household furniture – continued to work in entirely traditional ways, except for the use of novel materials here and there. At most they tried to meet the vastly expanded demand by the extension of something like the 'domestic system', which turned independent artisans into impoverished and increasingly specialized sweated labour in urban cellars and garret workshops. Industrialism produced not furniture and clothing factories, but skilled and organized cabinet-makers declining into slum-workers, and those armies of starving and turberculous seamstresses and shirtmakers which touched the hearts of middle-class opinion even in that extremely insensitive era.

Other industries applied some elementary mechanization and power – including steam power – to the small workshop, notably in the multitude of metal-using industries so characteristic of Sheffield and the Midlands, but without changing the character

*Output (in thousand tons)

Year	coal	iron
1830	16,000	600
1850	49,000	2,000

of their craft, or domestic production. Some of these complexes of small interlocking workshops were urban, as in Sheffield and Birmingham, some rural, as in the lost villages of the 'Black Country'; some of their workers were skilled, organized, almost guild-proud journeymen craftsmen (like the cutlery trades in Sheffield);* others increasingly degenerated into barbarized and murderous villages of men and women hammering out nails, chains and other simple metal goods. (In Dudley, Worcestershire, the average expectation of life at birth in 1841–50 was eighteen and a half years.) Yet others, like the pottery trades, developed something closer to a primitive factory system, or rather comparatively large-scale establishments based on an elaborate internal division of labour. On the whole, however, except for cotton, and the large-scale establishments characteristic of iron and coal, the development of production in mechanized factories, or in analogous establishments, had to wait until the second half of the nineteenth century, and the average size of plant or enterprise was small. Even in 1851, 1,670 cotton-masters included a considerably greater number of establishments employing a hundred or more men than the total put together of all the 41,000 tailors, shoemakers, engine- and machine-makers, builders, wheelwrights, tanners, woollen and worsted manufacturers, silk manufacturers, millers, lace manufacturers and earthenware manufacturers who reported the size of their establishments to the Census.

Yet an industrialization thus limited, and based essentially on one sector of the textile industry, was neither stable nor secure. We, who see the period from the 1780s to the 1840s in the light of later developments, see it simply as the initial phase of industrial capitalism. But might it not also be its final phase? The question seems absurd, because it so obviously was not. This is to underestimate the instability and tension of this initial phase – particularly of the three decades after Waterloo – and the malaise of both the economy and those who thought seriously about its prospects. Early industrial Britain passed through a crisis which reached its stage of greatest acuteness in the 1830s

* They were actually described as 'guild-organized' by a German visitor, who fancied that he recognized a familiar continental phenomenon there.

and early 1840s. That it was not in any sense a 'final' crisis, but merely one of growth, should not lead us to underestimate its seriousness, as economic (but not social) historians have persistently inclined to do.[6]

The most obvious evidence for this crisis is the high wind of social discontent which blew across Britain in successive gusts between the last years of the wars and the middle 1840s: Luddite and Radical, trade unionist and utopian-socialist, Democratic and Chartist. At no other period in modern British history have the common people been so persistently, profoundly, and often desperately dissatisfied. At no other period since the seventeenth century can we speak of large masses of them as revolutionary, or discern at least one moment of political crisis (between 1830 and the Reform Act of 1832) when something like a revolutionary situation might actually have developed. Some historians have tried to explain this discontent away, by arguing that the workers' conditions of life (except for a depressed minority) were merely improving less fast than the golden prospects which industrialism had led them to anticipate. But the 'revolution of rising expectations' is more familiar in books than in reality. We have yet to see many examples of peoples ready to mount the barricades because they have not yet been able to advance from owning bicycles to automobiles (though they are more likely to be militant if, once used to bicycles, they become too impoverished to afford them). Others have argued, more convincingly, that discontent arose simply out of the difficulties of adapting to a new type of society. But even these – as the records of migration to the USA should make clear – require an unusual amount of economic hardship to make men feel that they are gaining nothing in exchange for what they give up. Such discontent as was endemic in Britain in these decades cannot exist without hopelessness and hunger. There was enough of both.

The poverty of the British was in itself an important factor in the economic difficulties of capitalism, for it placed narrow limits upon the size and expansion of the home market for British products. This is obvious when we contrast the sharply rising per capita consumption of some goods of general use after the 1840s (during the 'golden years' of the Victorians) with the stagnation in their consumption earlier. Thus the average Briton between 1815 and 1844 consumed less than 20 lb. of sugar per year – in the 1830s and early forties nearer 16–17 lb.; but in the ten years after 1844 his consumption rose to 34 lb. a year; in the thirty years after 1844 to 53 lb., and by the 1890s he used between 80 and 90 lb. However, neither the economic theory not the economic practice of the early Industrial Revolution relied on the purchasing power of the labouring population, whose wages, it was generally assumed, would not be far removed from the subsistence level. When by any chance some section of them earned enough to spend their money on the same sorts of goods as their 'betters' (as happened from time to time during economic booms), middle-class opinion deplored or ridiculed such presumptuous lack of thrift. The economic advantages of high wages, whether as incentives to higher productivity or as additions to purchasing-power, were not discovered until after the middle of the century, and then only by a minority of advanced and enlightened employers like the railway contractor Thomas Brassey. It was not until 1869 that John Stuart Mill, the guardian of economic orthodoxy, abandoned the theory of the 'Wages Fund', that is of what amounted to a subsistence theory of wages.*

Conversely, both economic theory and economic practice stressed the crucial importance of capital accumulation by the capitalists, that is of the maximum rate of profit and the maximum diversion of income from the (non-accumulating) workers to the employers. Profits were what made the economy work and expand by reinvestment. They must therefore be expanded at all costs.† This view rested on two assumptions: that industrial progress required heavy investment and that insufficient savings were available for it without holding down the incomes of the

---

*Some economists, however, showed signs of dissatisfaction with this theory from at least the 1830s.

†How far they did expand as a share of the national income it is impossible to say in this period, but there is a little evidence for a fall in the share of wages in the national income between 1811 and 1842, and this at a time when the wage-earning population was increasing very rapidly as a proportion of the total population. However, the question is difficult and the material on which to base an answer entirely inadequate.

non-capitalist masses. The first of these was truer in the long run than in the short. The early phases of the Industrial Revolution (say 1780–1815) were, as we have seen, limited and relatively cheap. Gross capital formation may have amounted to no more than seven per cent of the national income by the early nineteenth century, which is below the rate of ten per cent which some economists have taken as essential for industrialization today, and far below the rates of up to thirty per cent which have been encountered in rapid industrializations of emerging, or the modernization of advanced, countries. Not until the 1830s and 1840s did gross capital formation in Britain pass the ten per cent threshold, and by then the age of (cheap) industrialization based on such things as textiles was giving way to the age of railways, coal, iron and steel. The second assumption that wages must be kept low was altogether wrong, but had some plausibility initially, because the wealthiest classes and greatest potential investors in this period – the great landlords, mercantile and financial interests – did not invest to any substantial extent in the new industries. Cotton-masters and other budding industrialists were therefore left to scrape together a little initial capital and expand it by ploughing back their profits, not because there was an absolute capital shortage, but simply because they had little access to the big money. By the 1830s, once again, there was no capital shortage anywhere.*

Two things therefore worried the early-nineteenth-century businessmen and economists: the rate of their profits and the rate of expansion of their markets. Both gave cause for concern, though we are today inclined to pay more attention to the second than the first. With industrialization, production multiplied and the prices of the finished goods fell dramatically. (Given the acute competition between small and medium-sized producers, they could rarely be kept up artificially by cartels or similar arrangements to fix prices or restrict output.) The costs of

* In Scotland, however, there was probably such a general shortage. This is why the Scottish banking system developed joint-stock organization and participation in industry far ahead of the English, for a poor country requires some mechanism for concentrating the many driblets of savings into a reservoir accessible to large-scale productive investment, whereas a rich country can rely on the numerous local springs and rivers to supply it.

production did not, and mostly could not, be reduced at the same rate. When the general economic climate changed from one of long-term inflation of prices to one of deflation after the end of the wars, the pressure on profit-margins increased, for under inflation profits enjoy an extra boost* and under deflation a slight lag. Cotton was acutely aware of this compression of its profit-rate:

COST AND SELLING PRICE OF I LB. OF SPUN COTTON [7]

Year	Raw materials	Selling cost	Margin for other costs and profits
1784	2s.	10s. 11d.	8s. 11d.
1812	1s. 6d.	2s. 6d.	1s.
1832	7½d.	11¼d.	3¾d.

Of course a hundred times 4d. amounted to more money than a single nine shillings, but what if the rate of profit fell to zero, thus bringing the vehicle of economic expansion to a stop through the failure of its engine and creating that 'stationary state' which the economists dreaded?

Given a rapid expansion of markets, the prospect strikes us as unreal, as indeed it increasingly (perhaps from the 1830s) did the economists. But markets were not expanding fast enough to absorb production at the rate of growth to which the economy had got used. At home, as we can see, they were sluggish, and probably became even more sluggish in the hungry thirties and early forties. Abroad the developing countries were unwilling to import British textiles (and British protectionism made them even less willing), and the undeveloped ones, on which the cotton industry relied, were simply not big enough, or did not expand fast enough as markets to absorb British output. In the post-Napoleonic decades the figures of the balance of payments show us the extraordinary spectacle of the only industrial economy in the world and the only serious exporter of manufactured goods unable to maintain an export surplus in its commodity trade (see Chapter 7). After 1826, indeed, the country

* Since wages tend to lag behind prices, and in any case the price-level when goods were sold tended to be higher than it had been earlier, when they were produced.

had a deficit not only on trade but also on its services (shipping, insurance commissions, profits on foreign trade and services, and so on).*

No period of British history has been as tense, as politically and socially disturbed, as the 1830s and early 1840s, when both the working class and the middle class, separately or in conjunction, demanded what they regarded as fundamental changes. From 1829 to 1832 their discontents fused in the demand for Parliamentary Reform, behind which the masses threw their riots and demonstrations, the businessmen the power of economic boycott. After 1832, when several of the demands of the middle-class radicals were met, the workers' movement fought and failed alone. From the crisis of 1837 on, middle-class agitation revived under the banner of the Anti-Corn-Law League, that of the labouring masses broadened out into the giant movement for the People's Charter, though the two now ran independently of and in opposition to each other. Yet both in their rival ways were prepared for extremes, especially during that worst of nineteenth-century depressions, 1841-2: Chartism for a general strike, the middle-class extremists for a national lock-out which would, by flooding the streets with starving labourers, force the government into action. Much of this tension of the period from 1829 to 1846 was due to this combination of working classes despairing because they had not enough to eat and manufacturers despairing because they genuinely believed the prevailing political and fiscal arrangements to be slowly throttling the economy. And they had cause for alarm. In the 1830s even the crudest accountants' criterion of economic progress, real income per head (which must not be confused with the average standard of living), was actually – and for the first time since 1700 – falling. If nothing was done, would not the capitalist economy break down? And might not, as observers increasingly began to fear around 1840 all over Europe, the impoverished, disinherited masses of the labouring poor revolt? As Marx and Engels rightly pointed out, in the 1840s the spectre of communism

---

*To be more precise, this balance was slightly negative in 1826–30, positive 1831–5, and negative again in all the quinquennia from 1836 to 1855.

haunted Europe. If it was relatively less feared in Britain, the spectre of economic breakdown was equally appalling to the middle class.

NOTES

1. See Further Reading and Note 1 to Chapter 2, p. 55. *P. Mantoux, *The Industrial Revolution in the 18th Century*, is still valuable; *T. S. Ashton, *The Industrial Revolution* (1948), brief and very clear. For cotton, A. P. Wadsworth and J. L. Mann, *The Cotton Trade and Industrial Lancashire* (1931), is basic but ends in 1780. N. Smelser, *Social Change in the Industrial Revolution* (1959), is actually about cotton, but the jargon is formidable. On entrepreneurs and engineering the works of Samuel Smiles, *Lives of the Engineers, Industrial Biography*, on the factory system, Marx's *Capital* remain indispensable. A. Redford, *Labour Migration in England 1800–1850* (1926), and S. Pollard, *The Genesis of Modern Management* (1965). See also Figures 1–3, 7, 13, 15–16, 22, 27–8, 37.
2. Fabriken-Kommissarius May, 1814, quoted in J. Kuczynski, *Geschichte der Lage der Arbeiter unter dem Kapitalismus* (Berlin, 1964),Vol. 23, p.178.
3. T. Barton, *History of the Borough of Bury* (1874), p. 59.
4. F. Harkort, 'Bemerkungen über die Hindernisse der Civilisation und die Emancipation der unteren Klassen' (1844), quoted in J. Kuczynski, op. cit., Vol 9, p. 127.
5. Andrew Ure, 'The Philosophy of Manufactures' (1835), quoted in Marx, *Capital* (British 1938 edition), p. 419.
6. S. G. Checkland, *The Rise of Industrial Society in England* (1964), discusses this; see also R. C. O. Matthews, *A Study in Trade Cycle History* (1954).
7. T. Ellison, *The Cotton Trade of Great Britain* (1886), p. 61.

4

THE HUMAN RESULTS OF THE INDUSTRIAL REVOLUTION
1750–1850[1]

ARITHMETIC was the fundamental tool of the Industrial Revolution. Its makers saw it as a series of sums of addition and subtraction: the difference in cost between buying in the cheapest market and selling in the dearest, between cost of production and sale price, between investment and return. For Jeremy Bentham and his followers, the most consistent champions of this type of rationality, even morals and politics came under these simple calculations. Happiness was the object of policy. Every man's pleasure could be expressed (at least in theory) as a quantity and so could his pain. Deduct the pain from the pleasure and the net result was his happiness. Add the happinesses of all men and deduct the unhappinesses, and that government which secured the greatest happiness of the greatest number was the best. The accountancy of humanity would produce its debit and credit balances, like that of business.*

The discussion of the human results of the Industrial Revolution has not entirely emancipated itself from this primitive approach. We still tend to ask ourselves: did it make people better or worse off, and if so by how much? To be more precise, we ask ourselves what quantities of purchasing power, or goods, services, and so on, that money can buy it gave to how many individuals, assuming that the woman with a washing machine will be better off than the one without (which is reasonable) but also (a) that private happiness consists in an accumulation of such things as consumer goods and (b) that public happiness consists in the greatest such accumulation by the greatest num-

---

* It is irrelevant for our purpose that the actual attempt to apply Bentham's 'felicific calculus' implies mathematical techniques greatly in advance of arithmetic, though not quite so irrelevant that it has been proved to be impossible on the Benthamite basis.

ber of individuals (which is not). Such questions are important but also misleading. Whether the Industrial Revolution gave most Britons absolutely or relatively more and better food, clothes and housing is naturally of interest to every historian. But he will miss much of its point if he forgets that it was not merely a process of addition and subtraction, but *a fundamental social change*. It transformed the lives of men beyond recognition. Or, to be more exact, in its initial stages it destroyed their old ways of living and left them free to discover or make for themselves new ones, if they could and knew how. But it rarely told them how to set about it.

There is, indeed, a relation between the Industrial Revolution as a provider of comforts and as a social transformer. Those classes whose lives were least transformed were also, normally, those which benefited most obviously in material terms (and vice versa), and their failure to grasp what was troubling the rest, or to do anything effective about it, was due not only to material but also to moral contentment. Nobody is more complacent than a well-off or successful man who is also at ease in a world which seems to have been constructed precisely with persons like him in mind.

The British aristocracy and gentry were thus very little affected by industrialization, except for the better. Their rents swelled with the demand for farm produce, the expansion of cities (whose soil they owned) and of mines, forges and railways (which were situated on their estates). And even when times were bad for agriculture, as between 1815 and the 1830s, they were unlikely to be reduced to penury. Their social predominance remained untouched, their political power in the countryside complete, and even in the nation not seriously troubled, though from the 1830s they had to consider the susceptibilities of a powerful and militant provincial middle class of businessmen. It may well be that after 1830 clouds began to appear on the pure sky of the gentlemanly life, but even they looked larger and darker than they were only because the first fifty years of industrialization had been so golden an era for the landed and titled Briton. If the eighteenth century was a glorious age for aristocracy, the era of George IV (as regent and king) was paradise. Their packs of hounds (the modern fox-hunting uniform still reflects its essentially Regency origins) criss-crossed the shires. Their pheasants, protected by spring-guns and keepers against all who had not the equivalent of £100 a year in rent, awaited the *battue*. Their Palladian and neo-classical country houses multiplied, more than at any time before or since except the Elizabethan. Since their economics, unlike their social style, were already adjusted to the business methods of the middle class, the age of steam and counting-houses posed no great problems of spiritual adjustment, unless perhaps they belonged to the backwoods of the lesser squirearchy, or their income came from the cruel caricature of a rural economy which was Ireland. They did not have to stop being feudal, for they had long ceased to be so. At most some rude and ignorant baronet from the hinterland faced the novel need to send his son to a proper school (the new 'public schools' were constructed from the 1840s to civilize them as well as the rising businessmen's offspring), or to adjust to more frequent spells of life in London.

Equally placid and prosperous were the lives of the numerous parasites of rural aristocratic society, high and low – that rural and small-town world of functionaries of and suppliers to the nobility and gentry, and the traditional, somnolent, corrupt and, as the Industrial Revolution proceeded, increasingly reactionary professions. The Church and the English universities slumbered on, cushioned by their incomes, their privileges and abuses, and their relations among the peerage, their corruption attacked with greater consistency in theory than in practice. The lawyers, and what passed for a civil service, were unreformed and unregenerate. Once again the old regime probably reached its peak in the decade after the Napoleonic Wars, after which a few waves began to form on the surface of the quiet backwaters of cathedral close, college, inns of court and the rest. From the 1830s on change came to them, though rather gently (except for the savage and contemptuous, but not notably effective, attacks upon them by outsiders, of which Charles Dickens' novels are the most familiar example). But the respectable Victorian clergy of Trollope's Barchester, though very far from the Hogarthian hunting parson/magistrates of the Regency, were the product of a carefully moderate adjustment, not of disruption. Nobody was as tender of the susceptibilities of weavers and farm-labourers as of parsons and dons, when it came to introducing them into a new world.

One important effect of this continuity – part reflection of the established power of the old upper class, part deliberate unwillingness to exacerbate political tensions among the men of money or influence – was that the rising new business classes found a firm pattern of life waiting for them. Success brought no uncertainty, so long as it was great enough to lift a man into the ranks of the upper class. He would become a 'gentleman', doubtless with a country house, perhaps eventually a knighthood or peerage, a seat in Parliament for himself or his Oxbridge-educated son, and a clear and prescribed social role. His wife would become a 'lady', instructed in her duties by a multitude of handbooks of etiquette which slid off the presses from the 1840s on. The older brand of businessman had long benefited from this process of assimilation, above all the *merchant* and financier – especially the merchant involved in overseas trade, who remained the most respected and most crucial form of entrepreneur long after the mills, factories and foundries covered the northern skies with smoke and fog. For him, too, the Industrial Revolution brought no major transformations, except perhaps in the commodities which he bought and sold. Indeed, as we have seen, it inserted itself into the powerful, world-wide and prosperous framework of trading which was the basis of British eighteenth-century power. Economically and socially their activities and status were familiar, whatever the rung on the ladder of success which they had climbed. By the Industrial Revolution the descendants of Abel Smith, banker of Nottingham, were already established in country seats, sitting in Parliament and intermarried with the gentry (though not yet, as later, with royalty). The Glyns had already moved up from a dry-salting business in Hatton Garden to a similar position, the Barings had expanded from the West Country clothing manufacture into what was soon to become a great power in international trade and finance, and their social ascent had kept step with their economic. Peerages were already achieved or round the corner. Nothing was more natural than that other types of businessmen – like Robert Peel Sen., the cotton-master – should climb the same slope of wealth and public honour, at the peak of which there beckoned government, or even (as for Peel's son and the son of Gladstone, the Liverpool merchant) the post of Prime Minister. Indeed the so-called 'Peelite' group in Parliament in the second third of the nineteenth century represented very much this group of business families assimilated into a landed oligarchy, though at odds with it when the economic interests of land and business clashed.

However, absorption into an aristocratic oligarchy is, by definition, available only for a minority – in this instance of the exceptionally rich, or those in businesses which had acquired respectability through tradition.* The great mass of men, rising from modest, though rarely from really poverty-stricken, beginnings to business affluence, the even greater mass of those pressing below them out of the labouring poor into the middle classes, were too numerous to be absorbed, and in the early stages of their progress unconcerned about absorption (though their wives might often feel less neutral in the matter). They recognized themselves increasingly – and after 1830 generally – as a 'middle class', and not merely a 'middle rank' in society. They claimed rights and power as such. Moreover – especially when, as so often, they came from non-Anglican stock, and from regions lacking a solid aristocratic traditional structure – they did not possess emotional attachments to the old regime. Such were the pillars of the Anti-Corn-Law League, rooted in the new business world of Manchester – Henry Ashworth, John Bright of Rochdale (both Quakers), Potter of the *Manchester Guardian*, the Gregs, Brotherton, the Bible Christian ex-cotton-master, George Wilson, the starch and gum manufacturer, and Cobden himself, who soon exchanged his not very brilliant career in the calico trade for the function of the fulltime ideologist.

Yet, though the Industrial Revolution fundamentally changed their – or perhaps their parents' – lives, setting them into new towns, posing them and the nation new problems, it did not

---

* As, for instance, retail trade and certain kinds of industry had not.

disorganize their lives. The simple maxims of utilitarian philosophy and liberal economics, broken down even further into the slogans of their journalists and propagandists, provided them with what guidance they needed, and if that was not enough, the traditional ethic – protestant or otherwise – of the aspiring and ambitious entrepreneur, thrift, hard work, moral puritanism, did the rest. The fortresses of aristocratic privilege, superstition and corruption, which had still to be razed to allow free enterprise to introduce its millennium, also still protected them against the sight of the uncertainties and problems which lay beyond their walls. Until the 1830s they hardly even had as yet to face the problem of what to do with more money than could be spent on a comfortable sufficiency and re-invested in an expanding business. The ideal of an individualist society, a private family unit supplying all its material and moral needs on the basis of a private business, suited them, because they were men who no longer needed traditions. Their efforts had raised them out of the rut. They were in a sense their own reward, the content of life, and if that was not enough, there was always the money, the comfortable house increasingly removed from the smoke of mill and counting-house, the devoted and modest wife, the family circle, the enjoyment of travel, art, science and literature. They were successful and respected. 'Denounce the middle classes as you may', said the Anti-Corn-Law agitator to a hostile Chartist audience, 'there is not a man among you worth a half-penny a week that is not anxious to elevate himself among them.'[2] Only the nightmare shadow of bankruptcy or debt sometimes lay over their lives, and we can still recognize it in the novels of the period: the trust in an unreliable partner, the commercial crisis, the loss of middle-class comfort, the womenfolk reduced to genteel penury, perhaps even emigration to that dustbin of the unwanted and the unsuccessful, the colonies.

The successful middle class and those who aspired to emulate them were satisfied. Not so the labouring poor – in the nature of things the majority – whose traditional world and way of life the Industrial Revolution destroyed, without automatically substituting anything else. It is this disruption which is at the heart of the question about the social effects of industrialization.

Labour in an industrial society is in many ways quite different from pre-industrial work. First, it is overwhelmingly the labour of 'proletarians', who have no source of income worth mentioning except a cash wage which they receive for their work. Pre-industrial labour, on the other hand, consists largely of families with their own peasant holdings, craft workshops, and so on, or whose wage-income supplements – or is supplemented by – some such direct access to the means of production. Moreover, the proletarian whose only link with his employer is a 'cash-nexus' must be distinguished from the 'servant' or pre-industrial dependant, who has a much more complex human and social relationship with his 'master', and one which implies duties on both sides, though very unequal ones. The Industrial Revolution replaced the servant and man by the 'operative' and 'hand', except of course the (mainly female) domestic servant, whose numbers it multiplied for the benefit of the growing middle class, for the safest way of distinguishing oneself from the labourers was to employ labour oneself.*

Second, industrial labour – and expecially mechanized factory labour – imposes a regularity, routine and monotony quite unlike pre-industrial rhythms of work, which depend on the variation of the seasons or the weather, the multiplicity of tasks in occupations unaffected by the rational division of labour, the vagaries of other human beings or animals, or even a man's own desire to play instead of working. This was so even in skilled pre-industrial wage-work, such as that of journeymen craftsmen, whose ineradicable taste for not starting the week's work until the Tuesday ('Saint Monday') was the despair of their masters. Industry brings the tyranny of the clock, the pace-setting machine, and the complex and carefully-timed interaction of processes: the measurement of life not in seasons ('Michaelmas term' or 'Lent term') or even in weeks and days, but in minutes, and above all a mechanized *regularity* of work which conflicts not only with tradition, but with all the

---

*Certain categories of workers were, however, not totally reduced to the simple cash-nexus, such as the 'railway servants' who paid the price of discipline and lack of rights for unusually good security, chances of gradual promotion, and even retirement pensions.

inclinations of a humanity as yet unconditioned into it. And since men did not take spontaneously to these new ways, they had to be forced – by work discipline and fines, by Master and Servant laws such as that of 1823 which threatened them with jail for breach of contract (but their masters only with fines), and by wages so low that only unremitting and uninterrupted toil would earn them enough money to keep alive, without providing the money which would take them away from labour for more than the time to eat, sleep and – since this was a Christian country – pray on the Sabbath.

Third, labour in the industrial age increasingly took place in the unprecedented environment of the big city; and this in spite of the fact that the most old-fashioned of industrial revolutions developed a good deal of its activities in industrialized villages of miners, weavers, nail- and chain-makers and other specialist workers. In 1750 there had been only two cities in Britain with more than 50,000 inhabitants – London and Edinburgh; in 1801 there were already eight, in 1851 twenty-nine, including nine over 100,000. By this time more Britons lived in town than in country, and almost one third of Britons lived in cities over 50,000 inhabitants. And what cities! It was not merely that smoke hung over them and filth impregnated them, that the elementary public services – water-supply, sanitation, street-cleaning, open spaces, and so on – could not keep pace with the mass migration of men into the cities, thus producing, especially after 1830, epidemics of cholera, typhoid and an appalling constant toll of the two great groups of nineteenth-century urban killers – air pollution and water pollution, or respiratory and intestinal disease. It was not merely that the new city populations, sometimes entirely unused to non-agrarian life, like the Irish, pressed into overcrowded and bleak slums, whose very sight froze the heart of the observer. 'Civilization works its miracles', wrote the great French liberal de Tocqueville of Manchester, 'and civilized man is turned back almost into a savage.'[3] Nor was it simply the steely unplanned concentration of those who built them on utility and financial profit, which Charles Dickens caught in his famous description of 'Coketown' and which built endless rows of houses and warehouses, cobbled streets and canals, but neither fountains nor public squares, promenades and trees, nor sometimes even churches. (The company which built the new railway town of Crewe graciously allowed its inhabitants to use a locomotive roundhouse for divine service now and then.) After 1848 the cities tended to acquire such public furniture, but in the first generations of industrialization they had very little of it, unless by chance they inherited traditions of gracious public building or open spaces from the past. The life of the poor man outside work was passed in the rows of cottages or tenements, the cheap improvised inns and the cheap improvised chapels which alone recorded that man is not content to live by bread alone.

But more than this: the city destroyed society. 'There is not a town in the world where the distance between the rich and the poor is so great or the barrier between them so difficult to be crossed,' wrote a clergyman about Manchester. 'There is far less *personal* communication between the master cotton spinner and his workmen, the calico printer and his blue-handed boys, between the master tailor and his apprentices, than there is between the Duke of Wellington and the humblest labourer on his estate.'⁴ The city was a volcano, to whose rumblings the rich and powerful listened with fear, and whose eruptions they dreaded. But for its poor inhabitants it was not merely a standing reminder of their exclusion from human society. It was a stony desert, which they had to make habitable by their own efforts.

Fourthly, pre-industrial experience, tradition, wisdom and morality provided no adequate guide for the kind of behaviour which a capitalist economy required. The pre-industrial labourer responded to material incentives, in so far as he wanted to earn enough to enjoy what was thought of as comfort at the social level to which it had pleased God to call him, but even his ideas of comfort were determined by the past, and limited by what was 'fitting' for one of his station, or perhaps the one immediately above his. If he earned more than the pittance he regarded as sufficient, he might – like the immigrant Irish, the despair of bourgeois rationality – take it out in leisure, in parties and alcohol. His sheer material ignorance of the best way to live in a city, or to eat industrial food (so very different from village food) might actually make his poverty worse than it 'need have been'; that is than it might have been if he had not been the sort of person he inevitably was. This conflict between the 'moral economy' of the past and the economic rationality of the capitalist present was particularly clear in the realm of social security. The traditional view, which still survived in a distorted way in all classes of rural society and in the internal relations of working-class groups, was that a man had a right to earn a living, and if unable to do so, a right to be kept alive by his community. The view of middle-class liberal economists was that men must take such jobs as the market offered, wherever and at whatever rate it offered, and that the rational man would, by individual or voluntary collective saving and insurance make provision for accident, illness and old age. The residuum of paupers could not, admittedly, be left actually to starve, but they ought not to be given more than the absolute minimum – provided it was less than the lowest wage offered in the market – and in the most discouraging conditions. The Poor Law was not so much intended to help the unfortunate as to stigmatize the self-confessed failures of society. The middle-class view of Friendly Societies was that they were rational forms of insurance. It clashed head-on with the working-class view, which also took them literally as communities of friends in a desert of individuals, who naturally spent their money also on social gatherings, festivities, and the 'useless' fancy-dress and ritual to which Oddfellows, Foresters and the other 'Orders' which sprang up all over the north in the period after 1815 were so addicted. Similarly the irrationally expensive funerals and wakes on which labourers insisted as a traditional tribute to the dead and communal reaffirmation of the living were incomprehensible to a middle class which observed that those who liked them were often unable to pay for them. Yet the first benefit paid by a trade union and friendly society was almost invariably funeral benefit.

In so far as social security depended on the labourers' own efforts, it therefore tended to be economically inefficient by middle-class standards; in so far as it depended on their rulers, who determined what little public assistance there was, it was an engine of degradation and oppression more than a means of material relief. There have been few more inhuman statutes than the Poor Law Act of 1834, which made all relief 'less eligible' than the lowest wage outside, confined it to the jail-like work-house, forcibly separating husbands, wives and children in order to punish the poor for their destitution, and discourage them from the dangerous temptation of procreating further paupers. It was never completely applicable, for where the poor were strong they resisted its extremes, and in time it became slightly less penal. Yet it remained the basis of English poor relief until the eve of the First World War, and the childhood experiences of Charlie Chaplin show that it remained very much what it had been when Dickens' *Oliver Twist* expressed the popular horror of it in the 1830s.* And in the 1830s – indeed until the 1850s – a minimum of ten per cent of the English population were paupers.

Up to a point – as with the Georgian merchant and industrialist – the experience of the past was not as irrelevant as it might have been in a country leaping more radically and directly from a non-industrial to a modern industrial age; and as in fact it was in Ireland or the Scottish Highlands. The semi-industrial Britain of the seventeenth and eighteenth centuries in some ways prepared and anticipated the industrial age of the nineteenth. For instance, the fundamental institution of working-class self-defence, the *trade union*, was already in being in the eighteenth century, partly in the unsystematic, but not ineffective, form of periodic 'collective bargaining by riot' (as among seamen, miners, weavers and framework knitters), partly in the much stabler form of craft societies for skilled journeymen, sometimes with loose national links through the practice of assisting unemployed members of the trade tramping in search of work or experience.

In a very real sense the bulk of British workers had adjusted itself to a changing, industrializing, though not yet revolutionized society. For some kinds of labour, whose conditions did not change fundamentally as yet – again miners and seamen come to mind – the old traditions could still suffice: sailors

* The Scottish Poor Law was somewhat different. See Chapter 15.

multiplied their songs about the new experiences of the
nineteenth century, such as the whaling off Greenland, but they
were traditional folksongs. An important group had even accepted, indeed welcomed, industry, science and progress
(though not capitalism). These were the 'artisans' or 'mech-
anics', the men of skill, expertise, independence and education,
who saw no great distinction between themselves and those of
similar social standing who chose to become entrepreneurs, or
to remain yeoman farmers or small shopkeepers: the body of
men who overlapped the frontiers between working and middle
classes.* The 'artisans' were the natural leaders of ideology
and organization among the labouring poor, the pioneers of
Radicalism (and later the early, Owenite, versions of Socialism),
of discussion and popular higher education – through Mech-
anics' Institutes, Halls of Science, and a variety of clubs,
societies and free-thinking printers and publishers – the nucleus
of trade unions, Jacobin, Chartist or any other progressive movements. The agricultural labourers' riots were stiffened by
village cobblers and builders; in the cities little groups of hand-
loom weavers, printers, tailors, and perhaps a few small businessmen and shopkeepers provided political continuity of leadership
on the left until the decline of Chartism, if not beyond. Hostile
to capitalism, they were unique in elaborating ideologies which
did not simply seek to return to an idealized tradition, but
envisaged a just society which would also be technically progressive. Above all, they represented the ideal of freedom and
independence in an age when everything conspired to degrade
labour.

Yet even these were only transitional solutions for the
workers' problem. Industrialization multiplied the number of
handloom weavers and framework-knitters until the end of the

---

*The family of Harold Wilson, British Prime Minister from 1964, is
almost a textbook illustration of this stratum. The eight paternal generations
run: smallholding farmer, smallholder, husbandman, cordwainer and
farmer, workhouse master, warehouse salesman, draper, works chemist.
The line intermarried in the nineteenth century with a generation of weavers
and spinners, another of cotton warp manufacturer, railway coalman,
railway engine fitter, and a third of railway clerk and schoolteacher (*Sunday
Times*, 7 March 1965).

Napoleonic Wars. Thereafter it destroyed them by slow strangulation: militant and thoughtful communities like the Dunfermline workers broke up in demoralization, pauperization and emigration in the 1830s. Skilled craftsmen were degraded into sweated outworkers, as in the London furniture trades, and even when they survived the economic earthquakes of the 1830s and 40s, they could no longer be expected to play so great a social role in an economy in which the factory was no longer a regional exception, but the rule. Pre-industrial traditions could not keep their heads above the inevitably rising level of industrial society. In Lancashire we can observe the ancient ways of spending holidays – the rush bearing, wrestling matches, cock-fighting and bull baiting – dying out after 1840; and the forties also mark the end of the era when folksong remained the major musical idiom of industrial workers. The great social movements of this period – from Luddism to Chartism – also died away: they had been movements which drew their force not merely from the extreme hardships of the age, but also from the force of these older methods of poor men's action. It was to take another forty years before the British working class evolved new ways of struggle and living.

Such were the qualitative stresses which racked the labouring poor in the first industrial generations. To these we must add the quantitative ones – their material poverty. Whether this actually increased or not has been hotly debated among historians, but the very fact that the question can be put already supplies a gloomy answer: nobody seriously argues that conditions deteriorate in periods when they plainly do not, such as the 1950s.*

There is, of course, no dispute about the fact that, *relatively*, the poor grew poorer, simply because the country, and its rich and middle class, so obviously grew wealthier. The very moment when the poor were at the end of their tether – in the early

---

*Indeed, during such periods, the large areas of existing poverty tend to be forgotten, and have to be periodically rediscovered (at least by those who are not poor), as happened in the 1880s, when the first social surveys revealed them to a surprised middle class. A similar rediscovery took place in the early and middle 1960s.

and middle forties – was the moment when the middle class dripped with excess capital, to be wildly invested in railways and spent on the bulging, opulent household furnishings displayed at the Great Exhibition of 1851, and on the palatial municipal constructions which prepared to rise in the smoky northern cities.

Secondly, there is – or ought to be – no dispute about the abnormal pressure on working-class consumption in the period of early industrialism, which is reflected in this relative pauperization. Industrialism means a relative diversion of national income from consumption to investment, a substitution of foundries for beefsteaks. In a capitalist economy this takes the form, largely, of a diversion of income from non-investing classes like peasants and labourers, to potentially investing ones, namely the owners of estates and business enterprises, that is from the poor to the rich. In Britain, there was never the slightest general shortage of capital, given the country's wealth and the relative cheapness of the early industrial processes, but a large section of those who benefited from this diversion of income – and the richest among them in particular – invested their money outside direct industrial development or wasted it, thus forcing the rest of the (smaller) entrepreneurs to press even more harshly upon labour. Moreover, the economy did not rely for its development on the purchasing capacity of its working population: indeed economists tended to assume that their wages would not be much above the level of subsistence. Theories advocating high wages as economically advantageous began to appear finally round the middle of the century, and the industries supplying the domestic consumer market – for example clothing and furniture – were not revolutionized until its second half. The Englishman who wanted a pair of trousers had the choice either of having them made to measure by a tailor, buying the cast-offs of his social superiors, relying on charity, going in rags, or making his own. Finally, certain essential requisites of life – food and perhaps housing, but certainly urban amenities – had the greatest difficulty in keeping pace with the expansion of the cities, or the population as a whole, and sometimes clearly did not keep pace. Thus the supplies of meat for London almost certainly lagged behind the city's population from 1800 until the 1840s.

Thirdly, there is no dispute about certain classes of the population whose conditions undoubtedly deteriorated. These were the agricultural labourers (about one million working men in 1851), at all events those in the south and east of England, and the smallholders and crofters in the Celtic fringe of Scotland and Wales. (The eight and a half million Irishmen, of course, mainly peasants, were pauperized beyond belief. Something not far short of a million of them actually starved to death in the Famine of 1846–7, the greatest human catastrophe of the nineteenth century anywhere in the world).* There were further the declining industries and occupations, displaced by technical progress, of whom the half-million handloom weavers are the best known example, but by no means the only one. They starved progressively in a vain attempt to compete with the new machines by working more and more cheaply. Their numbers had doubled between 1788 and 1814 and their wages risen markedly until the middle of the Wars; but between 1805 and 1833 they fell from 23 shillings a week to 6s. 3d. There were also the non-industrialized occupations which met the rapidly growing demand for their goods, not by technical revolution, but by sub-division and 'sweating' – for example the innumerable seamstresses in their garrets or cellars.

Whether, if we were to add up all the hard-pressed sections of the labouring poor and set against them those who managed somewhat to improve their incomes, we would find a net average gain or loss is an insoluble question, for we simply do not know enough about earnings, unemployment, retail prices and other necessary data to answer it decisively. There was, quite certainly, no significant general improvement. There may or may not have been deterioration between the middle 1790s and the middle 1840s. Thereafter, there was undoubted improvement – and it is the contrast between this (modest as it was) and the earlier period that really says all we need to know. After the early forties consumption rose markedly – until then it had crawled along without much change. After the 1840s – still, and rightly,

* That is, relative to the size of the population involved.

named the 'Hungry Forties' even though in Britain (but not in Ireland) things improved during most of them – unemployment undoubtedly declined sharply. For instance, no subsequent cyclical depression was even faintly as catastrophic as the slump of 1841–2. And above all, the sense of imminent social explosion, which had been present in Britain almost without interruption since the end of the Napoleonic Wars (except in most of the 1820s), disappeared. Britons ceased to be revolutionary.

Of course this pervasive social and political unrest reflected not merely material poverty but social pauperization: the destruction of old ways of life without the substitution of anything the labouring poor could regard as a satisfactory equivalent. But whatever the motives, waves of desperation broke time and again over the country: in 1811–13, in 1815–17, in 1819, in 1826, in 1829–35, in 1838–42, in 1843–4, in 1846–8. In the agricultural areas they were blind, spontaneous, and, in so far as their objectives were at all defined, almost entirely economic. As a rioter from the Fens put it in 1816: 'Here I am between Earth and Sky, so help me God. I would sooner lose my life than go home as I am. Bread I want and bread I will have.'[5] In 1816, all over the eastern counties, in 1822 in East Anglia, in 1830 everywhere between Kent and Dorset, Somerset and Lincoln, in 1843–4 once again in the east Midlands and the eastern counties, the threshing machines were broken, the ricks burned at night, as men demanded a minimum of life. In the industrial and urban areas after 1815 economic and social unrest was generally combined with a specific political ideology and programme – radical-democratic, or even 'cooperative' (or as we would now say, socialist), though in the first great movements of unrest from 1811–3 the Luddites of the East Midlands and Yorkshire smashed their machines without any specific programme of political reform and revolution. Phases of the movement stressing political and trade-unionist agitation tended to alternate, the former being normally by far the more massive: politics predominated in 1815–19, 1829–32, and above all in the Chartist era (1838–48), industrial organization in the early 1820s and 1833–8. However, from about 1830 all these movements became more self-consciously and characteristically proletarian.

The agitations of 1829–35 saw the rise of the idea of the 'general trades union' and its ultimate weapon, which might be used for political purposes, the 'general strike'; and Chartism rested firmly on the foundation of working-class consciousness, and in so far as it envisaged any real method of achieving its ends, relied on hopes of a general strike or, as it was then called, Sacred Month. But essentially, what held all these movements together, or revived them after their periodic defeat and disintegration, was the universal discontent of men who felt themselves hungry in a society reeking with wealth, enslaved in a country which prided itself on its freedom, seeking bread and hope, and receiving in return stones and despair.

And were they not justified? A Prussian official, travelling to Manchester in 1814, had made a moderately cheerful judgement:

> The cloud of coal vapour may be observed from afar. The houses are blackened by it. The river which flows through Manchester, is so filled with waste dye-stuffs that it resembles a dyer's vat. The whole picture is a melancholic one. Nevertheless, everywhere one sees busy, happy and well-nourished people, and this raises the observer's spirits.[6]

No observer of Manchester in the 1830s and 1840s – and there were many – dwelt on its happy, well-fed people. 'Wretched, defrauded, oppressed, crushed human nature lying in bleeding fragments all over the face of society', wrote the American, Colman, of it in 1845. 'Every day that I live I thank Heaven that I am not a poor man with a family in England.'[7] Can we be surprised that the first generation of the labouring poor in industrial Britain looked at the results of capitalism and found them wanting?

NOTES

1. See Further Reading, especially 4 (E. P. Thompson, F. Engels, N. Smelser), Note 1, Chapter 2 (K. Polanyi). On the 'standard of living' arguments see also E. J. Hobsbawm, *Labouring Men* (1964), Phyllis Deane, *The First Industrial Revolution* (1965). For labour movements, Cole and Postgate (Further Reading 2), A. Briggs (ed.), *Chartist Studies*

(1959). For social conditions, E. Chadwick, *Report on the Sanitary Conditions of the Labouring Population*, ed. M. W. Flinn (1965), A. Briggs, *Victorian Cities* (1963). See also Figures 2–3, 13, 20, 37, 45–6.

2. N. McCord, *The Anti-Corn Law League* (1958), pp. 57–8.

3. A. de Tocqueville, *Journeys to England and Ireland*, ed. J. P. Mayer (1958), pp. 107–8.

4. Canon Parkinson, quoted in A. Briggs, *Victorian Cities*, pp. 110–11.

5. William Dawson of Upwell, quoted in A. J. Peacock, *Bread or Blood* (1965).

6. Fabriken-Kommissarius May, 1814 (see Note 2, Chapter 3).

7. Quoted in A. Briggs, op. cit., p. 12.

5

AGRICULTURE
1750–1850[1]

EVEN in the mid eighteenth century agriculture no longer dominated the economy of Britain as it did that of most other countries, and by 1800 it probably occupied no more than a third of the population and provided about the same fraction of the national income. Yet it made a much larger public impression than its share of the economy might have suggested, and for two reasons. First, it was the indispensable foundation for industry, for there was no other regular source of the nation's food. Marginal imports of foodstuffs were possible, but until after the middle of the nineteenth century transport costs and technology did not permit the bulk of the nation – even a nation so accessible to maritime ports as Britain – to be fed regularly by imports from abroad. For a generation after Free Trade had been introduced (1846), British agriculture remained, for this reason, a haven of prosperous high prices, immune to foreign competition. British farmers *had* to feed a vastly expanded and rapidly expanding population. Though they did not feed it too well, they did not allow it to starve. As late as the 1830s over ninety per cent of the food consumed in Britain was grown in these islands. When we consider that in 1830 the British population was considerably more than double what it had been in 1750, and the proportion of families engaged in agriculture considerably less, we have a measure both of the task and the achievement of our food-growers.

The second reason for the prominence of agriculture was that the 'landed interest' dominated British politics and social life. To belong to the upper classes meant to own an estate and a 'seat'. Landownership was the price of entry into high politics. In Parliament the 'counties' and the small towns dominated by nobility and gentry overwhelmingly outweighed the cities. The very pattern and model of upper-class life were rural: the sports which were England's characteristic cultural export (before the urban and proletarian games like association football and the suburban and middle-class ones like tennis and rugby), the idealization of park and picturesque village, which still survives on *Times* calendars, the 'country members' of English clubs and libraries, the very schools which a new Victorian middle class built or took over for a suitably spartan education of its sons. The large landowners were rich and powerful, and the rich and powerful were landowners, though they could not all be Dukes. Any economic change which affected the land – or rather, since the rural poor were silent and, but for catastrophe or rebellion, unnoticed, the rural middle and upper classes – was bound to reverberate throughout politics. The British state was so constructed as to magnify and re-echo its noise.

But the Industrial Revolution inevitably imposed very fundamental changes on the land. The very size of the economic effort of British agriculture implied them. At first sight the strains on it might seem to be technical and economic, rather than social, for eighteenth-century rural society was (if we except parts of Scotland and Wales and the odd corner of England) already substantially geared to cash production for the market by means of the best technical and commercial methods. The fundamental structure of landownership and farming was already established by the mid eighteenth century, and certainly by the early decades of the Industrial Revolution. England was a country of mainly large landlords, cultivated by tenant farmers working the land with hired labourers. This structure was still partly hidden by an undergrowth of economically marginal cottager-labourers, or other small independents and semi-independents, but this should not obscure the fundamental transformation which had already taken place. By 1790 landlords owned perhaps three quarters of the cultivated land, occupying free-holders perhaps fifteen to twenty per cent, and a 'peasantry' in the usual sense of the word no longer existed. There was – or there seemed to be – merely a difference of degree between the partly modernized agriculture of this period and the more completely modernized farming of the early nineteenth century, not a difference in kind; all the more so since the bulk of the increase in productivity per man during the eighteenth century appears to have occurred before 1750.

Yet life is not so simple. Logically it seemed natural for agriculture to complete its conversion into an efficient commercial producer, rewarded for its efforts by the unlimited demand at rising prices of a population – especially an urban population – which constantly expanded just a little faster than the farmer could raise his output. Logically the British landlords and farmers had no objection to so profitable a course, and indeed pursued it. But unlike the manufacture of cotton in factories, 'the land' was not simply a way of making money for its owners and entrepreneurs, but a way of life. Economic logic implied putting not only agricultural products at the entire disposal of efficient farming and the market, but the land and the men upon it. The landlords drew the line at the first of these requirements, though raising no objections to large-scale transfers of land between farmers and changes of tenancies. Since 1660 they had mobilized both their political influence and the ingenuity of their attorneys to make forced land sales by large owners difficult, if not impossible. Both landlords and a large section of the farmers were disquieted and troubled by the social consequence of agricultural improvement, the creation of a growing surplus of the rural poor, the destruction of the stable traditional hierarchy of the countryside. It may be that if this surplus had drained quietly away into the cities and manufactures it would not have been so obtrusive. But it is a characteristic of agriculture in the early industrial era that its social disruption is in most cases greater than the initial capacity of the non-agricultural sector to absorb labour, and that the rural poor are slow to abandon the life of their ancestors, the life ordained by God and fate, the only life traditional communities know or can conceive. So long as no catastrophe brought the problem vividly before the rulers of the countryside, it might be overlooked. The hard times of the middle 1790s brought it before the most short-sighted eyes.

They were followed, twenty years later, by the collapse of the agricultural boom, which had risen to the most dizzy (and untenable) heights during the Napoleonic Wars, which, like all wars, were a golden era for farm prices. After 1815 not only the poor but the farmers themselves felt the strain of agricultural transformation. The 'landed interest' no longer faced the mere problem of its poor, which could be (and was) settled locally – by the nobility and gentry as magistrates, the rural middle strata as guardians and overseers of the poor, and so on – but their own troubles, which required national action. The city economists proposed solutions which they found entirely unacceptable: that uneconomic farms should go out of business until only economic ones were left, and that the surplus poor should not be uneconomically maintained, but driven out to find such employment as those who had jobs to offer would give them, at whatever wage the market determined. Against the first prospect the 'landed interest' used its political dominance to impose the Corn Laws, a policy of protectionism which bitterly alienated the urban and industrial interest and strained British politics, at times almost to snapping point, between 1815 and 1846. It was naturally less adamant about the second – and indeed yielded the point in 1834 by accepting the Poor Law of that year. Nevertheless, except for a handful of Scottish nobles who drove their dumbly loyal clansmen across the seas to Canada to make room for the profitable sheep, few were prepared for such extreme measures even at the expense of those they exploited. That the labourers crouched far below the farmers, and immeasurably below the squire, was natural; that they had no right to live on the land of their fathers was not. (Besides, if they went, what would happen to the rate of agricultural wages and the farmers' labour force?)

Two issues dramatized the social problem of agricultural change: 'enclosures' and the 'poor law'. Enclosures meant the rearrangement of formerly common or open fields into self-contained private land-units, or the division of formerly common but uncultivated land (woodlands, rough grazing, 'waste', and so on) into private property. Like the rationalization of private holdings – by exchanging, buying or leasing strips of land to make more compact units – they had long been practised; and since the middle of the seventeenth century with relatively little public fuss. From about 1760 landlords (once again exploiting their control of government) speeded up the process of converting the land into a patchwork of purely individual holdings, by the systematic use of Acts of Parliament; at first local and after 1801 general. The movement was largely confined to areas of England in which open fields had been common in the Middle Ages, and which specialized in field crops, especially grain, that is to an inverted triangle with its base along the Yorkshire, Lincolnshire and Norfolk coasts and its apex in Dorset. Enclosure of 'common' and 'waste' was rather more evenly distributed, except in the extreme south-east and south-west. Between 1760 and 1820 about half of Huntingdonshire, Leicester and Northampton, over forty per cent of Bedfordshire and Rutland, over a third of Lincolnshire, Oxford and the East Riding of Yorkshire, and a quarter of more of Berkshire, Buckingham, Middlesex, Norfolk, Nottingham, Warwick and Wiltshire were thus enclosed, mainly from open fields, though in some instances the law was merely coming into line with established facts.*

The case for enclosure was that it enabled uncultivated land to be brought into use and made the commercially minded 'improving' farmer independent of his more custom-bound and old-fashioned neighbours. This was undoubtedly so. The case against it is by no means so clear, because its opponents have only too often confused the specific device of the Enclosure Act with the general phenomenon of agricultural concentration of which it was one aspect. It was accused of throwing peasants off their holdings and labourers out of work. The second charge was true where enclosure transformed former tilled fields into pastures, which happened sometimes, but – in view of the booming demand for corn, especially during the Napoleonic Wars – by no means generally. Enclosure for tillage, or from uncultivated land, might actually mean more local work. How far enclosure acts threw small cultivators off the land is a matter of debate, but there is no special reason to suppose that they did

---

*On the other hand parliamentary enclosure was insignificant in counties like Cornwall (0·4 per cent), Devon (1·6 per cent), Essex (1·9 per cent), Kent (0·3 per cent) or Sussex (1·2 per cent), and, so far as fields were concerned, in the north and west.

so any more effectively than the buying-out or leasing of strips and smallholdings in the earlier period. The men who sold under an Act rather than by private agreement might of course resent being coerced by their richer and more powerful neighbours, but their economic loss or gain was not necessarily any different. On the other hand one class was undoubtedly a heavy loser by enclosure: the marginal cottagers and smallholders, eking out the produce of their little plots perhaps with wage-labour and certainly with the various petty – but to them crucial – advantages of common rights: pasture for animals and poultry, firewood, building material, timber to repair implements, fences and gates, and so on. Enclosure might well reduce them to simple wage-labour. More than this: it would transform them and the labourers from upright members of a community, with a distinct set of *rights*, into inferiors dependent on the rich. It was no insignificant change. A Suffolk clergyman wrote in 1844 of his villagers:

They have no village green or common for active sports. Some thirty years ago, I am told, they had a *right* to a playground in a particular field, at certain seasons of the year, and were then celebrated for their football; but somehow or other this right has been lost and the field is now under the plough. . . . Of late they have introduced a little cricketing and two or three of the farmers have *very kindly allowed* them to play in their fields. [*My italics*, EJH]²

It was a hard thing for free-born Englishmen to exchange their rights for the permission of their 'betters', however kind. By 1800 even passionate advocates of enclosure for productive improvement, like Arthur Young, began to flinch at what they considered their social results. 'I had rather', he wrote, 'that all the commons of England were sunk in the sea, than that the poor should in future be treated on enclosing as they have been hitherto.'³ Yet, in so far as this pauperization and landlessness was not due to enclosure, what was it due to?

It was due largely to the concentration and consolidation of farms, which made what passed for a 'small farm' in the England of 1830 as big as a small estate on the continent.

Enclosures were merely the most dramatic and, as it were,

official and political aspect of a general process by which farms grew larger, farmers relatively fewer, and the villagers more landless. It was this rather than the enclosures *per se* (which hardly touched some very pauperized areas of rural England) that accounts for the degradation of the village poor. 'The small farmers', wrote an expert at the end of the eighteenth century, 'were generally reduced in every county, and almost annihilated in some.' By this time a holding of twenty-five acres, unless in market gardens or something of the sort, could no longer keep a man; the foreign traveller, used to peasant holdings of ten or twelve acres, would rub his ears when he heard farms of upwards of a hundred acres described as 'small'. This concentration took place in open and enclosed country, among new or old enclosures, through expropriation, forced or voluntary sales, and especially on the very large new stretches of land brought into cultivation.* It would have pauperized a stable population. It was a disaster for a rapidly expanding one.

This surplus population lived by hiring out its labour. But in many parts of England (though less so in Scotland and the north) the nature even of this hired labour changed for the worse. 'The system of weekly wages', wrote a Norfolk observer in the 1840s, contrasting the situation with 'forty or fifty years ago', 'was the first blow towards weakening the ties which had hitherto bound the farm servant under all circumstances to his employer.'⁴ The traditional farm-servant was hired annually, at the great hiring-fairs, and, if unmarried, lived in and ate at the farmer's table. A large part of his income was in kind. He earned little, but enjoyed at least the security of regular employment. The man hired weekly, daily or by the task earned nothing when not actually working for someone – and in the slack winter season there was not much work. (This is why the labourers in 1816, 1822 and 1830 concentrated their dumb fury against the threshing machines, which took away the most

*For example, in 1724 there were sixty-five farms on the 4,400 acres of the Bagot estates in Staffordshire; sixteen of them above a hundred acres (average size 135 acres); in 1764 there were only forty-six farms on the 5,700 acres of the estates. Twenty-three of them were over a hundred acres (average size, 189 acres). G. Mingay, 'The Size of Farms in the 18th century', *Economic History Review*, XIV, p. 481.

commonly available winter work.) If he lived out, in his (or rather his employer's) cottage, the farmer owed him little but his miserable cash wage. If he had sense, he would raise a large family, for a wife and children meant extra earnings and, at certain times, an extra allowance from the Poor Law. Thus the breakdown of the traditional, semi-patriarchal farm encouraged the multiplication of local labour and consequently the decrease of its wages.

By the 1790s the consequent decay of the village poor had reached catastrophic proportions in parts of southern and eastern England.* It fell to the Poor Law to deal with it. The county notables of the eighteenth century were not philanthropists, but they found it difficult even to conceive of a community which did not provide a minimum wage for even its most inferior working members, and some kind of life for those unable to work; though not of course for 'foreigners', who were sent back to their own 'parish of settlement' when they could not earn their living. It was in the light of such vaguely defined but firmly held views that the magistrates of Berkshire, meeting at Speenhamland in 1795, attempted to change the Poor Law from an institution supplementing the normal run of the economy into a systematic device to ensure the labourers a living wage. A minimum rate was fixed, depending on the price of corn. If earnings fell below it, they were to be supplemented from the poor rates. In its more extreme forms the 'Speenhamland System' did not spread as widely as was once believed, but in the more moderate form of a systematic – and for the period, remarkably generous – children's allowance for men with large families† it became almost universal in many parts of the south and east.

What the effects of this spontaneously propagated system of social security were has been much argued about. There is little reason to dissent from the traditional view – that they were disastrous. It meant that *all* local ratepayers subsidized the

---

*In the industrial areas the drift of labour from the land already kept conditions up; and in Scotland and the extreme north the traditional system was not broken up to the same extent.

† 1s. 6d. or even 2s. per child (over three or four) was a substantial addition to a weekly wage of, say, 7s.

farmers (and especially the large farmers employing much labour) to the extent that they paid low wages. It pauperized, demoralized and immobilized the labourer, who could hope to be kept just above starvation in his own parish, but nowhere else on earth; and it discriminated sharply against the single or small-family man. It caused the poor rates to soar, without diminishing poverty: expenditure doubled from the mid-eighteenth century to the late 1780s, and again by the early 1800s, and yet again by 1817. The best that can be said for it is that, since industry could not yet absorb the rural surplus, something had to be done to maintain them in the village. But the significance of Speenhamland was social rather than economic. It was an attempt – a last, inefficient, ill-considered and unsuccessful attempt – to maintain a traditional rural order in the face of the market economy.

But the very men who made this attempt were wrecking what they wished to preserve. The inhuman economics of commercial and 'advanced' farming strangled the human values of a social order. What is more, the very wealth of the increasingly prosperous farmers, with their piano-playing daughters, made them ever more remote, even in spirit, from the pauperized labourers. The growing luxury of the landlords, symbolized in the new practice of preserving game for competitive massacre and the increasingly savage laws against poaching,* widened the chasm between the classes. The free-born Englishman degenerated into the 'servile and broken-spirited' Hodge, as an American visitor saw him in the 1840s. Meanwhile, however, agricultural output and productivity rose. Between 1750 and the later 1830s this was not, normally, due to any major technical innovations (except perhaps in Scotland, which set the pace for efficient and mechanized farming), but to the increase in the cultivated area, the greater efficiencies of larger farms, changes in crops and the wider spread of crop-rotations, methods of stockbreeding, implements, and so on, already well known before 1750. The

---

* 'Game-books' which recorded the number of birds shot, and strict preservation, seem to have come in the late eighteenth century; fox-hunting – the number of packs of hounds reached a peak in 1835 – became systematic in the first third of the nineteenth century.

Industrial Revolution, or science, hardly affected farming before the late 1830s – a moment marked by the foundation of the Royal Agricultural Society (1838) and the Rothamsted experimental station (1843). After that progress was remarkably rapid. 'Under-drainage' – essential to bring the heavy and soggy claylands into cultivation – spread from the 1820s; in 1843 the cylindrical clay drainpipe was invented. Fertilizers came into use rapidly: superphosphate was patented in 1842, and within the first seven years of the 1840s the import of Peruvian guano rose from virtually zero to over 200,000 tons. 'High Farming', with its heavy investment and relative mechanization, dominated the middle years of the century, and from about 1837 the increase in the yield of crops became rather striking. British farming, after seventy years of expansion before 1815 and two or three hesitant decades, entered its golden age. In the 1850s even the miserable labourer's lot improved sharply, though this was due not to any developments in agriculture, but to his mass 'flight from the land' – to railways, mines, cities and overseas – which produced a welcome rural labour shortage and slightly higher wages.

This improvement occurred when – in the teeth of bitter opposition from farmers and the squirearchy – the Corn Laws were abolished (1846) and British agriculture was thrown open to foreign competition. It had taken thirty years to break down this resistance, for the 'landed interest' defended not only its profits and rent-rolls, but its social and political superiority, as symbolized in a House of Lords of landed nobles and a House of Commons of squires. Admittedly this superiority was challenged not only by a new and self-conscious middle class which asked for its due place among – or even above – the former rulers of the kingdom, but by a middle class which regarded the landlord's rent as pure robbery anyway, and the artificial protection of high rents and high food prices after the Napoleonic Wars, at a time of business uncertainty (see pp. 75–8), as a gun pointed at the nation's economic heart. Yet – except on Free Trade – it was not unprepared to compromise. After the parliamentary reform of 1832 it insisted on the New Poor Law and on political control of the municipalities, but left local government in 'the counties' in the hands of lord and squire (until 1889), refrained from pressing its justified criticisms of ancient and aristocratic vested interests – the court, the civil service, the armed forces, the universities, the law, and so on – and even of the even greater vested interest of the Church. (However, the economic rights of the Church, which were exceedingly unpopular among farmers, were at least rationalized by the Tithe Commutation Act of 1836, though not abolished.)

On the other side, the nobility was equally inclined to compromise, even on Free Trade. The really large landlord did not necessarily depend on agricultural rents. He might enjoy the fruits of rising urban real-estate values, or the profits of mines and railways which a fortunate providence had placed under or on his land, or the interest of the share of their giant incomes invested in the past. The seventh Duke of Devonshire, left in a little temporary financial embarrassment of a million or so by an unusually free-spending sixth Duke, was not obliged to sell even the more outlying of his numerous seats, but could fall back on the development of Barrow-in-Furness and Buxton Spa. Socially, he was not yet threatened by the rivalry of wealthy industrialists, whose money would not buy them more than the status and estate of the wealthy gentry, though the occasional financier might already do rather better. In any case, the creation of new peers, though disquieting by the standards of the self-perpetuating two hundred of the eighteenth century, was as yet not very considerable by ours: 133 in the fifty years up to 1837 (that is an annual average of about 2·5), many of them admirals and generals, traditionally so rewarded. The nobility was open to settlement. Only the lesser gentry, rural and Tory, and the farmers, would fight in the last ditch. But long historical experience had shown that the squires alone were not a viable political force in the nation. Moreover, by the 1840s farming was distinctly a minority interest. It occupied no more than a quarter of the population and less than this share of the national income. When the nobility abandoned agriculture – as happened in 1846, and even more obviously in 1879 – all that was left was a minority pressure group stiffened by a bloc of fox-hunting back-bench MPs.

NOTES

1. See Further Reading, especially works by Carus-Wilson (ed.) and Glass and Eversley (ed.). There is now a useful and up-to-date textbook, *J. D. Chambers and G. E. Mingay, *The Agricultural Revolution 1750–1880* (1966). G. E. Mingay, *English Landed Society in the Eighteenth Century* (1963), is stronger on agriculture, *F. M. L. Thompson, *English Landed Society in the Nineteenth Century* (1963), on the nobility and gentry. For the farm labourers J. L. and B. Hammond, *The Village Labourer* (1911), and W. Hasbach, *A History of the English Farm Labourer* (1908), are still good starting-points, but the best book is the masterly M. K. Ashby, *The Life of Joseph Ashby of Tysoe* (1961). See also E. J. Hobsbawn and G. Rudé, *Captain Swing* (1969). K. Polanyi (Note 1, Chapter 2) is excellent on the Poor Law. See also Figures 4, 13.
2. Rev. J. S. Henslow, *Suggestions towards an enquiry into the present condition of the Labouring Population of Suffolk* (Hadleigh, 1844), pp. 24–5.
3. *Annals of Agriculture*, XXVI, p. 214.
4. R. N. Bacon, *History of the Agriculture of Norfolk* (1844), p. 143.

6

INDUSTRIALIZATION:
THE SECOND PHASE
1840–95[1]

THE first, or textile, phase of British industrialization had reached its limits or looked as though it might soon do so. Fortunately a new phase of industrialism was about to take over, and to provide a much firmer foundation for economic growth: that based on the capital goods industries, on coal, iron and steel. The age of crisis for textile industrialism was the age of breakthrough for coal and iron, the age of railway construction.

There were two converging reasons for this. The first was the growing industrialization in the rest of the world, which provided a rapidly increasing market for the kind of capital goods which could not be imported in any quantity except from the 'workshop of the world', and which could not yet be produced in sufficient quantity at home. The rate of expansion of British exports* was far higher between 1840 and 1860 (and especially in 1845–55, when the sale of home products abroad rose by 7·3 per cent *a year*) than ever before or since; notably greater for instance than in the pioneer period of cotton, 1780–1800. It benefited mainly the new capital goods. In 1840–2 they formed about eleven per cent of the value of our exports of manufactures, by 1857–9 twenty-two per cent, by 1882–4 twenty-seven per cent. Between 1840–2 and 1857–9 coal exports rose from less than three quarters of a million pounds to over three million, iron and steel exports from about three million to well over thirteen million, while those of cotton rose more slowly, though even they almost doubled. By 1873 they stood respectively at £13·2m., £37·4m. and £77·4m. The transport revolution of railway and steamship,

---

*That is, their growth in relation to the size of the British population. Cf. W. Schlote, *British Overseas Trade* (Oxford, 1952), pp. 41–2.

themselves major markets for British iron, steel and coal exports, gave an additional impetus to this opening of new markets and expansion of old ones.*

The second reason, however, has little to do with the growth of demand. It is the pressure of the increasingly vast accumulations of capital for profitable investment, which is best illustrated by the construction of the railways.

Between 1830 and 1850 some six thousand miles of railways were opened in Britain, mostly as the result of two extraordinary bursts of concentrated investment followed by construction, the little 'railway mania' of 1835–7 and the gigantic one of 1845–7. In effect, by 1850 the basic English railway network was already more or less in existence. In every respect this was a revolutionary transformation – more revolutionary, in its way, than the rise of the cotton industry because it represented a far more advanced phase of industrialization and one bearing on the life of the ordinary citizen outside the rather small areas of actual industry. It reached into some of the remotest areas of the countryside and the centres of the greatest cities. It transformed the speed of movement – indeed of human life – from one measured in single miles per hour to one measured in scores of miles per hour, and introduced the notion of a gigantic, nation-wide, complex and exact interlocking routine symbolized by the railway time-table (from which all the subsequent 'time-tables' took their name and inspiration). It revealed the possibilities of technical progress as nothing else had done, because it was both more advanced than most other forms of technical activity and omnipresent. The cotton-mills of 1800 were obsolescent by 1840; but by 1850 the railways had reached a standard of performance not seriously improved upon until the abandonment of steam in the mid twentieth century, their organization and

* Principal exports as a percentage of total domestic exports 1830–70.

	1830	1850	1870
Cotton yarn and goods	50·8	39·6	35·8
Other textiles	19·5	22·4	18·9
Iron, steel, machinery, vehicles	10·7	13·1	16·8
Coal, coke	0·5	1·8	2·8

methods were on a scale unparalleled in any other industry, their use of novel and science-based technology (such as the electric telegraph) unprecedented. They appeared to be several generations ahead of the rest of the economy, and indeed 'railway' became a sort of synonym for ultra-modernity in the 1840s, as 'atomic' was to be after the Second World War. Their sheer size and scale staggered the imagination and dwarfed the most gigantic public works of the past.

It seems natural to assume that this remarkable development reflected the needs of an industrial economy for transport, but (at least in the short run) this was not so. Most of the country was within easy access of water-transport by sea, river or canal,* and water-transport was then – and still is – by far the cheapest for bulk goods. Speed was relatively unimportant for non-perishable goods, so long as a regular flow of supplies was maintained, and perishable ones were virtually confined to agriculture and fisheries. There is no evidence that transport troubles seriously crippled industrial development *in general*, though they patently did in individual instances. Conversely, many of the railways actually constructed were and remained quite irrational by any transport criterion, and consequently never paid more than the most modest profits, if they paid any at all. This was perfectly evident at the time, and, indeed, hard-headed economists like J. R. McCulloch were publicly sceptical about all but a limited number of main lines or lines of specially heavy goods traffic, thus anticipating by more than a century the rationalization proposals of the 1960s.

Of course, transport needs gave birth to the railway. It was rational to haul coal-waggons along 'tramlines' from pithead to canal or river, natural to haul them by stationary steam-engines, and sensible to devise a *moving* steam engine (the locomotive) to pull or push them. It made sense to link an inland coalfield remote from rivers to the coast by an extended railway from Darlington to Stockton (1825), for the high costs of constructing such a line would more than pay for themselves by the sales of coal which it would make possible even though its own profits

---

*No point of the country is more than seventy miles from the sea and all industrial areas except some of the Midlands are considerably nearer.

were meagre.* The canny Quakers who found or mobilized the money for it were right; it paid two and a half per cent in 1826, eight per cent in 1832–3 and fifteen per cent in 1839–41. Once the feasibility of a profitable railway had been demonstrated, others outside the mining areas, or more precisely the north-eastern coalfields, naturally copied and improved upon the idea, such as the merchants of Liverpool and Manchester and their London supporters, who realized the advantages – for investors as well as for Lancashire – of breaking the bottleneck of a monopoly-priced canal (which had been constructed in its time for very similar reasons). They too were right. The Liverpool–Manchester line (1830) was virtually limited to a maximum dividend of ten per cent and had no difficulty in paying it. And this, the first of the general railway lines, in turn inspired other investors and businessmen anxious to expand the business of their cities and to get an adequate return on their capital. But only a small fraction of the £240 millions invested in railways by 1850 had any such rational justification.

Most of it was sunk into the railways, and much of it was sunk without trace, because by the 1830s there were vast accumulations of capital burning holes in their owners' pockets, that is seeking any investment likely to yield more than the 3·4 per cent of public stocks.† By the 1840s the annual surplus thus crying out for investment was estimated at sixty million pounds, or almost double the estimated total capital value of the cotton industry in the mid-1830s. The economy simply did not provide scope for industrial investment on this scale, and indeed the increasing readiness of hard-headed businessmen to dip into their pockets for quite unprofitable expenditures, for example for those gigantic, awful and very expensive municipal buildings with which the northern cities began to demonstrate their superiority over one another after 1848, bears witness not only to

---

*The Stockton–Darlington line was initially still operated like a real road, that is it merely provided a facility on which anyone could run a train against a toll.

† In fact, railway returns eventually settled down – the fact may not be insignificant – at just a little more than public stock, that is an average of about four per cent.

their increasing wealth, but to their increasing surplus of savings over what local industries needed for reinvestment. The most obvious outlet for such surplus capital as was available was investment abroad, and probably capital exports prevailed over capital imports even at the end of the eighteenth century. The wars provided loans to Britain's allies, the post-war era loans to re-establish reactionary continental governments. These operations were at least predictable, but the crop of loans raised in the 1820s for newly independent Latin American and Balkan governments were far otherwise. And so were the loans of the 1830s for equally enthusiastic and unreliable borrowers among the states of the USA. By this time too many investors had burnt their fingers to encourage further floods of capital into the pockets of foreign administrators. The money which the affluent Briton had 'in his youth . . . thrown into war loans and in his manhood wasted on South American mines', 'that accumulation of wealth which with an industrial people always outstrips the ordinary modes of investment' (to borrow the phrase of a contemporary historian of the railways)[2] was ready for investment in reliable Britain. In fact, it surged into railways for want of anything equally capital-absorbing, and turned a valuable innovation in transport into a major national programme of capital investment.

As always happens at times of capital glut, much of it was rashly, stupidly, some of it insanely invested. Britons with surpluses, encouraged by projectors, contractors and others whose profits were made not by running railways but by planning or building them, were undeterred by the extraordinarily swollen costs of railways, which made the capitalization per mile of line in England and Wales three times as high as in Prussia, five times as high as in the USA, seven times as high as in Sweden.* Much of it was lost in the slumps which followed the manias. Much of it was perhaps attracted less by rational calculations of profit and loss than by the romantic appeal of technological revolution, which the railway symbolized so marvellously, and which brought out the dreamer (or in economic terms, the

---

*The preliminary expenses and legal costs were estimated at £4,000 per mile of line, the cost of land in the 1840s could reach £8,000 per mile. The land for the London and Birmingham railway cost £750,000 alone.

speculator, in racing terms, the long-odds punter) in otherwise
solid citizens. Still, the money was there to be spent, and if it
did not on the whole produce much by way of profit, it produced
something more valuable: a new transport system, a new means
of mobilizing capital accumulations of all kinds for industrial
purposes, and above all, a vast new source of employment and a
gigantic and lasting stimulus to the capital goods industries of
Britain. From the individual investor's point of view the railways
were often merely another version of the American loans. From
the point of view of the entire economy, they were – by accident
rather than design – an admirable solution to the crisis of the
first phase of British capitalism. They were soon to be supplemented by the *steamship*, a form of transport pioneered in the
USA in the 1800s, but not seriously capable of competing with
the increasingly efficient sailing ship until the revolutionary
transformation in the capital-goods base of the industrial
economy which the railway era inaugurated.*

The balance sheet of the railway construction of the 1840s is
impressive. In Britain: over two hundred millions invested,
direct employment – at the peak of construction (1846–8) – of
something like 200,000, and an indirect stimulus to employment
in the rest of the economy which cannot be calculated.† The
railways were largely responsible for the doubling of British iron
output between the middle 1830s and the middle 1840s, and at
their peak – 1845–7 – accounted for perhaps forty per cent of the
country's entire domestic consumption, settling down thereafter
to a steady fifteen per cent of its output. Such a vast economic
stimulus, coming at the very moment when the economy was
passing through its most catastrophic slump of the century
(1841–2), could hardly have been better timed. Outside Britain:
a major stimulus to the export of capital goods for the

*Until the mid-1830s annual construction of steamships rarely exceeded
3,000 tons; 1835–45 it ran, roughly at an annual level of 10,000 tons; in
1855 81,000 (against ten times as much in sailing tonnage). Not until the
1880s was more steam than sail-tonnage built in Britain. However, though a
ton of steam cost more than one of sail it also performed more.

†The number of men occupied in mining, metallurgy, machine and
vehicle building, and so on, which were largely affected by the railway
revolution, rose by almost forty per cent between 1841 and 1851.

construction of railways abroad. The Dowlais Iron Company, for instance, between 1830 and 1850 supplied twelve British but sixteen foreign railway companies.

But the stimulus was not exhausted with the 1840s. On the contrary, world railway construction continued on an increasingly massive scale, at least until the 1880s, as the following table makes clear; the railways were built to a large extent with British capital, British materials and equipment, and often by British contractors:

WORLD RAILWAY MILEAGE OPENED, PER DECADE
(TO NEAREST THOUSAND MILES)

Year	UK	Europe (including UK)	America	Rest of world
1840–50	6,000	13,000	7,000	—
1850–60	4,000	17,000	24,000	1,000
1860–70	5,000	31,000	24,000	7,000
1870–80	2,000	39,000	51,000	12,000

This remarkable expansion reflected the twin process of industrialization in the 'advanced' countries and economic opening-up of the undeveloped areas, which transformed the world in these mid-Victorian decades, turning Germany* and the USA into major industrial economies soon to be comparable to the British, opening areas like the North American prairies, the South American pampas, the South Russian steppes to export agriculture, breaking down with flotillas of warships the resistance of China and Japan to foreign trade, laying the foundations of tropical and subtropical economies based on the export of mines and agrarian products. The consequences of these changes were not felt in Britain until after the crisis of the 1870s. Until then their main effects were patently beneficial to the greatest and in some parts of the world the only exporter of industrial products and capital (see Chapter 7).

Three consequences of this change in the orientation of the British economy may be noticed.

*Or rather, the area which became Germany in 1871.

The first is the Industrial Revolution in the heavy industries, which for the first time provided the economy with abundant supplies of iron, and more important, steel (which had hitherto been produced by rather old-fashioned methods and in tiny quantities):*

PRODUCTION OF PIG-IRON, STEEL AND COAL (IN THOUSAND TONS)

1850	2,250	49	49,000
1880	7,750	1,440	147,000

In coal this increase was achieved substantially by familiar methods, that is without any significant labour-saving devices, which meant that the expansion of coal output produced a vast increase in the number of coalminers. In 1850 there were rather more than 200,000 of them in Britain, around 1880 about half a million, and by 1914 well over 1·2 million, working in some three thousand mines, or almost as many as the entire agricultural population and the (male and female) textile workers. This was to be reflected not only in the character of the British labour movement but in national politics, for miners, concentrated in single-industry agglomerations of villages, were one of the few groups of manual workers – and in the countryside almost the only ones – capable of determining the fortunes of parliamentary constituencies. That the British Trades Union Congress committed itself to the socialist slogan of the nationalization of industries as early as the 1890s was largely due to the pressure of the miners, which was in turn due to their general, and amply justified, dissatisfaction, especially with the owners' gross neglect of the men's safety and health in that dark and murderous occupation.†

The vast increase in iron output was also due to unrevolutionary improvements – chiefly a remarkable increase in the

* In 1850 the total steel output of the Western world may not have amounted to more than 70,000 tons, of which Britain supplied five sevenths.

† About 1,000 miners were killed annually in accidents in 1856–86, with occasional giant disasters such as those of High Blantyre (200 dead, 1877), Haydock (189 dead, 1878), Ebbw Vale (268 dead, 1878), Risca (120 dead, 1880), Seaham (164 dead, 1880), Pen-y-Craig (101 dead, 1880).

capacity or productivity of blast-furnaces, which, incidentally, tended to keep the capacity of the industry running well ahead of actual output, thus producing a constant tendency to bring down the price of iron though it also suffered wide price fluctuations for other reasons: in the mid-eighties the actual British output was considerably less than half of potential capacity. Steel production, on the other hand, was revolutionized by the invention of the Bessemer converter in 1850, the open-hearth furnace in the 1860s, and the basic process in the late 1870s. The new ability to mass-produce steel reinforced the general impetus given to the capital goods industries by transport, for as soon as it was available in quantity a large-scale process of substituting it for the less durable iron began, so that railways, steamships and so on in effect required two inputs of iron within little more than a generation. Since the productivity per man of these industries rose very sharply, and they never required very much manual labour anyway, their effect on employment was not so great. But like coal, and of course like the vast expansion of transport which went with iron, steel and coal, they provided jobs for the hitherto unemployed or least employable: unskilled men drawn from the agricultural surplus population (British or Irish). The expansion of these industries was therefore doubly useful: they gave unskilled labour better-paid work, and, by drawing off the rural surplus, improved the condition of the remaining farm workers, which began to improve markedly, even dramatically, in the 1850s.*

However, the rise of the capital goods industries provided a comparable stimulus to the employment of skilled labour in the vast expansion of engineering, the building of machines, ships, and so on. The number of workers in these industries also just about doubled between 1851 and 1881, and unlike coal and iron they have continued to expand ever since. By 1914 they formed the largest single category of British male workers – considerably more numerous than all workers, male or female, in textiles. They thus greatly reinforced an aristocracy of labour which

---

*The numbers employed in transport more than doubled in the 1840s, and doubled again between 1851 and 1881, when they stood at almost 900,000.

regarded itself as – and was – much better off than the bulk of the working class.

The second consequence of the new era, it is therefore evident, was a remarkable improvement in employment all round, and a large-scale transfer of labour from worse- to better-paid jobs. This accounts largely for the general sense of improvement in living standards and the lowering of social tension during the golden years of the mid-Victorians, for the actual wage-rates of many classes of workers did not rise significantly, while housing conditions and urban amenities remained shockingly bad.

A third consequence was the remarkable rise in the export of British capital abroad. By 1870 something like £700 million were invested in foreign countries, more than a quarter of it in the rising industrial economy of the USA, so much so that the subsequent and striking growth of British foreign holdings could have been achieved without much further capital export, merely by the reinvestment of the interest and dividend from what was already being held abroad. (Whether this is what actually happened is another question.) This emigration of capital was, of course, merely one part of the remarkable flow of profits and savings in search of investment; and, thanks to the transformations of the capital market in the railway era, prepared to seek it not just in old-fashioned real estate or government stock, but in industrial shares. In turn, businessmen and promoters (contemporaries would probably have said 'unsound businessmen and shady promoters') were now better able to raise capital not only from potential partners or other informed investors, but from a mass of quite uninformed ones looking for a return on their capital anywhere in the golden world economy, and finding it through the agency of family solicitors and stockbrokers, who often paid the solicitors for steering such funds their way. New legislation which made joint stock companies with limited liability possible encouraged more adventurous investment, for if such a company went bankrupt the shareholder lost only his investment but not, as he had been liable to, his entire fortune.*

*Of course, before the coming of general limited liability special provisions had been made for certain kinds of joint stock investment.

Economically the transformation of the capital market in the railway era – the stock exchanges of Manchester, Liverpool and Glasgow were all the products of the 'mania' of the 1840s – was a valuable, though almost certainly not an essential, means of mobilizing capital for large undertakings beyond the scope of partnerships, or for enterprises in remote parts of the world. Socially, however, it reflected another aspect of the mid-Victorian economy: the growth of a class of *rentiers*, who lived on the profits and savings of the previous two or three generations' accumulations. By 1871 Britain contained 170,000 'persons of rank and property' without visible occupation – almost all of them women, or rather 'ladies'; a surprising number of them unmarried ladies.* Stocks and shares, including shares in family firms formed into 'private companies' for this purpose, were a convenient way of providing for widows, daughters and other relatives who could not – and no longer needed to be – associated with the management of property and enterprise. The comfortable avenues of Kensington, the villas of spas and the growing seaside resorts of the middle class, and the environs of Swiss mountains and Tuscan cities welcomed them. The era of railway, iron and foreign investment also provided the economic base for the Victorian spinster and the Victorian aesthete.

*

With the railways Britain therefore entered the period of full industrialization. Its economy was no longer dangerously poised on the narrow platform of two or three pioneer sectors – notably textiles – but broadly based on a foundation of capital goods production, which in turn facilitated the advance of modern technology and organization – or what passed for modern in the mid nineteenth century – into a wide variety of industries. It had the skills to produce not everything, but anything it chose to produce. It had surmounted the original crisis of the early

*Of the shareholders in the Bank of Scotland and the Commercial Bank of Scotland in the 1870s about two fifths were women, and of these in turn almost two thirds were single.

Industrial Revolution, and not yet begun to feel the crisis of the pioneer industrial country which ceases to be the only 'workshop of the world'.

A fully industrialized industrial economy implies permanence, if only the permanence of further industrialization. One of the most impressive reflections of the new state of affairs – in economics, in social life and in politics – is the new readiness of Britons to accept their revolutionary ways of living as natural or at least irreversible, and to adapt themselves to them. Different classes did so in different ways. We must look briefly at the two most important, the employers and the workers.

Establishing an industrial economy is not the same thing as operating one already in existence, and the very considerable energies of the British 'middle class' in the half-century from Pitt to Peel had been primarily devoted to the first of these objects. Politically and socially this meant a concentrated effort to give themselves confidence and pride in their historic task – the early nineteenth century was the first and last when ladies wrote little pedagogic works on political economy for other ladies to teach to their children, or better still, to the poor * – and a long battle against 'the aristocracy' to reshape the institutions of Britain in a manner suitable to industrial capitalism. The reforms of the 1830s and the installation of Free Trade in 1846 more or less achieved these objects, at least in so far as this could be done without running the risk of a perhaps uncontrollable mobilization of the labouring masses. (See Chapters 4 and 12.) By the 'golden years' these battles had been won, though a few actions against the rearguard of the old regime remained to be fought. The very Queen herself was a visible pillar of middle-class respectability, or seemed to be, and the Conservative Party, organ of all that was out of sympathy with industrial Britain, was for several decades a permanent political minority lacking

---

* Such as Mrs Marcet, Harriet Martineau and the novelist Maria Edgeworth, much admired by Ricardo and read by the young Princess Victoria. A recent writer observes very acutely that the apparent neglect of the French Revolution and the Napoleonic Wars in the novels of Jane Austen and Maria Edgeworth may have been a deliberate exclusion of subject matter which should be of no interest to the respectable middle class.

an ideology or a programme. The formidable movement of the labouring poor – Jacobin, Chartist, even in its primitive way socialist – disappeared, leaving foreign exiles like Karl Marx disconsolately trying to make what they could of the liberal-radicalism or the respectable trade unionism which took its place.

But economically the change was quite as striking. The capitalist manufacturers of the first phase of industrial revolution were – or saw themselves as – a pioneering minority seeking to establish an economic system in an environment by no means entirely favourable to it: surrounded by a population deeply distrustful of their efforts, employing a working class un-accustomed to industrialism and hostile to it, struggling – at least initially – to build their factories out of modest initial capital and ploughed-back profits by abstinence, hard work and grinding the faces of the poor. The epics of the rise of the Victorian middle class, as preserved in the works of Samuel Smiles, looked back to an often quite mythical era of heroes of self-help, expelled by the stupid progress-hating multitude yet returning later in triumph and top hats. What is equally to the point, they were themselves men formed by their past – all the more so as they lacked scientific education and prided themselves above all on empiricism. Hence they were only incompletely aware of the most rational way of running their enterprises. It may seem grotesque now that economists could argue, as Nassau Senior did against the Ten Hours Bill of 1847, that the employers' profit was made in the last hour of work, and that therefore a reduction of hours would be fatal to them, but there were plenty of hard-headed men who took the view that the only way to make profits was to pay the lowest money-wages for the longest hours.

The employing class itself was therefore incompletely familiar with the rules of the industrial game, or disinclined to abide by them. These rules decreed that economic transactions were essentially governed by the free play of forces in the market – by all men's unrestricted and competitive pursuit of their economic advantage – which would automatically produce the best results all round. But, quite apart from their own reluctance to compete when it did not suit them,* they did not regard these considerations as applicable to the workers. These were still sometimes bound by long and inflexible contracts, such as the coalminers' 'yearly bond' in the north-east, more often milked for supplementary profit by the non-economic compulsion of 'truck' (payments in kind, or forced purchases in company shops), or fines, and in general held tight by a law of contract (codified in 1823) which made them liable to imprisonment for breach of employment, while their masters went free or were merely fined for their own breaches. Economic incentives – such as payment by results – were by no means common, except in some industries or for certain kinds of labour, though (as Karl Marx was to argue convincingly) 'piece-work' was at this time the form of wage-payment most suitable to capitalism. The only incentive generally recognized was profit; and those who earned no profits as entrepreneurs or subcontractors of various kinds were left to work to the pace dictated by the machine, or discipline, or the driving of subcontractors, or – where too skilled to be driven – to their own devices. Though it was already known that higher wages and shorter hours might raise productivity, employers continued to distrust them, seeking instead to depress wages and lengthen hours. Rational cost-accounting or industrial management were rare, and those who recommended them, like the scientist Charles Babbage (pioneer of the computer), were regarded as unpractical eccentrics. Trade unions were seen as either doomed to almost immediate failure, or as engines of economic catastrophe. Though they ceased to be formally illegal in 1824,† every effort was made to destroy them where possible.

In these circumstances it was not surprising that the workers should also refuse to accept capitalism, which, as we have seen, was far from attracting them in the first place. It offered them

---

*Though cartels, price-fixing arrangements, and so on were at this time rarely lasting or effective, except in such fields as government contracting.

†Thanks to the efforts of the Philosophic Radicals, who argued that, if legal, their total ineffectiveness must soon become obvious, and the workers would therefore cease to be tempted by them.

little in practice. Contrary to the apologists of the system, it offered them little even in theory, at any rate, *so long as they remained workers* – which most of them were destined to do. Until the railway era it did not even offer them its own permanence. It might collapse. It might be overthrown. It might be an episode and not an epoch. It was too young to have established its permanence by sheer duration, for as we have seen, outside a few pioneer areas, even in textiles the main weight of industrialization occurred after the Napoleonic Wars. At the time of the great Chartist general strike of 1842 every adult person in, say, Blackburn could remember the time when the first spinning factory and power-loom had been introduced in the town, less than twenty-five years earlier. And if the 'labouring poor' hesitated to accept the system as permanent, even less were they likely – unless forced, often by extra-economic coercion – to adapt themselves to it, even in their struggles. They might seek to by-pass it, as the early socialists did by free communities of cooperative production. They might seek, in the short run, to evade it, as the early trade unions did by sending their unemployed members 'on tramp' to some other city, until they discovered that 'bad times' in the new economy were periodic and universal. They might seek to forget about it, dreaming of a return to peasant proprietorship. It is no accident that the greatest mass leader of this era, the Chartist tribune Feargus O'Connor, was an Irishman whose positive economic programme for the masses who swore by him was a plan for land settlement.

Some time in the 1840s all this began to change, and to change rapidly, though by local and unofficial action rather than by any large national legislation or organization. Employers began to abandon 'extensive' methods of exploitation such as lengthening hours and shortening wages for 'intensive' ones, which meant the opposite. The Ten Hours Act of 1847 made this a necessity in the cotton industry, but without any legislative pressure we find the same tendency spreading in the industrial north. What the continentals were to call the 'English week', a free weekend, at all events from Saturday midday, began to spread in Lancashire in the 1840s, in London in the 1850s. Payment by results (that is incentive payments to workers) undoubtedly became more popular, while contracts tended to shorten and to become more flexible, though both these developments cannot yet be fully documented. Extra-economic compulsion diminished, the readiness to accept legal supervision of working conditions – as by the admirable Factory Inspectors – increased. These were not so much victories of rationality, or even of political pressure, as relaxations of tension. British industrialists now felt rich and confident enough to be able to afford such changes. It has been pointed out that the employers who advocated policies of relatively high wages and conciliating workers by reforms in the 1850s and 1860s frequently represented old-established and flourishing businesses no longer threatened with bankruptcy by any fluctuation of trade. The 'New Model' employers – commoner outside Lancashire than inside – were men like the Bass brothers (brewing), Lord Elcho (coal and iron), Thomas Brassey (railway contracting), Titus Salt, Alfred Illingworth, the Kell Brothers from round Bradford, A. J. Mundella and Samuel Morley (hosiery). Is it an accident that Bradford, which produced several of these, set off the status-competition in the West Riding for municipal monuments by constructing an opulent structure (with a restaurant 'for the accommodation of mercantile men', a hall for 3,100 people, a vast organ and illumination by a continuous line of 1,750 gas jets), thus spurring its rival Leeds to the titanic expenditure of £122,000 on its town hall? Bradford began – like so many other cities – to plan its break with municipal stinginess in 1849.

By the end of the 1860s these changes became more visible, because more formal and official. In 1867 factory legislation was for the first time seriously extended beyond the textile industries, and even began to abandon the fiction that its only purpose was to protect children – adults being theoretically capable of protecting themselves. Even in textiles, where the general business view had been that the Acts of 1833 and 1847 (the Ten Hours Act) were wanton and ruinous interferences with private enterprise, opinion was reconciled to them. No one, wrote the *Economist*, 'had any doubt *now* of the wisdom of those measures'.[3] Progress in the mines was slower, though the yearly bond in the north-east was abolished in 1872 and the right of the miners to check the honesty of their payment by results through an elected 'checkweighman' was theoretically recognized. The unjust Master and Servant code was finally abolished in 1875. More important, trade unions were given what amounted to their modern legal status, that is they were henceforth accepted as permanent and not in themselves noxious parts of the industrial scene. This change was all the more startling because the Royal Commission of 1867, which initiated it, was the result of some dramatic, and entirely indefensible, acts of terrorism by small craft societies in Sheffield (the 'Sheffield Outrages') which were expected to lead, and twenty years earlier would probably have led, to strong anti-union measures. In fact the Acts of 1871 and 1875 gave the unions a degree of legal freedom which conservative-minded lawyers have since, at intervals, attempted to whittle away.

But the most obvious symptom of the change was political: the Reform Act of 1867 (followed, as we have seen, by a whole crop of important legislative changes) accepted an electoral system dependent on working-class votes. It did not introduce parliamentary democracy, but it implied that the rulers of Britain reconciled themselves to its eventual introduction, which subsequent reforms (in 1884-5, 1918 and 1928) achieved with diminishing amounts of fuss.* Twenty years earlier Chartism had been resisted because democracy was believed to imply social revolution. Fifty years earlier it would have been unthinkable, except by the masses and a handful of extremist middle-class radicals. George Canning in 1817 had thanked God 'that the House of Commons is not sufficiently identified with the people to catch their every nascent wish. . . . According to no principle of our Constitution was it ever meant to be so . . . it never pretended to be so, nor can ever pretend to be so without bringing ruin and misery upon the kingdom.'[4] A Cecil, arguing for the rearguard in those debates of 1866-7 which reveal so much about the attitudes of the British upper classes, still warned his hearers that democracy meant socialism. The rulers of Britain did not welcome the Reform. On the contrary, but for

*But *The Times* did not regard democracy as acceptable until 1914.

the mass agitations of the poor, they would not have yielded anything like so much – though their readiness to yield in 1867 contrasts strikingly with their mass mobilization of force against Chartism in 1839, 1842 and 1848. However, they were prepared to accept it, because they no longer regarded the British working class as revolutionary. At all events they now saw it as divided into a politically moderate aristocracy of labour, ready to accept capitalism, and a politically ineffective, because unorganized and leaderless, proletarian plebs, which presented no major danger. For the great mass movements which mobilized all the labouring poor against the employing class, like Chartism, were dead. Socialism had disappeared from the country of its birth.

My sorrowful impressions [wrote an old Chartist in 1870] were confirmed. In our old Chartist time, it is true, Lancashire working men were in rags by the thousands; and many of them often lacked food. But their intelligence was demonstrated wherever you went. You would see them in groups discussing the great doctrine of political justice. . . . *Now* you will see no such groups in Lancashire. But you will hear well-dressed working men talking, as they walk with their hands in their pockets, of 'Co-ops' and their shares in them, or in building societies. And you will see others, like idiots leading small greyhound dogs.[5]

Affluence – or what men used to starvation regarded as comfort – had extinguished the fires in hungry bellies. Equally important, the discovery that capitalism was not a temporary catastrophe, but a permanent system which allowed some improvement, had altered the objective of their struggles. There were no Socialists to dream of a new society. There were trade unions, seeking to exploit the laws of political economy in order to create a scarcity of their kind of labour and thus increase their members' wages.

*

The British middle-class citizen who surveyed the scene in the early 1870s might well have thought that all was for the best in the best of all possible worlds. Nothing very serious was likely to go wrong with the British economy. But it did. Just as phase one of industrialization stumbled into self-made depression and crisis, so phase two bred its own difficulties. The years between 1873 and 1896 are known to economic historians, who have discussed them more eagerly than any other phase of nineteenth-century business conjuncture, as the 'Great Depression'. The name is misleading. So far as the working people are concerned, it cannot compare with the cataclysms of the 1830s and 1840s, or the 1920s and 1930s. (See below, pp. 207–10.) But if 'depression' indicates a pervasive – and for the generations since 1850 a new – state of mind of uneasiness and gloom about the prospects of the British economy, the word is accurate. After its glorious advance, the economy stagnated. Though the British boom of the early 1870s did not crash into ruins quite so dramatically as in the USA and Central Europe, amid the debris of bankrupt financiers and cooling blast-furnaces, it drifted inexorably downwards. Unlike in other industrial powers, the British boom would not really revive. Prices, profits and rates of interest fell or stayed puzzlingly low. A few feverish little booms did not really halt this long and frustrating descent, which was not reversed until the middle 1890s. And when the economic sun of inflation once more broke through the prevailing fog, it shone on a very different world. Between 1890 and 1895 both the USA and Germany passed Britain in the production of steel. During the 'Great Depression' Britain ceased to be the 'workshop of the world' and became merely one of its three greatest industrial powers; and in some crucial respects, the weakest of them.

The 'Great Depression' cannot be explained in purely British terms, for it was a world-wide phenomenon, though its effects varied from one country to another and in several – notably the USA, Germany and some new arrivals on the industrial scene such as the Scandinavian countries – it was on balance a period of extraordinary advance rather than stagnation. Yet in all, it marks the end of one phase of economic development – the first, or if we prefer, the 'British' phase of industrialization – and the start of another. Broadly speaking, the mid-century boom was due to the initial – or virtually initial – industrialization of the main 'advanced' economies outside Britain and the opening-up of hitherto unexploited, because inaccessible or undeveloped, areas of primary production and agriculture.* So far as the industrial countries were concerned, it was something like an extension of the British Industrial Revolution and the technology on which it was based. So far as the primary producers were concerned, it was the construction of a global system of transport based on the railway and improved – and increasingly steam-driven – shipping, capable of linking regions of relatively easy economic utilization and various mining areas to their markets in the urbanized and industrial sector of the world. Both processes immensely stimulated the British economy without as yet doing it any noticeable harm. (See p. 115.) Yet neither could continue indefinitely.

For one thing, the sharp reduction in costs both in industry and (through the transport revolution) in primary products was bound to make itself felt sooner or later – when the new plants produced, the new railroads operated, the new farming regions had come under cultivation – as a fall in prices. In fact it took the form of that spectacular twenty-year deflation which reduced the general price-level by about a third and was what most businessmen meant when they talked about persistent depression. Its effects were most dramatic, indeed catastrophic, in parts of agriculture, fortunately a relatively minor part of the British economy though not elsewhere. As soon as the massive flows of cheap foodstuffs converged upon the urbanized areas of Europe – in the 1870s – the bottom fell out of the agricultural market, not only in the receiving areas, but in the competing regions of overseas producers. The flaring discontent of Populist farmers on the North American Continent, the more dangerous rumble of agrarian revolutionism in the Russia of the 1880s and 1890s, not to mention the spurt of agrarian and nationalist unrest in Ireland in the era of Parnellism and Michael Davitt's

---

*This is not to deny the industrial development outside Britain before the 1840s, but its comparability with British industrialization. Thus in 1840 the value of all US and German hardware manufactures was each about one sixth of the British; the value of all textile manufactures somewhat over one sixth and one fifth respectively; the output of pig-iron a little over one fifth and about one eighth.

Land League* testify to its effect on regions of peasant agriculture or family farming, which were at the direct or indirect mercy of world prices. Importing countries ready to protect their farmers by tariffs, as several did after 1879, thought they had some defence. British agriculture was, as we shall see, devastated in so far as it had specialized in grain-crops, which now became quite uncompetitive, but was too unimportant to win itself protection, and eventually shifted to products not challenged, or challengeable, by overseas producers. (See p. 199.)

Again, the immediate benefits of the first phase of industrialization wore off. The possibilities of the technological innovations of the original (British) industrial era tended to exhaust themselves, and most notably so in the countries most completely transformed during this phase. A new phase of technology opened new possibilities in the 1890s, but in the meantime a certain faltering is understandable. It was all the more troubling, because both new and old industrial economies ran into problems of markets and profit-margins analogous to those which had shaken British industry forty years earlier. As the vacuum of demand was filled, markets tended to be glutted, for though they had obviously increased, they had not increased fast enough – at least at home – to keep pace with the multiple expansion of output and capacity in manufactured goods. As the titanic profits of the industrial pioneers declined, squeezed between the upper millstone of price-reducing competition and the lower of increasingly expensive and mechanized plant, with increasingly large and inelastic overheads, businessmen searched anxiously for a way out. And as they searched, the growing masses of the labouring classes in the industrial economies joined the agrarian population in agitations for improvement and change, as they had done in the corresponding era of British industrialization. The era of the Great Depression was also the era of the emergence of mass socialist (that is mainly Marxist) working-class parties all over Europe, organized in a Marxist International.

* It had fainter, because much more localized, echoes in the few peasant regions of Great Britain, notably in the crofter agitation of the Scottish highlands and the analogous movements of the Welsh hill-farmers.

In Britain the effect of these global changes was both greater and smaller than elsewhere. The agrarian crisis affected this country (but not Ireland) only marginally, and indeed the flood of increasingly cheap imports of food and raw material had its advantages. On the other hand what was elsewhere a mere stumble and change of footing in the progress of industrialization was much more serious in Britain. In the first instance this was because the British economy had been largely geared to an un-broken expansion abroad, and especially in the USA. The construction of the world network of railways was far from complete in the 1870s; yet the break in the mad construction boom in the early 1870s* had sufficient effect on the British exports of capital in money and goods to make at least one historian explain the Great Depression in the phrase 'What happened when the Railways were built'.[5] British *rentiers* had got so used to the flow of income back from North America and the undeveloped parts of the world that the defaults of their foreign debtors in the 1870s – for example the collapse of Turkish finance in 1876 – brought the laying-up of carriages and the temporary slump of building in places like Bournemouth and Folkestone. (More to the point, it mobilized those militant consortia of foreign bondholders or governments acting for their investors, which were to turn nominally independent governments into virtual or actual protectorates and colonies of the European powers – as in Egypt and Turkey after 1876.)

But the break was not merely temporary. It revealed that other countries were now able to produce for themselves, perhaps even for export, what had hitherto been available in practice only from Britain. And it also revealed that Britain was not ready for all but one of the possible methods of dealing with this situation. Unlike other countries, which now turned to tariffs protecting both their agriculture and their industrial home markets (for example France, Germany and the USA), Britain held firmly to free trade. (See Chapter 12.) She was equally disinclined to take the path of systematic economic concentration – the formation of trusts, cartels, syndicates, and so on – which was so characteristic

*Both in the USA and Germany the 1873 crash was largely a crash of railway promotion.

of Germany and the USA in the 1880s. (See Chapter 9.) She was too deeply committed to the technology and business organization of the first phase of industrialization, which had served her so well, to advance enthusiastically into the field of the new and revolutionary technology and industrial management which came to the fore in the 1890s. This left her with only one major way out – a traditional one for Britain, though one also now adopted by the competing powers – the economic (and increasingly the political) conquest of hitherto unexploited areas of the world. In other words, imperialism.

The era of the Great Depression thus also initiated the era of imperialism; the formal imperialism of the 'partition of Africa' in the 1880s, the semi-formal imperialism of national or international consortia taking over the financial management of weak countries, the informal imperialism of foreign investment. Political historians have professed to find no economic reasons for this virtual division of the world between a handful of West European powers (plus the USA) in the last decades of the nineteenth century. Economic historians have had no such difficulty. Imperialism was not a new thing for Britain. What was new was the end of the virtual British monopoly in the un-developed world, and the consequent necessity to mark out regions of imperial influence formally against potential competitors; often ahead of any actual prospects of economic benefits, often, it must be admitted, with disappointing economic results.*

One further consequence of the era of the Great Depression, that is of the emergence of a *competing group* of industrial and economically advanced powers, must be noted. It is the fusion of political and economical rivalry, the fusion of private enterprise with government backing, which is already visible in the growth of protectionism and imperialist friction. Increasingly business, in one way or another, called on the state not only to give it a free hand, but to save it. A new dimension entered

---

*But even this was not new. British businessmen had great hopes of Latin America in the 1820s, when they hoped to create an informal empire there by the setting-up of independent republics. They were, at least initially, disappointed.

international politics. And, significantly, after a long period of general peace, the great powers moved once again into an age of world wars.

Meanwhile the end of the age of unquestioned expansion, the doubt about the future prospects of the British economy, began a fundamental change in British politics. In 1870 Britain had been Liberal. The bulk of the British bourgeoisie, the bulk of the politically conscious working class, and even the old Whig section of the landed aristocracy found their political and ideological expression in the party of William Ewart Gladstone, who looked forward to peace, retrenchment and reform, the total abolition of the income tax and national debt. Those who did not had no real alternative programme or perspective. By the middle of the 1890s the great Liberal Party was split, virtually all of its aristocrats and a large section of its capitalists having seceded to the Conservatives or the 'Liberal Unionists' who were to fuse with the Conservatives. The City of London, a Liberal stronghold until 1874, had acquired its Conservative colouring. An independent Labour Party backed by the trade unions and inspired by socialists was about to appear. Already the first cloth-capped proletarian socialist was sitting in the House of Commons. A few years, but a historic era, earlier, a shrewd observer had still (1885) written about the British workers:

There is less tendency to socialism here than among other nations of the Old World or of the New. The English working man . . . makes none of those extravagant demands upon the protection of the State in the regulation of his daily labour and of the rate of his wages, which are current among the working classes of America and of Germany, and which cause a certain form of socialism to be equally the pest of both countries.[7]

By the end of the Great Depression things had changed.

NOTES

1. Checkland, Chambers, Clapham, Landes (see Further Reading 3). There are unfortunately no modern histories of any of the basic industries. M. R. Robbins, *The Railway Age* (1962), is a useful introduction to its subject. L. H. Jenks, *The Migration of British Capital to 1875* (1927), is wider than its title suggests. C. Erickson, *British Industrialists: Steel and Hosiery* (1959), is useful on businessmen; S. Pollard, *A History of Labour in Sheffield* (1959), virtually unique as a regional study of labour. Royden Harrison, *Before the Socialists* (1965), throws light on the social politics of the period. On migrations, Brinley Thomas, *Migration and Economic Growth* (1954), and J. Saville, *Rural Depopulation in England and Wales* (1957). The bibliography of the 'Great Depression' is large. Ashworth (Further Reading 3) may introduce the facts; C. Wilson, 'Economy and Society in late Victorian Britain' (*Economic History Review*, XVIII, 1965), and A. E. Musson in *Journal of Economic History*, 1959, the arguments. See also Figures 1, 3, 5, 7, 13–17, 21–2, 24, 26–8, 31–2, 37, 50–1.

2. John Francis, *A History of the English Railway* (1851), II, p. 136.

3. Quoted in J. H. Clapham, *An Economic History of Modern Britain*, II, p. 41.

4. Quoted in W. Smart, *Economic Annals of the 19th Century* (1910), I, p. 54.

5. *The Life of Thomas Cooper, Written by Himself* (1872), p. 393.

6. W. W. Rostow, *British Economy in the 19th Century* (1948), p. 88.

7. T. H. S. Escott, *England* (1885 edn), pp. 135–6.

7

BRITAIN IN THE WORLD ECONOMY[1]

THE mid-Victorian period is a good vantage-point from which to survey the characteristic and crucial system of Britain's economic relations with the rest of the world.

In the literal sense Britain was perhaps never the 'workshop of the world', but her industrial dominance was such in the middle of the nineteenth century that the phrase is legitimate. She produced perhaps two thirds of the world's coal, perhaps half its iron, five sevenths of its small supply of steel, about half of such cotton cloth as was produced on a commercial scale, and forty per cent (in value) of its hardware. On the other hand even in 1840 Britain possessed only about one third of the world's steam power and produced probably something less than one third of the world's total of manufactures. The chief rival state, even then, was the USA – or rather the northern states of the USA – with France, the German Confederation and Belgium. All these, except in part little Belgium, lagged behind British industrialization, but it was already clear that, if they and others continued to industrialize, Britain's advantage would inevitably shrink. And so it did. Though the British position was pretty well maintained in cotton, and may actually have been strengthened in pig-iron, by 1870 the 'workshop of the world' possessed only between one quarter and one fifth of the world's steam power, and produced much less than half its steel. By the end of the 1880s the relative decline was visible even in the formerly dominant branches of production. By the early 1890s the USA and Germany both passed Britain in the production of the crucial commodity of industrialization, steel. From then on Britain was one of a group of great industrial powers, but not the leader of industrialization. Indeed, among the industrial powers it was the most sluggish and the one which showed most obvious signs of relative decline.

Such international comparisons were not merely a matter of

national pride (or uneasiness), but of urgent practical importance. As we have seen the early British industrial economy relied for its expansion chiefly on international trade. It had to, for with the exception of coal its domestic supplies of raw material were not very impressive, and some crucially important industries such as cotton relied entirely on imports. Moreover, from the middle of the nineteenth century the country was no longer able to feed itself from its own agricultural production. Furthermore, though the British population rose fast, it was originally too small to maintain an industrial and trading apparatus of the size actually developed, all the more so because the greater part of it – the labouring classes – were too poor to provide an intensive market for anything but the absolute essentials of subsistence: food, housing, and a few elementary pieces of clothing and household goods. Poor as it was, the home market might have been developed more effectively, but – largely because of Britain's reliance on overseas trade – it was not. This intensified the dependence on the international market even more.

More important than this, Britain was also in a position to develop its international trade to an abnormal extent, simply because of the monopoly of industrialization, and of relations with the underdeveloped overseas world which she succeeded in establishing between 1780 and 1815. In a sense her industry expanded into an international vacuum, though parts of it were empty because they had been cleared by the activities of the British navy, and were kept empty because rival trading powers were unable to leap across the British-controlled high seas.

The British economy therefore developed a characteristic and peculiar pattern of international relations. It relied heavily on foreign trade, that is to say, broadly speaking, on exchanging its own manufactures and other supplies and services of a developed economy (capital, shipping, banking, insurance, and so on) for foreign primary products (raw materials and food). In 1870 British trade per capita (excluding the 'invisible' items) stood at £17 7s. od. as against £6 4s. od. for each Frenchman, £5 6s. od. for each German and £4 9s. od. for each citizen of the USA. Only little Belgium, the other pioneer of industry, had at this time comparable figures among the industrial states. Overseas markets for products and overseas outlets for capital played an important and growing part in the economy. By the end of the eighteenth century domestic exports amounted to about thirteen per cent of the national income, by the early 1870s to about twenty-two per cent and thereafter they averaged between sixteen and twenty per cent except in the period between the 1929 slump and the early 1950s. Until the 'Great Depression' of the nineteenth century, exports normally grew faster than the real national income as a whole. In the major industries the foreign market played an even more decisive role. This is most obvious in cotton, which exported over half the total value of its output at the beginning of the nineteenth century and almost four fifths at the end, and iron and steel, which relied on overseas markets for about forty per cent of its gross production from the mid nineteenth century.

The 'ideal' result of this massive interchange would have been to transform the world into a set of economies dependent on and complementary to the British, each exchanging the primary products for which its geographical situation fitted it (or so the more naïve economists of the period argued) for the manufactures of the world's workshop. In fact several such complementary economies did develop at various times, mainly on the basis of some specialized local products for which the British were the main buyers: cotton in the southern states of the USA until the American Civil War, wool in Australia, nitrates and copper in Chile, guano in Peru, wine in Portugal, and so forth. After the 1870s the growth of a massive international trade in foodstuffs added various other countries to this economic empire, notably Argentina (wheat, beef), New Zealand (meat, dairy products), the agrarian sector of the Danish economy (dairy products, bacon) and others. Meanwhile South Africa developed a similar relationship on the basis of its gold and diamond exports, the world market being controlled from London, and various tropical countries on the basis of different vegetable products (for example palm-oil, rubber).

Obviously, the entire world could not be turned into this kind of planetary system circling round the economic sun of Britain, if only because Britain was not the only already developed or industrializing economy. The other advanced economies, each with its own pattern of international relationships, were of course Britain's trading partners, and indeed potentially more important customers for her goods than the undeveloped world, being both richer and more dependent on the purchase of manufactures. It is a commonplace that trade between two developed countries is normally more intense than between a developed and a backward, or between backward ones. However, this type of trade was far more vulnerable, because it was protected by neither economic nor political control. An advanced country in the process of industrialization would initially need Britain, because – in the early stages at all events – it would benefit by drawing on the unique supply of capital, machinery and technical skill of Britain, and sometimes it had no alternative. Time and again we find on the continent of Europe the first factories or machine-workshops started by some Englishman, the first native machines copied from some British design (illegally smuggled if before 1825, legally acquired thereafter). Europe was full of Thorntons (Austria and Russia), Evans and Thomas (Czechoslovakia), Cockerills (Belgium), Manbys and Wilsons (France) or Mulvanys (Germany), and the universal spread of football in the twentieth century is largely due to the works teams started by British owners, managers or skilled operatives in all parts of the continent. Inevitably we find the first railways – and often the bulk of railways – built by British contractors, with British locomotives, rails, technical staff and capital.

However, equally inevitably, an industrializing economy would attempt to protect its industries against the British, for if it did not they were unlikely to develop to the point of being able to compete with the British at home, let alone abroad. National economists in the USA and Germany never had much doubt about the value of protection, and industrialists in fields competitive with the British had even less. Even firm believers in Free Trade like John Stuart Mill accepted the legitimacy of discriminating in favour of 'infant industries'. However, legitimate or not, there was nothing to stop sovereign and economically as well as politically independent states from doing so, as the (northern) USA did from 1816 and most other advanced countries from the 1880s. And even without discrimination, once a local economy was on its feet, its need of Britain diminished rapidly, except perhaps in so far as the international trading and financial mechanism happened to be located in London. From the middle of the nineteenth century this began to be obvious. British exports of goods to the 'advanced world' were and remained large, but static or declining. In 1860–70, fifty-two per cent of British capital investments had also gone to Europe and the USA. By 1911–13 only twenty-five per cent of them were still in these areas.

The British hegemony in the underdeveloped world was thus based on a permanent complementarity of economies; British hegemony in the industrializing world on potential or actual competition. The one was therefore likely to last, the other was in its nature temporary. Even when other 'advanced' economies were small and struggling, their interest was divided between the urge to speed their own development by drawing on the resources of Britain and the urge to protect themselves against British industrial supremacy. Once they had made what use they could of Britain, they would inevitably tend to veer towards protectionism, unless of course they had advanced so far as to be able to undersell the British. In this case the British might well have to think of protecting themselves and their markets in third countries against them.

Broadly speaking, there was only one comparatively brief historical period when both developed and underdeveloped sectors of the world had an equal interest in working with and not against the British economy, or when they had no choice in the matter: the decades between the abolition of the Corn Laws in 1846 and the outbreak of the Great Depression in 1873. Many underdeveloped areas had virtually no one except Britain to sell to, since Britain was the only modern economy.* The

* For instance, even in 1881–4 Britain, with more than twice the per capita consumption, used almost half of all the sugar consumed in Europe, and, since several continental countries covered much of their requirements from domestic production (beet-sugar), by far the greater part of the overseas cane-sugar imported into Europe.

advanced countries were entering the period of rapid industrialization, when their demands for imports, especially of capital and capital goods, were virtually unlimited. And any countries which did not care to enter into relations with the advanced world (that is largely with Britain) were forced to do so by gunboats and marines: the last 'closed' countries of the world, China and Japan, were thus forced into unrestricted intercourse with the modern economies between 1840 and 1860.

Both before and after this brief period the situation of Britain in the economic world was in important respects dissimilar. Before the 1840s the size and scale of international economic operations were comparatively modest, the scope for massive international flows limited, partly because of the absence of adequate surpluses of production for export (except in Britain), or because of the technical or social difficulty of transporting men and goods in sufficient bulk or quantity, or because of the relatively modest balances for investment abroad accumulated up to this point, even in Britain. Between 1800 and 1830 total international trade increased by a modest thirty per cent from about £300 million to about £400 million; but between 1840 and 1870 it multiplied five times over, and by the latter date had passed £2,000 million. Between 1800 and 1840 a little over a million Europeans migrated to the USA, which we may use as a convenient yardstick of the general flow of migration; but between 1840 and 1870 almost seven million moved across the North Atlantic. By the early 1840s Britain had accumulated perhaps about £160 million in credits abroad, by the early 1850s around £250 million; but between 1855 and 1870 she invested abroad at the average rate of £29 million a year and by 1873 her accumulated balances had almost reached £1,000 million. All this is merely another way of saying that before the age of the railway and the steamship the scope of the world economy was limited, and with it the scope of Britain.

After 1873 the situation of the 'advanced' world was one of rivalry between developed countries; and what is more countries of whom only Britain had a built-in interest in total freedom of trade. Neither the USA, nor Germany nor France relied to any substantial extent on massive imports of food and raw materials;

indeed, except for Germany, they were substantial exporters of foodstuffs. Nor did they rely to anything like the British extent on exports for the market of their industries; indeed the USA relied almost entirely on its domestic market and Germany did so to a large extent. An all-embracing world system of virtually unrestricted flows of capital, labour and goods never actually existed, but between 1860 and 1875 something not too far removed from it came into being. 'By 1866,' a historian has written, 'the greater part of Western Europe was in a situation very close to free trade, or at all events closer to free trade than at any other time in history.'[2] The USA was the only major economic power which remained systematically protectionist, but even this state went through a period of lowering its duties in 1832–60 and again after the Civil War (1861–5) until 1875. At the same time – again with the partial exception of the USA – the general adoption of a gold-standard by the currencies of the chief European nations between 1863 and 1874 simplified the operations of a single free and multilateral system of world trading, increasingly pivoting on London.

It did not last. The free flow of goods was the first to be inhibited by the tariff barriers and other discriminatory measures which were erected with increasing frequency and height after 1880. The free flow of men remained unimpeded until the First World War and its aftermath.* The free flow of capital and payments alone survived until 1931, though increasingly shaken after 1914, and with it the supremacy of London and the will-o'-the-wisp of a wholly liberal world economy. But if this had ever been a practical possibility, which is doubtful, it was dead by the end of the 1870s.

*

The chief measure of an economy's relations with the rest of the world is its balance of payments, that is the balance of its income and capital from abroad and its outgoings to foreign countries. Whatever this figure actually means – and like all forms of book-keeping it requires very expert interpretation – it throws light

*This was not of major importance to Britain.

on the nature and pattern of a country's international dealings. This balance consists of 'visible' and 'invisible' items. The 'visible' items on the credit side are the exports of merchandise (including goods imported into Britain and re-exported), and the sales of bullion. The 'invisible' items consist of the profits of foreign trade and services (for example by British firms handling British and other marketing and buying abroad), earnings from insurance, brokerage, and so on, from shipping, from personal expenditures of foreigners in Britain (for example tourism) and remittances by emigrants, and from genuinely invisible and often unmeasurable items like the earnings of smugglers. In addition 'invisible' income consists of interests and dividends received from abroad. The items on the debit side are the converse: the cost of imports of merchandise, of paying foreign firms and shippers, remittances of dividend and interests abroad and so on. In the extreme situation the two sides should exactly balance, though this hardly ever happens, and indeed is probably undesirable. If there is a surplus or a deficit, the classical theory of international trade requires sooner or later some transfers of bullion (if that is the standard of international payments), but the gap can, of course, be filled by borrowing or lending. Ideally, once again, the balance of payments with the world implies a system of world clearing and settlement, that is of setting off the surpluses in dealings with some countries against the deficits in dealing with others. It is extremely unlikely that the account with all countries will be in balance. Indeed, there had been traditionally areas of the world with which British (visible) trade had been fairly consistently in deficit – for instance France, the Baltic and Eastern Europe, and especially India – and in the pre-liberal era this had seriously worried economists and politicians.

The (visible) balance reflects not merely the quantities of goods and so on imported and exported, but their prices, that is the so-called *terms of trade*. If they 'improve' a ton of exports will buy more imports, if they 'worsen' it will buy less.* For a

---

*They are normally measured by taking the relation between exports and imports for a base-year as 100 and expressing other years as a percentage of it.

country of Britain's character these express essentially the relation between the price of (British) industrial products and (foreign) raw materials and foodstuffs. For – at all events during Britain's industrial supremacy – well over ninety per cent of our net imports consisted of primary products, while between seventy-five and ninety per cent of our home-produced exports consisted of manufactured goods, and a good deal of our re-exports of commodities processed by British industry (refined, distilled, and so on). But here a curious situation arises.

Suppose the terms of trade moved in Britain's favour, that is we got our primary products more cheaply than before, or manufacturing exports cost more, or both. The main purchasers of British goods, the primary producing countries, would then be able to buy *less* British goods, having less income to pay for them. But a worsening of the terms of trade would not necessarily have the converse effect, since Britain depended on importing a fairly inelastic quantity of food and raw materials whatever happened to keep its population fed and its factories running. There would be a tendency for imports to stay high whatever happened: if the terms of trade favoured us we tended to buy more, if they went against us we might not import less. There would also be a natural tendency for our exports to rise when the terms of trade worsened. And this was indeed so. When they moved against us, the proportion of our industrial production exported rose; and the other way round. From the point of view of British industrial supremacy it was desirable that we should buy expensively rather than cheaply.

Now broadly speaking, industry underwent a continuous process of cheapening because of the continuous technological revolution, but agricultural production, which until the end of the century produced the bulk of both food and industrial raw materials – up to the early 1880s between sixty and seventy per cent of them were materials for the textile industry – underwent intermittent cheapening, but not yet anything comparable to industrial revolution. On the whole, until the industrial revolution in the form of railways and steamships (which opened up new and cheap sources of supply like the American Middle West), individual applications of machinery to agriculture (like the steam-driven sugar mill), and a growing demand for non-agricultural raw materials, such as the products of mining and oilwells, transformed the primary producing sector, the terms of trade therefore tended to move against the rapidly cheapening industrial goods. But agriculture was not transformed until the last third of the nineteenth century. Hence for the first sixty years of the century the mechanism for boosting British exports worked well. Thereafter it ceased, not only because of changes on the primary side, but also because of changes on the British side. British exports ceased to be based essentially on textiles, and increasingly shifted to more expensive capital goods and raw materials – iron, steel, coal, ships, machinery. Textiles, which had formed seventy-two per cent of our manufactured exports in 1867–9, fell to fifty-one per cent at the eve of the First World War, while capital goods rose from twenty to thirty-nine per cent. The growth of the home market – due largely to a rise in the standard of living to cheaper food imports and the proportional fall in the importance of cotton – reduced the proportion of net imported raw materials from over seventy to around forty per cent and increased the import of foodstuffs from under twenty-five per cent to around forty-five per cent; the major change occurring quite rapidly after 1860. There was naturally a greater incentive to keep vast food-imports cheaper than raw materials; for high food prices could not, like high raw material prices, be made good by improvements in industrial efficiency. A third factor affected the relations between the two price levels. Henceforth in the periodic slumps primary prices were likely to collapse more dramatically than industrial prices, whereas in the first half of the nineteenth century, if anything, the opposite had been the case.* Lastly, the growth of satellite and dependent colonial or semi-colonial economies producing primary

* Various reasons may be suggested for this important phenomenon. Two relevant ones are (*a*) that until the second half of the century slumps often still began in the agricultural sector – for example with bad harvests – but later on in the industrial sector, and (*b*) that the 'degree of monopoly' – that is the ability to maintain stable prices and meet slumps by cutting production or in some other way – was increasingly greater in the industrial sector than in agriculture. Indeed, agriculture might actually tend to meet slumps by *increasing* output.

commodities put their terms of trade very much under the control of the dominant industrial economies, and especially Britain.

So a period when the terms of trade had moved against Britain was succeeded, after 1860, by one in which they rapidly and then slowly moved in her favour till 1896–1914, and after the First World War a period in which they moved our way very sharply indeed. Since the Second World War they have tended to worsen again. Consequently over this long period the export-booster ceased to operate as strongly as before, though of course from time to time heavy British investment overseas gave our customers more funds to buy, and reductions in other costs (for example freight charges) also improved the situation. However, the incentive for British industry, when not committed to exports, to prefer the home to the foreign market grew.

We would, therefore, expect to find, and do find, an increasingly large excess of imports over exports after 1860. But we also find – and this is rather odd – that at *no* time in the nineteenth century did Britain have an export surplus in goods, in spite of her industrial monopoly, her marked export-orientation, and her modest domestic consumer market.* Before 1846 Free Traders argued that this was because the Corn Laws prevented our potential customers from earning enough through their exports to pay for ours, but this is doubtful. The buyers of our exports reflect the limits of the markets to which Britain exported, which were essentially countries which either did not want to take much more British textiles or were too poor to have more than a very tiny per capita demand. But it also reflects the traditional 'underdeveloped' slant of the British economy, and also to some extent the luxury demand of the British upper and middle classes. As we have seen, between 1814 and 1845 about

---

*The interpretation of these statistics is a very controversial matter. Some students deny that there was no export surplus. They argue that as the goods went in British ships they should logically be measured at foreign ports, and then the value of exported goods is often greater than that of imports. On the other hand there may have been advantages in not having a continuous surplus on visible and invisible transactions. Had there been, we would have accumulated a vast gold reserve or caused a liquidity crisis, unless we had financed the export surplus by even more lending abroad than we actually seem to have done. I owe this point to K. Berrill.

seventy per cent of our net imports (in value) were raw materials, about twenty-four per cent foodstuffs – overwhelmingly tropical or similar products (tea, sugar, coffee) – and alcohol. There is not much doubt that Britain consumed so much of these because we had a traditionally important re-export trade in them. Just as cotton production grew, as it were, as a by-product of a large international entrepot trade, so did the unusually large consumption of sugar, tea, and so on, which accounts for a large part of the deficit on current account.

Nowadays governments would worry acutely over such a deficit. In the nineteenth century they did not, and not only because in the earlier part of it they were not aware that it existed.* In fact, Britain's 'invisible' dealings procured her a large surplus, and not a deficit with the rest of the world. Probably the most important of these earnings came initially from *British shipping*, which amounted to between one third and half of the world tonnage. (It tended to decline relatively in the first half of the century, mainly because of the rising American merchant fleet, but recovered all and more of its supremacy after 1860 in the age of the iron steamship.) Until the early 1870s its earnings exceeded the *interests and dividends* from British investments abroad. This source of income, which became increasingly the major means of filling the gap between imports and exports, started modestly after the Napoleonic Wars, but by the later 1840s had become of about equal importance to the third major source of invisible income, the *profits on foreign trade and services*, and by the later 1860s had overhauled these. By the middle decades of the century a fourth source, the earnings from *insurance, brokerage commissions*, and so on – in brief, from the dominant financial position of the City of London – had also become reasonably important.

Broadly speaking, the invisible income other than interests and dividends more than covered the trading deficit in the first quarter of the century, but between 1825 and 1850 – the difficult years of the early industrial economy, as we have seen (cf. pp. 76–7 above) – they did not quite do so, and after 1875 they

* Because of the peculiar and misleading way in which the trade statistics were drawn up.

were not normally adequate any longer. However, in the earlier period income from capital previously exported already produced a modest surplus, and after 1875, as the dividends from the vast earlier investments rolled in, an increasingly large one. The international position of the British economy therefore became increasingly dependent on the British inclination to invest or lend their accumulated surpluses abroad.

But this, like Britain's visible trade, became increasingly tied up with the underdeveloped world, and especially with that sector of it which was under effective economic or political control by Britain: the formal or informal Empire. Or, to be more exact, the peculiar position of Britain made both visible and invisible transactions naturally flow in this direction.

British visible trade, as we have seen, had after 1820 always found it easier to penetrate further into the underdeveloped world than to break into the more lucrative, but also more resistant and rival developed markets. This was so whether British industry was dynamic and world-leading or not, as can be seen from the following table:

EXPORTS OF COTTON PIECE GOODS (MILLION YARDS) – % OF TOTAL

Year	Europe and USA	Underdeveloped world	Other countries
1820	60·4	31·8	7·8
1840	29·5	66·7	3·8
1860	19·0	73·3	7·7
1880	9·8	82·0	8·2
1900	7·1	86·3	6·6

The pattern of Britain's exports in general was similar, though not so extreme as in cotton: a steady flight from the modern, resistant and competitive markets into the undeveloped. Two areas of the world were of special importance to Britain in this respect.

The first was Latin America, which, it is not unfair to say, saved the British cotton industry in the first half of the nineteenth century, when it became the largest single market for its exports – reaching thirty-five per cent of them in 1840, mainly to Brazil. Later on in the century it became somewhat less important, though towards the end the British informal colony of Argentina became an important market. The second was the East Indies (which soon became important enough to split into India and the Far East). This soon became absolutely crucial. From six per cent of our cotton exports after the Napoleonic Wars these regions came to absorb twenty-two per cent in 1840, thirty-one per cent in 1850 and an absolute majority of them – anything up to sixty per cent – after 1873. India took most of this – about forty to forty-five per cent after the onset of the Great Depression. Indeed, in this period of difficulty Asia saved Lancashire, even more decisively than Latin America had done in the early part of the century. There are, as we see, good reasons why British foreign policy in the first half of the nineteenth century favoured the independence of Latin America and the 'opening' of China. There are even more convincing reasons why India was vital to British policy throughout this period.

Capital exports, including those to the undeveloped world and the British Empire in particular, became important somewhat later. Before the 1840s they consisted essentially of government loans, after that of government loans, railways and public utilities. Around 1850 Europe and the USA still accounted for over half of them, but between 1860 and 1890, as one might expect, the proportion of Europe fell drastically (from twenty-five to eight per cent) and that of the USA sagged slowly until it also fell dramatically during the First World War (from 19 to 5·5 per cent). Latin America and India stepped into the breach, as usual, but – if we except the disappointing investments there after the fight for independence – in reverse order. In the 1850s India, thanks to heavy and (against *laissez-faire* theory) government-guaranteed railway and other issues, took the lead with about twenty per cent of our total investment; thereafter it dropped quite sharply. Latin America, however, thanks to the development of Argentina and other dependent economies, doubled its share of British holdings by the 1880s and thereafter

represented about twenty per cent in its turn.* But the really
striking increase was in the *developing* rather than the backward
areas of the underdeveloped world, and especially of the British
Empire. The 'white' dominions (Canada, Australia, New
Zealand, South Africa) raised their share from twelve per cent
in the 1860s to almost thirty per cent in the 1880s; and if we
include Argentina, Chile and Uruguay as 'honorary' dominions
– their economies were not dissimilar – the rise in these outlets
for capital export is even more striking. After the First World
War, the share of the dominions became even more important –
getting on for forty per cent. Taking the Empire and Latin
America as a whole, their share went up as follows:

Year	Empire (%)	Latin America (%)	Total (%)
1060s	36	10·5	46·5
1880s	47	20	67
1900–13	46	22	68
1927–9	59	22	81

With one major exception these developments were, at least
to begin with, independent of policy. The character of Britain's
pioneer economic hegemony established, as it were, a certain
slope in the international economic landscape, and Britain slid
naturally down it. The one exception was India. Its abnormality
leaps to the eye. It was, for one thing, the only part of the British
Empire to which *laissez-faire* never applied. Its most enthusiastic
champions in Britain became bureaucratic planners when they
went there, and the most committed opponents of political
colonization rarely, and then never seriously, suggested the
liquidation of British rule. And the 'formal' British Empire
expanded in India even when no other part of it did. The
economic reasons for this anomaly were compelling.

As we have seen, India was an increasingly vital market for

* In 1890 out of about £424 million invested there Argentina represented
about £157 million, Brazil – formerly the biggest item – about £69 million,
Mexico £60 million, Uruguay £28 million, Cuba £27 million, and Chile
£25 million.

the staple export, cotton goods; and it became so because in the first quarter of the nineteenth century British policy destroyed the local textile industry as a competitor with Lancashire. In the second place India controlled the trade of the Far East through its export surplus with that area; the exports consisting largely of opium, a state monopoly which the British fostered systematically (mainly for revenue purposes) almost from the start. As late as 1870 almost half China's total imports consisted of these narcotics, kindly supplied by the liberal economy of the West. Both these surpluses and the rest of India's trading surplus with the world were naturally siphoned off from Britain's benefit through the (politically established and maintained) Indian trading deficit with Britain, through the 'Home Charges' – that is India's payments for the privilege of being administered by Britain – and through the increasingly large interest-payments on the Indian Public Debt. Towards the end of the century these items became increasingly important. Before the First World War 'the key to Britain's whole payments pattern lay in India, financing as she probably did more than two fifths of Britain's total deficits'.[3] As another writer has put it:

> Thus not only the funds for investment in India but a large part of the total investment income from overseas, that gave Britain her balance-of-payments surplus in the last quarter of the nineteenth century, was provided by India. India was in truth the jewel in the imperial diadem.[4]

It is not surprising that not even the free-traders wished to see this gold-mine escape from British political control, and that a great part of British foreign and military or naval policy was designed essentially to maintain safe control of it.

In India, the formal Empire never ceased to be vital to the British economy. Elsewhere it appeared to become increasingly vital after the 1870s, when foreign competition became acute, and Britain sought to escape from it – and largely did escape from it – by a flight into her dependencies. From the 1880s 'imperialism' – the division of the world into formal colonies and 'spheres of influence' of the great powers, generally combined with the attempt to establish deliberately the sort of economic satellite system which Britain had evolved spontaneously – became universally popular among the large powers. For Britain this was a step back. She exchanged the informal empire over most of the underdeveloped world for the formal empire of a quarter of it, plus the older satellite economies. Nor was the change particularly easy or inviting. The really valuable satellite economies were (except for India) either beyond political control – like the Argentine – or they were white settler 'dominions' with their own economic interests, which did not necessarily coincide with Britain's. They required compensatory concessions for their own products in Britain, if they were to hand over their markets entirely to the mother country, and it was on this point that Joseph Chamberlain's plans for imperial integration broke down in the early 1900s. There was some point in annexing all the backward areas possible in order to secure control of the raw materials in them, which even at the end of the nineteenth century increasingly looked as though they would be vital for modern economies, and which indeed became vital. By the end of the Second World War, the rubber and tin of Malaya, the rich mining deposits of central and southern Africa, and above all the oil deposits of the Middle East had become the major international assets of Britain, and the mainstay of her balance of payments. But at the end of the nineteenth century the economic case for annexing large tracts of jungle, bush and desert was not overwhelming. However, it was not Britain which took the initiative, and where her rivals led, she had to follow suit. And, as we have seen, between the wars, after the collapse of the pre-1914 structure of her international economic relations, the Empire was there to provide a cushion in an increasingly hard world.

In terms of visible trade the collapse came suddenly after the First World War. This was due both to the general crisis of the world economy which contracted the scope of international economic transactions, and with it of Britain which lived by them, and to the delayed but inevitable revelation that British industry had become obsolete and inefficient. Only for a brief period after the war (1926–9) did world trade regain the level of 1913, and at the worst periods it fell about a quarter below it:

a startling change from the years from 1875 to 1913 when it had trebled. But if during this hard period British exports fell by half, it was not merely because of the general contraction, but because they were no longer competitive.

Britain had escaped from the Great Depression (1873–96) – the first international challenge – not by modernizing her economy, but by exploiting the remaining possibilities of her traditional situation. She had exported more to the backward and satellite economies (as in cotton), and made what she could from the last of the great technical innovations she had pioneered, the iron steamship (as in shipbuilding and coal exports). When the last great receptacles of cotton goods developed their own textile industries – India, Japan and China – the hour of Lancashire tolled. For not even political control could permanently keep India non-industrial, though as late as the 1890s the Lancashire pressure-group had prevented the imposition of duties to protect the Indian cotton industry.* The war, which interrupted the normal course of international trade and stimulated industrial growth in many countries which had to be protected afterwards, revealed the new situation brutally. Before it, Indian industry had provided only twenty-eight per cent of the local textile supply; after it, it provided over sixty per cent. Rival and more efficient suppliers and the oil-fired ships cut down the exports of coal. They had rocketed from about twenty million tons in the early 1880s to seventy-three million in 1913. In the 1920s they averaged forty-nine million, in the 1930s forty. The deficit on visible trade – the gap between imports and exports – was rarely less than twice as large as in the worst years before 1913.

Britain's invisible income, on the other hand, appeared more than adequate to fill this gap. As her industry sagged, her finance triumphed, her services as shipper, trader and intermediary in the world's system of payments became more indispensable. Indeed if London ever was the real economic hub of the world, the pound sterling its foundation, it was between 1870 and 1913.

As we have seen, foreign investments increased by leaps and

* In effect such duties were not imposed until after 1917.

bounds, mainly in the 1860s and 1870s, later by the reinvestment of their own interest and dividends. By 1913 Britain owned perhaps £4,000 million worth abroad, as against less than £5,500 million owned by France, Germany, Belgium, Holland and the USA put together. In the later 1850s British ships had carried about thirty per cent of the cargoes entering French or US ports: by 1900 they carried forty-five per cent of the French, fifty-five per cent of the American ones.* Paradoxically the very process which weakened British production – the rise of new industrial powers, the enfeeblement of the British competitive power – reinforced the triumph of finance and trade. The new industrial powers expanded their imports of primary products from the undeveloped world, but they had not Britain's traditional symbiotic arrangements with it, and therefore ran up a heavy joint deficit. Britain filled this deficit (*a*) by her own increasing imports of manufactures from the industrial states, (*b*) by her 'invisible' income from shipping services and the like, and (*c*) by the income which came to her as the world's greatest lender. The threads of the world's web of trading and financial settlements ran through London, and increasingly they had to run through London, because London alone could fill the holes in it.

The First World War tore this web, though British governments made desperate efforts to maintain it. Britain ceased to be the world's great creditor nation, mainly because she was obliged to liquidate a large part of her investments in the USA (say about £500 million, mainly in railway securities) and in turn became heavily indebted to the USA, which ended the war as the greatest creditor nation in its turn. After 1919 Britain appeared to recover – and a heroic attempt was made by her governments to re-create the conditions of 1913 and thus to restore that lost paradise. By 1925 investment earnings and other invisible earnings were – in contemporary values – higher than ever before. But this was an illusion. Gross investment income had risen from about 4·5 per cent of the national income

*Only Germany, which started a deliberate course of maritime rivalry with Britain in the 1890s, cut down her use of British shipping from then on.

in the 1870s to about nine per cent in 1910–13; after the First World War the percentage was back, on average, to where it had been in the 1870s; after the Second World War to where it had been in the 1860s. The slump of 1929 destroyed the illusion of a return to the *belle époque* before 1913, the Second World War buried it. Britain now had neither adequate visible nor adequate invisible income. The recurrent 'balance of payments' crises, which first caused British governments systematic insomnia in 1931, are the tangible symptoms of this predicament.

NOTES

1. *Ashworth, Landes, Deane and Cole (see Further Reading 3). *M. Barratt Brown, *After Imperialism* (1963), is an excellent introduction. S. B. Saul, *Studies in British Overseas Trade 1870–1914* (1960), and A. Imlah, *Economic Elements in the Pax Britannica* (1958), Charles Feinstein, 'Income and Investment in the UK 1856–1914', *Economic Journal*, 1961, are more technical. L. H. Jenks (see Chapter 6, Note 1) remains indispensable. The basic material on trade is in W. Schlote, *British Overseas Trade* (English edn, 1952). *W. A. Lewis, *Economic Survey 1919–1939* (1949), for the inter-war period. On British industrial influence abroad, W. O. Henderson, *Britain and Industrial Europe 1750–1870* (1954). M. Greenberg, *British Trade and the Opening of China* (1951), and H. S. Ferns, *Britain and Argentina in the 19th Century* (1960), are case-studies. See also Figures 23–26.

2. Hauser, Maurain, Benaerts, *Du Libéralisme à l'Impérialisme* (1939), pp. 62–3.

3. S. B. Saul, op. cit., p. 62.

4. M. Barratt Brown, op. cit., p. 85.

8

STANDARDS OF LIVING
1850–1914[1]

LET us stop and take a different sort of look round Britain at the high point of its capitalist career, three or four generations after the Industrial Revolution. It was, first and foremost, a country of workers. R. Dudley Baxter, calculating the size of the various British classes in 1867, reckoned that over three quarters – seventy-seven per cent – of the 24·1 million inhabitants of Great Britain belonged to the 'manual labour class'; and he included among the 'middle class' all office-workers and shop-assistants, all shopkeepers, however tiny, all foremen and supervisory workers, and the like. Not more than fifteen per cent of these belonged to a skilled or moderately well-paid aristocracy of labour – say, with wages of 28 shillings a week to £2 – rather over half to the unskilled, agricultural, women and other underpaid– say with wages of 10–12 shillings a week – and the balance to intermediate ranges. At work a part of them – the textile workers, the various other 'factories and workshops' which were just being brought into the system of factory legislation in the 1860s, even to some extent the coalminers – were already enjoying some legal regulation of their conditions, and more rarely of their hours of labour. From 1871 they even achieved the first legal recognition of non-religious leisure, the Bank Holidays. But overwhelmingly their wages and conditions depended on the bargains they could make with their employers, alone or through their trade unions. By the early 1870s trade unionism was officially accepted and recognized, where it had succeeded in establishing itself. Thanks to the archaic structure of the British economy, this was not only among the skilled craftsmen of manual trades (for example the builders, tailors, printers, and so on), but also in the core of the basic industries, such as the cotton mills and the coal mines, and the great complex of machine- and ship-building, in which most of the skilled work remained essentially that of manual craftsmen. Even so, this amounted to no more than a small minority of British workers, except in certain localities and trades. Even the great trade-union expansion of 1871–3 only raised the number of organized workers to something like half a million. Vast sectors of the economy – for instance transport – were still virtually unorganized. However, the fact that a rather old-fashioned trade unionism, often of the craft type, had succeeded in establishing a permanent base for further advance in some of the chief sectors of industrial Britain was significant. It had the advantage of giving the labour movement very considerable potential power, but also the disadvantage (which it shared with British industry as a whole), of saddling it with a rather old-fashioned and unadaptable structure, from which the later advocates of more rational and effective union organization (for example by 'industrial' unions) have never since been able to liberate it.

When workers lost their employment – which they might do at the end of the job, of the week, of the day or even of the hour – they had nothing to fall back upon except their savings, their friendly society or trade union, their credit with local shopkeepers, their neighbours and friends, the pawnbroker or the Poor Law, which was still the *only* public provision for what we now call social security. When they grew old or infirm, they were lost, unless helped by their children, for effective insurance or private pension schemes covered only a few of them. Nothing is more characteristic of Victorian working-class life, and harder for us to imagine today, than this virtually total absence of social security. Skilled workers, or those in expanding industries, would probably enjoy some of the benefits of being in short supply, except in the recurring economic crises. They would also benefit from trade unions, friendly societies, cooperatives and even modest private savings. Unskilled ones would be lucky to make ends meet, and would probably bridge the empty part of each week by pawning and repawning their miserable belongings. In the Liverpool of the 1850s sixty per cent of all pawnbrokers' pledges were for 5 shillings or less, twenty-seven per cent for 2s. 6d. or less.

Unlike other countries hardly any 'lower middle class'

separated them – or linked them – to the middle classes. In fact the term 'lower middle class' as then used covered the labour aristocracy as well as the small shopkeepers, innkeepers, small employers, and so on, who were often recruited from this stratum, in addition to the remarkably thin layer of white-collar workers and other employed but clean-handed occupations. In 1871 there were a mere 100,000 'commercial clerks' and 'bank clerks' to conduct the business of the greatest commercial and banking nation in the world – not much more than a third of the number of coalminers. Their position was respected, though they were not necessarily very affluent, for until after 1870, when a national system of elementary education was set up (it did not become effectively compulsory until 1891), even literacy was by no means universal. The way of life of the middle class was visibly the model of such families as the Pooters of 'The Laurels', Holloway – the white-collar suburbs were only gradually emerging, notably from the 1870s – though the relatively well-off labour aristocrat or small shopkeeper might combine an imitation of middle-class material standards (such as the purchase of gold watches and pianos) with other habits which maintained his solidarity with the rest of the manual working class among whom he mostly continued to live. If he became economically independent or an employer – as was quite possible in small-scale industries like building and various sorts of metalwork, and through small shopkeeping – he might leave his trade union, though the heavy risk of bankruptcy and relapse into the proletariat would make him disinclined to. But so long as he remained a worker, affluence brought political moderation, but not *embourgeoisement*.

Self-satisfied observers might talk of mid-Victorian Britain as a middle-class nation, but in fact the genuine middle class was not large. In terms of income it might broadly coincide with the 200,000 English and Welsh assessments over £300 a year for income tax under Schedule D (profits of business, the professions and investments) in 1865–6, of which 7,500 were for incomes of over £5,000 a year – very substantial wealth in those days – and 42,000 for incomes of £1,000–5,000. This relatively small community would include the 17,000-odd merchants and bankers of 1871, the 1,700-odd 'ship-owners', the unknown number of factory and mine-owners, most of the 15,000 doctors, the 12,000 solicitors and 3,500 barristers, the 7,000 architects and 5,000 civil engineers – a profession which expanded very rapidly during these decades, but, regrettably and significantly, ceased to expand towards the end of the century.* It would not contain many of what are today called intellectuals or 'creative' occupations. There were a mere 2,148 'authors, editors and journalists' (compared with 14,000 on the eve of the First World War), no scientists classed separately as such, and a static number of university teachers, for Victorian Britain was a philistine society.

The widest definition of the middle class or those who aspired to imitate them was that of keeping domestic servants. Their numbers, it is true, increased very substantially from 900,000 in 1851 to 1·4 million in 1871, almost their maximum.† But in 1871 there were only about 90,000 female cooks and not many more housemaids, which gives a more precise – though probably too narrow – measure of the real size of the middle class; and as a gauge of the even more affluent, 16,000 private coachmen. Who were the rest of the servant-keepers? Perhaps mainly the aspiring members of the 'lower middle class', striving for status and respectability, and just then discovering in birth-control a way of accelerating its achievement; for, as recent research has shown, it was the choice between a higher living standard, which was now more readily available, and a large family, which determined the decline in the (upper- and middle-class) birth rate which became observable from the 1870s.

Such was the mid-Victorian social pyramid. It was increasingly an urban phenomenon, or perhaps, so far as its middle layers were concerned, a suburban one, for the migration of the non-proletarians to the outskirts of the cities gathered speed; particularly in the 1860s and later in the 1890s. Townsmen outnumbered countrymen for the first time in 1851. What is more to

*It grew from 3,329 in 1861 to 7,124 in 1881; but in 1911, *including mining engineers*, its numbers were only 7,208.

† Omitting inn- and hotel-servants, who were then still classed with them.

the point, by 1881 perhaps two out of every five Englishmen and Welshmen lived in the six giant built-up areas ('conurbations') of London, south-east Lancashire, the west Midlands, west Yorkshire, Merseyside and Tyneside. And the rural areas were only very partly agricultural. In 1851 only two million out of over nine million occupied Britons were engaged in agriculture, by 1881 only 1·6 out of 12·8 million, on the eve of the First World War fewer than eight per cent. The cities which now constituted the real Britain were no longer the totally abandoned and neglected money-making deserts of the first half of the century. The horrors of that period, dramatized in the growing epidemics which did not even spare the middle class, led to systematic sanitary reform from the 1850s (drainage, water-supply, street-cleaning, and so on), affluence produced municipal building and, combined with radical agitation, even managed to save some open spaces and parks for the public in those fortunate areas where they had not already been built up. On the other hand railways, sidings and stations tore wide strips into the centres of cities, pushing the population which had previously lived there into other slums, and covering those that remained with that dense layer of soot and grime which may still be seen in some corners of northern towns to this day. The acrid fog which foreigners found so characteristic wrapped itself ever more firmly round Victorian Britain.

The mid-Victorian city was in most respects, except perhaps beauty, a distinct improvement on the towns of the 1830s and 40s, though this was due rather to general spending on basic urban equipment and amenities than to any public effort to improve the conditions of life of the working class as such. Still, there was a current of municipal reform which benefited them, and an even stronger commercial movement to exploit the unsatisfied desire of the labouring poor for entertainment and vicarious comfort by such institutions as the cut-glass-and-mirrored gin palace and the sham opulence of the Victorian music-hall, whose stylistic home is still often, and recognizably, in the 1860s. If the British city nevertheless remained an appalling place to live in, exceeded only by the grimly rectilinear streets of low cottages in the British industrial and mining village, it was because urban and industrial expansion still outstripped the spontaneous or planned attempts at urban improvement. London grew from just over two million inhabitants in 1841 to just under five million in 1881; Sheffield from 111,000 to 285,000, Nottingham from 52,000 to 187,000, Salford from 53,000 to 176,000, though already the Lancashire cities grew more slowly. Unquestioned improvement (except, perhaps, once again in the field of aesthetics) occurred only in the growing middle-class suburbs – Kensington is largely a creation of the 1860s and 1870s – and the new middle-class or *rentier* seaside resorts and spas, which developed – generally when the railways reached them, often on the initiative of landowners anxious to develop their real estate* – rapidly in the 1850s and 1860s.

*

Taken by and large the lives of most Britons improved in the 'golden years', though perhaps not so much as contemporaries thought. They improved even more, and more strikingly, during the 'Great Depression', though for rather different reasons. So far as real incomes are concerned, they probably stopped improving around 1900, and by 1914 there had been a perceptible stagnation or even decline in real wages, which is probably the chief reason why the last years before the First World War saw extremely acute and widespread labour unrest. Yet in other respects it is probable that improvement continued.

The 1870s marked a distinct turning-point. Up to that time, whatever happened to incomes, such reliable indices of social well-being as death rates (and especially infantile death rates) did not fall significantly. Indeed it is probable that in urban areas they may have risen during parts of the 'golden decades'. After then they began that almost continuous fall which is so characteristic of developed countries: slow but visible at first, faster

---

*The Duke of Devonshire developed Eastbourne from 1851. The famous 'piers' were constructed at Southport in 1859–60, at Bournemouth (which had only 1,000 inhabitants in 1851) in 1861, and enlarged at Brighton in 1865–6.

from the beginning of the twentieth century.* As the birth rate also began to fall, at least in the middle and lower middle classes – owing to birth control and higher living standards (see p. 157) – the growth of population now depended not so much on the gap between a high death rate and an even higher birth rate, but increasingly on the gap between a falling death rate and a less rapidly declining birth rate.

In these respects the 'golden years' were evidently by no means golden. However, in terms of real incomes and consumption they already showed a distinct advance. Average real wages (allowing for unemployment) remained pretty unchanged from 1850 until the early 1860s, but rose by about forty per cent between 1862 and 1875. They sagged for a year or two in the late 1870s, but were back to the old level by the mid-eighties and after that climbed rapidly. By 1900 they were one third above 1875 and eighty-four per cent higher than in 1850. Then, as we have seen, they ceased to rise.

Even if we regard these general averages as reliable (which is doubtful), they do not, of course, give a realistic picture of the situation. When the first serious social surveys were made towards the end of the century – by Booth in London and Rowntree in York – they suggested that about forty per cent of the working class lived in what was then called 'poverty' or even worse, that is to say on a family income of 18–21 shillings,† a miserable mass of whom two thirds would, at some time or other in their lives – generally in old age – become actual

*Deaths per 1,000

Years	Males	Females	Live births (deaths from 0–1 years)
1838–42	22·9	21·2	150
1858–62	22·8	21	149·4
1868–72	23·5	20·9	155·8
1878–82	21·5	19·1	142·2
1888–92	20·2	17·9	145·6
1898–1902	18·6	16·4	152·2
1908–12	15·1	13·3	111·8
1914	15	13·1	105

† See opposite page.

paupers. At the other end of the working class a maximum of fifteen per cent, probably rather less, lived in what was then regarded as comfort, with incomes of, say, £2 or above. In other words, the Victorian and Edwardian working classes were divided into the labour aristocracy, which normally lived in a sellers' market – that is could make themselves sufficiently scarce to command higher wages – the unskilled or unorganized mass which could command only a subsistence or near-subsistence wage from its buyers, and an intermediate stratum.

This explains the rather different movements of the standard of living in the 'golden years', the Great Depression and the Edwardian years. In periods of inflation such as the first and the last, those who could raise their money-wages faster than prices could improve their lot. And so they did:

Unstinted food, clothes of the same pattern as the middle class, when house rents permit, a tidy parlour, with stiff, cheap furniture which, if not itself luxurious or beautiful, is a symptom of the luxury of self-respect, and an earnest of better things to come, a newspaper, a club, an occasional holiday, perhaps a musical instrument.[2]

In such terms did an informed observer describe their condition in the middle 1880s. Not so the bottom forty per cent or those who could not make themselves scarce enough. Their situation improved only when unemployment declined (as it pretty certainly did from the 1840s on) and when they moved from lower- to higher-paid, from stagnant to expanding industries (as we

---

†Rowntree calculated the minimum weekly cost of maintaining a couple and three children in 1899 as 21s. 8d., made up as follows:

Food for husband and wife	6s.	
Food for three children	6s.	9d.
Rent	4s.	
Clothing for adults	1s.	
Clothing for children	1s.	3d.
Fuel	1s.	10d.
Sundries (light, household equipment, soap, etc.)	10d.	

The food included *no* butcher's meat, and was deliberately less generous than the diets prescribed for able-bodied paupers. This was indeed a bare subsistence standard.

have seen that many of them did in the 'golden years'). However, it is fairly clear that no startling general improvement took place before the 1860s, except perhaps among the farm labourers, whose mass flight from the land bettered the condition of those who stayed behind as well as of those who went. The stagnant mass of poverty at the bottom of the social pyramid remained nearly as stagnant and as nauseous as before. In the early 1900s, an old man has recalled

. . . it will give you some idea of conditions in Liverpool, it was quite common for a farthing's worth of milk to be sold; not merely bought and sold, but carried to the house too. At the end of the week you would collect a penny three farthings for seven farthings' worth of milk. This was in the poorest part of Liverpool. . . . I remember once I was working from the Smithdown Road depot on the tram to Pier Head and I had seventy-five passengers and they all paid twopence, and when I came to cash up, I had only one threepenny bit, all the rest was in coppers. That was a sign of the poverty.[3]

The Great Depression brought important changes. Probably the most rapid general improvement in the conditions of life of the nineteenth-century worker took place in the years 1880–95, mitigated only by the somewhat higher unemployment of this period. This is because falling living-costs benefit the poorest as well as the rest, indeed proportionately more than the rest, and the 'Depression' was, as we have seen, primarily a period of falling prices – but they fell largely because an entire new world of cheap, imported, foodstuffs opened before the British people. Between 1870 and 1896 their meat consumption per head went up by almost a third, but the proportion of imported meat they ate trebled. From the end of the century until after the First World War about forty per cent of the meat eaten in Britain came from abroad.

In fact, after 1870 the food and the eating habits of the British people began to be transformed. They began, for instance, to eat fruit, previously a luxury. To begin with working-class fruit consumption took the form of jam; later also of the novel and imported banana, which supplemented or replaced apples as the only fresh fruit eaten by the urban poor. Even so characteristic a landmark of the British proletarian scene as the fish-and-chip shop first appears in this period. It spread outwards from its original home in, probably, Oldham, after 1870.

What is more, from the 1870s not only the food supplies but the entire consumer-goods market of the poor began to be transformed by the rise of the shop (especially the multiple shop), and of factory production for a specific working-class public. A favoured stratum of workers, especially in the north, had begun to make their own distributive mechanism from the 1840s on, the 'Co-ops', which grew modestly at first – in 1881 they had only half a million members – but much more rapidly thereafter. By 1914 there were three million Co-operators. More striking was the rise of the multiple shop and chain store: from ten branches of multiple butchers in 1880 to 2,000 in 1900, from twenty-seven branches of grocery firms to 3,444 (they grew more slowly in the 1900s). Even more significant, for the early multiples were aimed mainly at the working-class market, was the rise of the clothing and footwear shop, the by-product of the rise of factory boot- and shoe-making in the 1860s, of factory tailoring in the 1880s. Footwear led the way – there were already three hundred shoe-chain shops in 1875, but twenty-five years later there were 2,600, half of them founded in the 1890s – men's wear shops followed more modestly and continued to expand fast even in the difficult 1900s, women's wear shops followed most slowly of all. Their time had not yet arrived.

Equally significant for the future, though not yet very important, industrialism now began to produce, in the wake of the USA, comparatively cheap consumer durables like the sewing machine (sold at £4 in the 1890s), which also pioneered hire-purchase, and the bicycle. This new and exciting machine almost immediately entered popular folklore, through the music-halls, and ideological folklore, through the Clarion Cycling Clubs of the enthusiastic young socialists, and the knickerbockered Mr Bernard Shaw. The bicycle was not available to the very poor, but this period gave them the first means of public transport specifically aimed at the working class, the tram. It had scarcely existed in 1871, but employed over 18,000 men by 1901: the average tram fare in the 1880s was just under 1½d. Lastly, and here again the 1880s mark a turning-point, popular entertainment was transformed. In Britain revolutionary devices like the phonograph and the cinema were still in the nursery stage, even in 1914, but the music-hall – at all events in London – had its first major boom in the 1880s and its years of glory in the 1890s. After 1900 it tended to play safe for the growing family public. Increasingly opulent variety palaces moved from the proletarian suburbs where they had begun their career to the very centres of the cities. At the same time sport, and especially association football, became the national institution we know. In 1885 professionalism was legalized.

In a word, between 1870 and 1900 the pattern of British working-class life which the writers, dramatists and TV producers of the 1950s thought of as 'traditional' came into being. It was not 'traditional' then, but new. It came to be thought of as age-old and unchanging, because it ceased in fact to change very much until the major transformation of British life in the affluent 1950s, and because its most complete expression was to be found in the characteristic centres of late-nineteenth-century working-class life, the industrial north or the proletarian areas of large non-industrial cities like Liverpool and south or east London, which did not change very much, except for the worse, in the first half of the twentieth century. It was neither a very good nor a very rich life, but it was probably the first kind of life since the Industrial Revolution which provided a firm lodging for the British working class within industrial society.

Clearly the last quarter of the nineteenth century was a time when life became very much easier and more varied for the working class, though the Edwardian age brought a setback. Nevertheless, trends are not achievements, and the picture of social conditions which the surveys of the time revealed – often to the shocked surprise of the inquirers – was horrifying. It was a picture of a working class stunted and debilitated by a century of industrialism. In the 1870s eleven- to twelve-year old boys from the upper-class public schools were on average *five inches taller* than boys from industrial schools, and at all teen-ages three inches taller than the sons of artisans. When the British people was for the first time medically examined *en masse* for military service in 1917, it included 10 per cent of young men totally unfit for service, 41·5 per cent (in London 48–9 per cent) with 'marked disabilities', 22 per cent with 'partial disabilities' and only a little more than a third in satisfactory shape. Ours was a country filled with a stoic mass of those destined to live all their lives on a bare and uncertain subsistence until old age threw them on to the scrapheap of the Poor Law, underfed, badly housed, badly clothed. By the standards of 1965, or even of 1939, the rise of the working-class standard to a modest human level had barely begun.

Fortunately the unemployment, the uncertainty, and perhaps above all the declining faith in the automatic advance of British capitalism made the people less inclined to accept their fate passively, and gave them more effective means of improving it. Socialism reappeared in the 1880s, and recruited an elite of active and able workers who in turn created or transformed the broader-based mass labour movements: the trade unions and the novel independent working-class parties, which converged to form the Labour Party in the early 1900s. The harder times of Edwardian England prepared the way for a more massive political transformation, which the war accelerated. The trade-union movement leaped to something like one and a half million members in the great 'explosion' of 1889–90, grew more slowly to about two million, doubled again to about four million in the great 'labour unrest' of 1911–13, and doubled yet again to reach a temporary peak of eight million at the end of the First World War. Much of this was due to the growth of unions in hitherto unorganized industries, such as transport by water, rail and road, or unorganized sections of older industries, such as the unskilled and semi-skilled in the metal trades. Much of it was also due to the expansion of the older unions.

The political declaration of independence by the workers had less dramatic results, though by 1914 there were forty Labour MPs. Fortunately the extension of the vote in 1884–5 gave the working class considerably increased political leverage on the older parties, especially the Liberals, normally anxious to retain their proletarian following. For the first time public authorities and the state thought seriously about social improvement. By 1914 the outline of a system of social security – the result of

Liberal legislation after 1906 – was already visible. However, the public sector was not yet of serious practical importance. Old Age Pensions (five shillings a week at the age of seventy) introduced in 1908, were the only form of social payment which was genuinely redistributive, if we except the Poor Law. The National Insurance Act of 1914 was, as its name implies, supposed to be an actuarially sound insurance scheme, paid for by premiums, and while its medical services were scant but useful, its capacity to provide against unemployment revealed itself as distinctly limited after 1920. Central government still spent only tiny sums on directly social objects other than education: £17 million in 1913, out of a total gross expenditure of £184 million, on Old Age Pensions, Labour Exchanges and Unemployment Insurance. By 1939 the analogous expenditures were to be £205 million out of £1,006 million. Local government expenditure was relatively even less important. It ran at about £13 million out of £140 million (in England and Wales, 1913), which was actually a much smaller percentage than fifty years earlier, for Poor Law payments, the chief item, had not even doubled, whereas the total local government expenditure had increased about five times over since 1868. Public housing was quite negligible. In 1884, when figures begin, about £200,000 were spent out of rates and loans for this purpose; in 1913 about £1 million. For comparison we may note that in the 1930s public expenditure on housing never fell below £70 million per year. On balance, indeed, the poor paid more in taxes than they received back in social services.

The situation of the upper classes was very different, and the immensity of the gap between the top and bottom of society was merely underlined by the orgy of conspicuous waste into which a section of the rich, headed by that symbol of a luxury class, King Edward VII, launched itself in the decades before 1914. Biarritz, Cannes, Monte Carlo and Marienbad – the international luxury hotel was very much the product of this age and found in the 'Edwardian' style its best architectural form – steam yachts and large racing stables, private trains, massacres of game-birds and opulent country-house weekends stretching into weeks: these consoled the increasingly lengthy leisure hours of the rich. Only six per cent of the population left any property worth mentioning at all when they died. Only four per cent left more that £300. But in 1901–2 just under 4,000 estates paid duty on a capital value of £19 million, and 149 of them were proved for £62·5 million. The rich were still rich, for the pound sterling was still very much the pound sterling. The Duke of Bedford, reeling (as all landowners claimed they were) under the effects of the agricultural depression, was not too bankrupt to offer his agent an ample salary and pension, together with the free occupancy of a country house, staffed at ducal expense with three indoor, seven outdoor servants and three gamekeepers, the use of another country house, plus game, garden produce, cream, milk, butter and whisky as free allowances.

Below them were the middle and lower middle classes, a large body comprising – if we define those who kept servants – perhaps thirty per cent of the population, at all events in York. In the middle of the Edwardian era perhaps 1¾ million belonged to families earning (or at any rate receiving) more than £700 a year, which was comfortable, and perhaps 3¾ millions to families getting between £160 and £700 a year, which was reasonable. In 1913–14 the average adult man earned roughly thirty shillings for a working week of fifty-four hours (or an annual income, if fully employed, of £77), and the average adult woman in industry earned 13s. 6d. for a working week of the same length (or, if fully employed, about £35 a year). These middle strata ate well, and indeed too much. They lived well, and increasingly in those middle- and lower-middle-class suburbs which surrounded the less smoky sides of the cities, ranging from the modest terraced or semi-detached house-and-gardens of districts like Tooting, through the more opulent zones like Wimbledon towards the stockbroker belt in the green countryside beyond: fortresses of political conservatism from which their defenders sallied in the mornings, armed with the new newspapers of the *Daily Mail* type (1896), to reach the offices in which a rapidly growing number of them worked.

By 1906 perhaps half a million *employees* earned over £160 a year (or something like half the lower middle class), though the bulk of the rising population of clerks had only their aspirations in common with the higher ranges of the middle class. Over three quarters of the men clerks in commerce and all the women earned less than £3 a week in 1910. (Over three quarters of the women clerks, still very much a minority, earned less than £1 a week.) Only in banking and insurance were earnings rather better. The poor white-collar worker, especially if he insisted – as he naturally did – on a middle-class style of life, was not much better off than the well-paid worker, though in the last decades of the century he made his income go further by cutting down the size of his family through birth-control – mainly through abstention from intercourse or *coitus interruptus*.* As A. J. P. Taylor has said: 'The historian should bear in mind that between about 1880 and 1940 he has on his hands a frustrated people,'[4] and of no class was this more true than the late Victorian and Edwardian lower middle class.

However, beside such measurable changes in the British ways of living, there were equally significant but unquantifiable ones. The first was the conservatism – as yet mainly of complacency – which, as we have seen, increasingly fossilized the British rich. The tendency for the Conservatives to replace the Liberal Party as the united expression of the British rich after 1874 reflects this, though it was briefly interrupted in the early twentieth century. The decline of religious nonconformity – especially middle-class nonconformity – was masked by the growing electoral weight of the 'nonconformist conscience', never more powerful than in the last decades of the nineteenth century, and by the continued rise of nonconformist businessmen to affluence and influence. But in fact, from the 1870s on, nonconformity ceased to expand much, and with it there declined one powerful force making for Liberalism and competitive private enterprise.

The assimilation of the British business classes to the social pattern of the gentry and aristocracy had proceeded very rapidly from the mid nineteenth century, the period when so many of the so-called 'public schools' were founded, or reformed by finally excluding the poor for whom they had originally been

---

* Mechanical means for men were not widely used until the inter-war period, for women not until the 1930s.

intended.* In 1869 they were more or less set free from all government control and set about elaborating that actively anti-intellectual, anti-scientific, games-dominated tory imperialism which was to remain characteristic of them. (It was not the Duke of Wellington but a late-Victorian myth which claimed that the battle of Waterloo was won on the playing-fields of Eton, which did not exist in his time.)

Unfortunately the public school formed the model of the new system of secondary education, which the less privileged sectors of the new middle class were allowed to construct for themselves after the Education Act of 1902, and whose main object was to exclude from higher education the children of the working class, which had unfortunately won the right to universal primary education in 1870. Knowledge, especially scientific knowledge, therefore took second place in the new British educational system, to the maintenance of a rigid division between the classes. In 1897 less than seven per cent of grammar-school pupils came from the working class. The British therefore entered the twentieth century and the age of modern science and technology as a spectacularly ill-educated people.

The somnolence of the economy was already obvious in British society in the last decades before 1914. Already the rare dynamic entrepreneurs of Edwardian Britain were, more often than not, foreigners or minority groups (the increasingly important German-Jewish financiers who provided the excuse for much of the pervasive anti-semitism of the period, the Americans so important in the electrical industry, the Germans in chemicals, Quakers and late-flowering provincial dissenters like Lever, who exploited the new resources of tropical empire). Conversely the flourishing activities of the 'City' were already – even when so obviously the product of provincial nonconformist enterprise as the rising business of life insurance and building societies – enmeshed in a pseudo-baronial network of gentlemanly non-competition. The 'guinea-pig' director, an aristocrat put on the board of an often *louche* company for the

* Cheltenham, Marlborough, Rossall, Haileybury, Wellington, Clifton, Malvern, Lancing, Hurstpierpoint and Ardingly were all founded, and Uppingham transformed, between the early 1840s and the middle 1860s.

publicity value of his name, became common. His obverse was the genuine bourgeois who, unlike his predecessors in the Anti-Corn Law days, imagined himself, and indeed became, the 'gentleman' of the Forsyte saga type.

The characteristic mythical Britain of travel posters and *Times* calendars emerged in consequence. The heavy incrustation of British public life with pseudo-medieval and other ritual, like the cult of royalty, date back to the late Victorian period, as does the pretence that the Englishman is a thatched-cottager or country squire at heart. But, as we have seen, at the other end of the social scale the same period saw the emergence of a very different social phenomenon, the characteristic 'traditional' way of life of the British urban working class. However, unlike the developments among the upper classes, its emergence reflected not merely regression and fossilization, but – in spite of its narrowness and rigidity – modernization. The socialism which increasingly dominated the labour movement may have been extremely vague. Often, as in its pacifist and internationalist aspects, it was little more than a proletarian prolongation of the nonconformist, radical-liberal Little Englandism which the business classes were rapidly abandoning. Yet it *was* committed to a fundamental structural change in the economy. It was based on an economic analysis which took account, as the increasingly ossified economic orthodoxy of the 'Treasury Mind' did not, of new factors such as the tendency towards concentration, and the need for an increasingly systematic public intervention in the affairs of the economy. This was perhaps the reason why small and as yet unrepresentative groups of technocratic and managerial thinkers like the Fabians found themselves operating within the labour movement. The tragedy of the movement was that in practice it did not live up to its theory.

NOTES

1. Briggs, Cole and Postgate, Kitson Clark (Further Reading 2), Clapham, Checkland, Ashworth (Further Reading 3). The basic material on working-class living standards is in articles by G. H. Wood in *Journal of the Royal Statistical Society*, 1899 and 1909. Asa Briggs, *Victorian Cities*, S. Pollard, *History of Labour in Sheffield*, H. J. Dyos, *Victorian Suburb* (1961), for urban problems. E. Phelps Brown, *Growth of British Industrial Relations* (1959), for social legislation and conditions, K. W. Wedderburn, *The Worker and the Law* (1965), for labour law. J. B. Jefferys, *Retail Trading in Great Britain 1850–1950* (1954), is good, but statistical. H. Pelling. *A History of Trade Unionism* (1963) and *The Origins of the Labour Party* (1965), must be complemented by R. Tressell, *The Ragged-Trousered Philanthropists* (novel). G. and W. Grossmith, *Diary of a Nobody*, for the lower middle class. On education, Brian Simon, *Education and the Labour Movement 1870–1920* (1965). W. S. Adams, *Edwardian Portraits* (1957), is excellent on the upper classes. E. P. Thompson, 'Homage to Tom Maguire' (in A. Briggs and J. Saville, ed., *Essays in Labour History*, 1960), is a superb introduction to the revival of socialism. See also Figures 2–3, 7, 10, 14, 21, 32, 37, 41, 43, 45–6, 49–52.

2. Pollard, op. cit., p. 105.

3. *Tom Barker and the IWW* (ed. E. C. Fry, Australian Society for Labour History, 1965), pp. 5, 7.

4. A. J. P. Taylor, *English History 1914–45* (1965), p. 166.

9

THE BEGINNINGS OF DECLINE[1]

SINCE the Industrial Revolution the transformation of industry has become continuous, but every now and then the cumulative results of these changes become so obvious that observers are tempted to talk about a 'second' industrial revolution.* The last decades of the nineteenth century were such a time. And the break appeared all the greater, because the earlier phase of industrialism had been unusually and visibly archaic, and because Britain, its pioneer, apparently remained wedded to this archaic pattern, while other and newer industrial economies did not.

The first and in the long run most profound change was in the role of science in technology. In the first phase of industrialism this was, as we have seen, small and secondary. The important inventions were simple, the products of skill, practical experience and a readiness to try anything new and see whether it worked, rather than of sophisticated theory or esoteric knowledge, the crucial sources of power (coal, water) were old and familiar, the crucial raw materials were no different from those long familiar, though of course (like iron) used on a much larger scale than ever before and with certain improvements. Technologically more revolutionary devices already existed – for instance in the chemical industry – and sometimes attracted attention by their public prominence, like gas-lighting; but their importance in production was ancillary. The greatest technological triumphs of the archaic phase of industrialization, the railway and the steamship, were pre-scientific or at any rate only semi-scientific in this sense.

Yet the very scale of the railway, and the transport revolution

* Curiously enough, there is rarely a 'third' or 'fourth'. As times goes on the 'second revolution' becomes assimilated to the changes of the past, and in due course another 'second' industrial revolution is discovered – maybe in the 1920s, and then again in the age of experiments in ambitious automation after the Second World War.

it inaugurated, made scientific technology more necessary, and the expansion of the world economy increasingly presented industry with strange natural raw materials which required scientific processing for effective use (for example rubber and petroleum). One major tool of scientific technology, classical physics (including acoustics), had long been available, another, inorganic chemistry, came of age during the first phases of the Industrial Revolution. In the 1830s and 1840s two more became industrially available: electro-magnetism and organic chemistry. The basic institution of science, the research laboratory – especially the university research laboratory – had also developed between, say, 1790 and 1830. Scientific technology not only became more desirable, but also possible.

The major technical advances of the second half of the nineteenth century were therefore essentially scientific; that is to say they required at the very least some knowledge of recent developments in pure science for original inventions, a far more consistent process of scientific experiment and testing for their development, and an increasingly close and continuous link between industrialists, technologists and professional scientists and scientific institutions. An inventor who had never heard of Newton could devise something like the spinning-mule; but even the technically least qualified inventors of the age of electricity – say the American Samuel Morse, of the electric telegraph, after whom the Morse Code is named – had at least to have listened to some scientific lectures. (His British equivalent, Sir Charles Wheatstone, was actually a university professor and FRS.) Increasingly the scientific environment was the one in which even 'accidental' inventions were made – like the colour mauve, the first of the aniline dyes, discovered by W. H. Perkin in 1856 while a young student at the Royal College of Chemistry. Increasingly science actually suggested not merely solutions but problems, as to Gilchrist-Thomas: a police-court clerk whose lectures at evening classes drew his attention to the difficulty of using phosphoric iron ores in metallurgy, while providing him with the chemical knowledge to surmount it in 1878. Fortunately Gilchrist-Thomas also had a cousin who was a chemist in a Welsh ironworks and therefore in a position to test his solution – which consisted of lining a Bessemer converter with basic slag.

Two major growth-industries of the new phase of industrialism, the electrical and the chemical, were entirely based on scientific knowledge. The third, the development of the internal combustion engine, though not in itself raising any scientific problems of great novelty, was dependent on at least two branches of the chemical industry: those which refined and processed the natural material of oil and rubber, which were comparatively intractable in their crude state. Lesser industries, which did not reach their full development until the twentieth century, such as the complex of those based on photography, rested even more firmly on a scientific foundation of chemistry and optics. Indeed the famous German optical industry actually produced one major firm – Zeiss – which was the planned offspring of the academic research laboratories at the University of Jena. And by the end of the nineteenth century it was already clear, especially from the experience of the German chemical industry which led the world, that the output of technological progress was a function of the input of scientifically qualified manpower, equipment and money into systematic research projects. In the USA Thomas Alva Edison (1847–1931) demonstrated the results of large-scale laboratories for technological invention in a more empirical manner at Menlo Park from 1876.

The second major change was less revolutionary. It simply consisted in the systematic extension of the factory system – the division of manufacture into a large series of simple processes each carried out by a specialized machine operated by power — to areas hitherto untouched by it. The most important of these in the long run was the manufacture of machinery itself, or in modern times of 'durable consumer goods', which are largely machinery for personal rather than productive use. This is the development – part technical, part organization – which we know as 'mass-production' and which, when the application of human labour to the actual process of production is reduced to vanishing point, we call 'automation'. There was nothing revolutionary in it, in principle. The original cotton factory already strove after the ideal of becoming a gigantic, complex and 'self-acting' (as it was then called) automaton, and each technical innovation brought it a little closer towards this object. With some exceptions like the Jacquard loom it remained pretty remote from it, by modern standards, because the incentives to eliminate skilled labour were not strong enough, but above all because the implications in terms of labour management and the organization of production were not yet systematically thought out. But it was visibly mass-production and on the road to automation, and certain forms of early chemical production, with their continuous operation, automatic control of temperature (a thermostat was patented in 1831) and virtual elimination of all process-work, were even closer.

The mechanization of machine-making depended on a vast, standardized demand for the same sort of machine. That is why it was first pioneered in armaments (the manufacture of ammunition-casing and small-arms) until the sheer size of the potential market in industry and among sufficiently wealthy private consumers made it commercially attractive. The pioneer products of this development were, for evident reasons, mainly American: the sewing machine of Elias Howe (1846), better known through the adaptation of the commercial developer Isaac Singer (1850), the typewriter, first invented in 1843 and commercially successful after 1868, the Yale lock (1855), the Colt revolver of 1835, and the machine-gun (1861). It was also the USA which introduced the mass-production of self-propelled vehicles, though in fact the motor-car was a European – chiefly a French and German – invention, and the most modest of mechanical vehicles, the bicycle (1886), never really became a major force in the New World. But behind these visible products was a far more important transformation in machine-tools: the turret-lathe (*c.* 1845), the universal milling machine (1861), the automatic lathe (*c.* 1870); and with – or rather a little after – them the development of steel alloys (and in the twentieth century other alloys such as tungsten-carbide) sufficiently hard and sharp to cut steel at the high mechanical speeds – and incidentally, perhaps in the late nineteenth century chiefly – to produce more formidable armaments. Substances hitherto merely known as curiosities to the field geologist or the chemist – tungsten, manganese, chromium, nickel, and others – became essential components of metallurgy after 1870, thus initiating a revolution in this field.

The other aspect of this development was the systematic *organization* of mass-production by means of the planned flow of processes and the 'scientific management' of labour, that is the actual analysis and breakdown of human as well as mechanical jobs. Here again the USA was the pioneer, mainly because of its acute shortage of skilled labour. The very earliest experiments in continuous production lines go back to the ingenious Yankee technicians of the late eighteenth century, such as Oliver Evans (1755–1819), who constructed an entirely automatic flour-mill and invented the conveyor-belt, though it was not until the 1890s that the technique was seriously developed in the Chicago meat-packing industry and elsewhere, and not until the early 1900s that it reached maturity in Henry Ford's motor works.* 'Scientific management' became both a programme and a reality in the 1880s, chiefly under the impact of F. W. Taylor of the USA. By 1900, therefore, the foundations of modern large-scale industry had been laid.

The third major change is closely connected with the second: it consisted of the discovery that the largest potential market was to be found in the rising incomes of the mass of the working citizens in economically developed countries. Here again the USA was in the lead, partly because of the sheer potential size of its domestic market, partly because of the relatively high average incomes of people in a country with a permanent labour shortage; or at all events in the economically dynamic sectors of that country. The American motor industry, to take the obvious example, was built on the assumption that a sufficiently cheap automobile, expensive though it was, would find a mass market.† In the archaic era of industrialism this was inconceivable. The

---

*The government enterprises working for the British Navy had, however, evolved perhaps the first working assembly-line in the famous biscuit-bakery at Deptford in the early nineteenth century.

†Though the USA did have a mass market in the countryside for the horse-and-buggy, which Ford to some extent aimed at.

demand for elaborate and expensive goods was then confined to a large, but numerically restricted, middle class and the few rich. The demand of the masses was confined to the elements of food, shelter (including some rudimentary household goods) and clothing. The market for mass-production was therefore extensive and not intensive, and even so, it was confined to the simplest and most standardized articles. And since their wages were low, and ought to be low, they could not only buy little, but the incentive to mechanize the manufacture of goods for their needs was limited. Where servants are plentiful and cheap, the demand for vacuum cleaners is small.

The last major change was the increase in the *scale* of economic enterprise, the concentration of production and ownership, the rise of an economy composed of a handful of great lumps of rock – trusts, monopolies, oligopolies* – rather than a large number of pebbles. That concentration was the logical result of competition had long been suspected by some. Karl Marx made this tendency into one of the corner-stones of his economic analysis. In Germany and the USA this process became clearly visible as early as the 1880s. Economists of almost all political tendencies took a poor view of it. Since it conflicted with the ideal of a freely competitive business economy it must, they felt, be not merely socially undesirable (because it favoured the big over the little, the rich over the poor), but economically retrograde. However, there is every reason to believe that 'big business' was in fact *better* business than little business, at least in the long run: more dynamic, more efficient, better able to undertake the increasingly complex and expensive tasks of development. The real case against it was not that it was big, but that it was anti-social. This did not apply to the biggest business of all, government and other public enterprise. While in this period the growth in the scale of economic operations took the form of the rise of private business giants and

---

* When one firm virtually or wholly controls a field of economic activity, it is a monopoly. When a small number of firms between them do so (as in the American motor industry, which is dominated by General Motors, Ford and Chrysler), this is oligopoly. The second case is more usual than the first, but not in practice very different.

combinations rather than government enterprise, indirectly the role of government became increasingly decisive. For the mid-Victorian ideal of a state which abstained deliberately from economic management and interference was generally abandoned after 1873.

*

However strongly the winds of change blew elsewhere, as soon as they crossed the Channel to Britain they grew sluggish. In every one of the four aspects of the economy we have just sketched, Britain fell behind her rivals; and this was all the more striking, not to say painful, when these occupied fields which Britain had herself been the first to plough before abandoning them. This sudden transformation of the leading and most dynamic industrial economy into the most sluggish and conservative, in the short space of thirty or forty years (1860–90/1900), is the crucial question of British economic history. After the 1890s we may ask why so little was done to restore the dynamism of the economy, and we may blame the generations after 1890 for not doing more, for doing the wrong things, or even for making the situation worse. But essentially these are discussions about bringing the horse back into the stable after it has gone. It went between the middle of the century and the 1890s.

The contrast between Britain and more modern industrial states is particularly striking in the new 'growth-industries', and it becomes even more marked when we compare their very feeble performance with the achievements of British industry in those branches in which the archaic structure and technique could still produce the best results. The chief of these was shipbuilding, the last and one of the most triumphant assertions of British supremacy. During the age of the traditional wooden sailing ship Britain had been a great, but by no means unchallenged, producer. Indeed her weight as a shipbuilder had been due not to her technological superiority, for the French designed better ships and the USA built much better ones; as witness the almost consistent triumphs of American sailing ships from the famous grain races of the 'clippers' to the yacht races between millionaire syndicates of our own day. Between American independence and the outbreak of the Civil War American shipbuilding expanded at a far faster rate, gained upon British shipbuilding steadily, and had by 1860 almost caught it up.* British ship-builders benefited rather because of the vast weight of Britain as a shipping and trading power and the preference of British shippers (even after the abrogation of the Navigation Acts, which protected the industry heavily) for native ships. The real triumph of the British shipyards came with the iron and steel steamship. As the rest of British industry fell behind, they drew ahead: in 1860 British tonnage had been a little larger than American, six times as large as the French, eight times as large as the German; in 1890 it was over twice as large as the American tonnage, ten times as large as the French, and still roughly eight times as large as the German.

Now none of the advantages of modern productive technique and organization applied to ships, which were built in giant single units, of largely unstandardized materials and with a vast input of the most varied and highest manual skills. They were no more mechanized than palaces. On the other hand the ad-vantages of specialization in small units were immense, for they achieved, in effect, what the systematic subdivisions of processes now does in giant firms, and what could certainly not then have been achieved any other way in the construction of such complex products. Moreover, they multiplied the possibilities and mini-mized the costs of technical innovation. A specialized marine engineering firm in a competitive market had every incentive to produce better engines, nor would the process of shipbuilding be held up because the firms specializing in ships' plumbing were not keeping pace with their own innovations. It was not until after the Second World War, when the technical ad-vantages of integration had become much more decisive, that British shipbuilding lost its lead.

In the growth-industries of the scientific-technological type, and where integration and large-scale production paid off, the

---

*In 1800 British tonnage (including colonial) was 1·9 millions – about twice the American; in 1860 it was 5·7 millions as against 5·4 millions for the USA.

story was sadly different. Britain pioneered the chemical industry and the invention of aniline dyes, though even in the 1840s already partly on the basis of German academic chemistry. But by 1913 we accounted for only eleven per cent of world output (as against thirty-four per cent for the USA, twenty-four per cent for Germany), while the Germans exported twice as much as we did and – most significant of all – supplied the British home market with ninety per cent of its synthetic dyes. And what there was of the British chemical industry rested largely on the enterprise of immigrant foreigners, such as the firm of Brunner-Mond, which later became the nucleus of Imperial Chemical Industries.

Electro-technics were, both in theory and in practice, a pioneer achievement of the British. Faraday and Clerk Maxwell laid its scientific foundations, Wheatstone (of the electric telegraph) first made it possible for the Victorian father in London to discover immediately whether or not his daughter had eloped to Boulogne with 'the tall handsome man with the dark moustache and military cloak' (to quote an illustration of the benefits of this invention in a contemporary technical handbook).[2] Swann began to think about a carbon-filament incandescent lamp in 1845, two years before Edison was born. Yet by 1913 the output of the British electrical industry was little more than a third of the German, its exports barely half. And once again, it was the foreigners who invaded Britain. Much of the domestic industry was initiated and controlled by foreign capital – mainly American, such as Westinghouse – and when in 1905 the London underground was to be electrified and the first 'tube' constructed, the enterprise and finance were largely American.

No industry was more British in origins than that of machines and machine-tools.

'The change thus effected', wrote Sir William Fairbairn, one of its pioneers, of 'self-acting machines' in 1853, 'and the improvements introduced into our constructive machinery are of the highest importance; and it gives me pleasure to add that they chiefly belong to Manchester, are of Manchester growth, and from Manchester they have had their origin.'[3] Yet nowhere did foreign countries – and again chiefly the USA – leap ahead more decisively than in this field. As early as 1860 the American advances were watched with a little anxiety, though hardly yet with much real fear. But in the 1890s it was from the USA that the impetus to introduce automatic machine-tools came, it was an American, Colonel Dyer, who led the associated British employers in their (incompletely successful) attempt to break down the hold of the skilled craftsman in the industry, and an American company which obtained a monopoly of the machinery for the manufacture of the first fully mechanized consumer-goods industry, the manufacture of boots and shoes.

The saddest case was perhaps that of the iron and steel industry, for we see it losing its pre-eminence at the very moment when its role in the British economy was greatest, and its dominance in the world most unquestioned. Every major innovation in the manufacture of steel came from Britain or was developed in Britain: Bessemer's converter (1856), which first made the mass-production of steel possible, the Siemens-Martin open-hearth furnace (1867), which greatly increased productivity, and the Gilchrist-Thomas basic process (1877–8), which made it possible to use an entire range of new ores for steel manufacture. Yet, with the exception of the converter, British industry was slow to apply the new methods – Gilchrist-Thomas benefited the Germans and French far more than his countrymen – and they utterly failed to keep up with subsequent improvements. Not only did British production fall behind that of Germany and the USA in the early 1890s, but also British productivity. By 1910 the USA produced almost twice as much basic steel alone as the total steel production of Great Britain.

*

Why all this was so has been much debated. Clearly, the British did not adapt to new circumstances. They could have done so. There is no reason why British technical and scientific education should have remained negligible, in a period when a wealth of rich amateur scientists and privately endowed research laboratories or of practical experience in production clearly no longer compensated for the virtual absence of university education and the feebleness of formal technological training. There was no compelling reason why Britain in 1913 had only nine thousand university students compared to almost sixty thousand in Germany, or only five day students per ten thousand (in 1900) compared to almost thirteen in the USA; why Germany produced three thousand graduate engineers per year while in England and Wales only 350 graduated in *all* branches of science, technology and mathematics with first- and second-class honours, and few of these were qualified for research. There were plenty of people throughout the nineteenth century to warn the country of the dangers of its educational backwardness; there was no shortage of funds, and certainly no lack of suitable candidates for technical and higher training.

It was no doubt inevitable that British pioneer industries should lose ground relatively as the rest of the world industrialized, and that their rate of expansion should decline; but this purely statistical phenomenon need not have been accompanied by a genuine loss of impetus and efficiency. Still less was it predetermined that Britain should fail in industries in which she started with the arguable disadvantages neither of the older pioneer, nor of the late-comer, but substantially at the same time and point as the rest. There are economies whose lag can be explained by purely material weakness: they are too small, their resources too scarce, their supply of skills too meagre. Britain clearly was not one of them, except in the vague sense that any country of her size and population had, in the long run, more limited possibilities of economic development than much vaster and richer countries like the USA or the USSR; but certainly not significantly more limited possibilities than the Germany of 1870.

Britain then failed to adapt to new conditions, not because she could not, but because she did not wish to. The question is, why not? An increasing popular explanation is the sociological one, which puts it down to lack (or decline) of enterprise among businessmen, to the conservatism of British society, or to both. This has the advantage for the economists of throwing the burden of explanation on the historians and sociologists, who are even less capable of bearing it but just as willing to try. There are various versions of such theories, all quite unconvincing, but the most familiar runs something like this: the British capitalist aimed at eventual absorption into the socially more respected and higher stratum of the 'gentlemen' or even the aristocrats, and when he achieved it – and the British hierarchy was only too willing to accept him as soon as he had made his pile, which in the outlying counties might be quite a modest one – he ceased to strive. As an entrepreneur he lacked that built-in urge to maintain a constant rate of technical progress almost for its own sake which is believed to be characteristic of American industrialists. The small family firm, which was the characteristic type of enterprise, was fairly effectively insulated against excessive growth, which risked the loss of family control. Consequently each generation became less enterprising, and, sheltered behind the vast ramparts of pioneer profits, had less need to be.

There is some truth in such explanations. The aristocratic scale of values, which included amateur status and not apparently trying too hard among the criteria of the 'gentleman', and inculcated them in the 'public schools' which indoctrinated the sons of the risen middle class, was indeed dominant. Being 'in trade' was indeed an awful social stigma; though 'trade' in this sense meant small-scale shopkeeping much more than any activity in which really big money – and therefore social acceptance – could be gained.* The wealthy capitalist could certainly, upon shedding his more provincial crudities – and from Edwardian times even without shedding so much as his accent – win his knighthood or peerage; and his children slid into the leisure class without any difficulty whatever. The small family firm certainly predominated. The ramparts of profit were indeed high. A man might have to work hard to raise himself into the middle class, but once in a moderately flourishing line of business, he could take things very easily indeed, unless he made some appalling miscalculation, or hit an abnormally bad patch

---

* So long as the aristocracy actually remained *richer* than the middle class, it had no need to mitigate its contempt; and locally it often continued to remain much richer. In Cambridge (1867) the gentlemen and clergymen at their death left median property to the value of £1,500–2,000; the professors and masters of colleges a mean of £26,000 each; but the local businessmen only a median of £800, the shopkeepers of £350.

in the course of an unusually bad slump. Bankruptcy was, according to economic theory, the penalty of the inefficient businessman, and its spectre haunts the novels of Victorian England. But in fact the risks of incurring it were extremely modest, except for the very tiny and marginal man in such occupations as small shopkeeping, the fringes of the building trade, and the underside of a few still dynamic industries such as metals. In Edwardian England, including two years of crisis, the average bankruptcy was for liabilities of no more than £1,350. Indeed the risk of loss through bankruptcies* became steadily less during the last thirty years before the First World War. In important industries it was negligible. Thus in 1905–9 (which includes a depression) out of the 2,500 or so firms in cotton manufacture an annual average of only eleven went bankrupt – something less than one half per cent.

Freed from the spectre of sudden impoverishment and social ostracism – the very horror of bankruptcy is itself a symptom of its comparative rarity – the British businessman did not need to work much. Frederick Engels may not perhaps be a typical specimen; but there is no sign that until his retirement at the age of forty-nine with a comfortable life income for himself and the Marx family he failed to pull his weight in the flourishing firm of Ermen and Engels, cotton-merchants of Manchester, though the world knows that he spent as little time as he could on their business.

It is equally true that British business lacked certain non-economic spurs to enterprise; a nation which is already at the top politically and economically, and tends to look down on the rest of the world with self-satisfaction and a little contempt, inevitably does. Americans and Germans might dream of making their destiny manifest; the British knew that it had manifested

---

*Estimated loss to creditors in England and Wales through bankruptcy proceedings: annual average in £

1884–8	8,662,000	1899–1903	6,017,000
1889–93	7,521,000	1904–9	5,965,000
1894–8	6,417,000		

It should be remembered that the total number of business enterprises during this period pretty certainly increased.

itself already. There is no doubt, for instance, that a nationalist desire to catch up with the British was largely responsible for the systematic German reinforcement of industry by scientific research: the Germans said so. Nor can one reasonably deny that the typically American desire to have the latest and most up-to-date piece of mechanical equipment, while providing a constant impetus to technical progress, is also often – perhaps mostly – quite economically irrational in origin. The average firm which installs elaborate computer-equipment today gets less benefit from it even than the average man who exchanges the simple, small, adaptable, cheap and superior razor-blade for the electric razor. An economy which makes capital as well as con-sumer goods into social status-symbols – perhaps because it has no others – has an undoubted advantage in the matter of technical progress over one which has not.

Nevertheless, the value of these observations is limited, if only because very many British businessmen did not conform to them. Before the twentieth century the average British business-man was not a 'gentleman' and never became either a knight, a peer, or even the owner of a country house. It was Lloyd George who made provincial towns into 'cities of dreadful knights'. The absorption of the sons of grocers and cotton-spinners into the aristocracy was a *consequence* of the loss of impetus in British business, not its cause; and even today, the actual management of medium-sized firms (the sort of people who would in 1860–90 certainly have been owner-managers) contains not more than one in five who have been to a university, not much more than one in four who have been to a public school, including not more than one in twenty who have been to one of the top twenty or so public schools.*

Sociologically, the incentive to make money fast was by no means weak in Victorian Britain, the attraction of the gentry and

*The figures apply to 1956. We may take education at a public school and/or one of the two ancient universities as the criterion of absorption into the 'upper class', at least in England. But the interesting thing in the late Victorian and Edwardian period is that a *growing* percentage of public-school boys went into business, though a *declining* one into the expert professions. The public-school ethos did not discourage money-making, only technological and scientific professionalism.

aristocracy by no means overwhelming, especially not to the cohorts of middle-class conscious and often nonconformist (that is deliberately anti-aristocratic) Northerners and Midlanders, their heads filled with mottoes like 'where there's muck there's brass', and solid pride in their productive achievements. They were proud of the soot and smoke in which they drenched the cities in which they made their money.

Moreover, earlier in the nineteenth century, Britain had certainly not lacked that acute, even irrational, joy in technical progress as such, which we think of as characteristically American. One can hardly imagine the railways being developed, let alone built, in a country or by a business community which was not *excited* by their sheer technical novelty; for as we have seen their actual business prospects were known to be relatively modest. It is true that the large literature of popular science and technology petered out after the 1850s, and that perhaps it had always aimed at a public of 'artisans' rather than at the middle class: at those who wanted to, or ought to, rise rather than at those who had already risen. And yet these were precisely the recruits to the bourgeois army most likely to finger the field-marshal's baton in their knapsack. And even in the second half of the century there were enough of them to make the fortune of Samuel Smiles, the bard of the engineers. His *Self Help* came out in 1859. Within four years it had sold 55,000 copies. The romance of technology remained strong enough to make engineering the choice of seventy-five per cent of boys in at least one large public school of the 1880s.

What is more, there were plainly sectors of the British economy to which few of the complaints of torpor and conservatism applied. There were the West Midlands, whose capital was Birmingham: a jungle of small firms producing essentially consumer goods – often durable metal goods – for the home market. The Midlands did transform themselves after 1860, having previously been very incompletely captured by the Industrial Revolution. Old and declining industries were replaced, and sometimes actually transformed themselves, as in Coventry, where textiles went down after 1860, but the local watch-makers became the nucleus of the bicycle industry, and through it later of the motor industry. If Lancashire in 1914 was recognizably what it had been in 1840, Warwickshire certainly was not. There were industries, such as parts of the increasingly important engineering and metals manufacture, which had all the bubbling instability of the dynamic private enterprise of the theorists; where men rose and fell, and were on the move. While an average of only eleven firms in the cotton industry went bankrupt every year in 1905-9, an annual average of 390 were bankrupted in the metal industries in the same period, mainly small men attempting independent production with inadequate resouces. And there were parts of the economy, like the distributive trades, where no one could conceivably speak of stagnation. These also were based on the home market and not on exports.

Simple sociological explanations therefore will not do. In any case, economic explanations of economic phenomena are to be preferred if they are available. There are indeed several, all resting tacitly or openly on the assumption that in a capitalist economy (at all events in its nineteenth-century versions) businessmen will be dynamic only in so far as this is rational by the criterion of the individual firm, which is to maximize its gains, minimize its losses, or possibly merely to maintain what it regards as a satisfactory long-term rate of profit. But since the rationality of the individual firm is inadequate, this may not work out to the best advantage of the economy as a whole, or even of the individual firm. This is partly because the interest of the firm and the economy may diverge in the short run or the long, because the individual firm is to some extent powerless to achieve the objects it would wish to, because it is impossible for the accountancy of the individual firm to determine its best interests, or for other analogous reasons. All these are merely different ways of expressing the proposition that a capitalist economy is not planned, but emerges from a multitude of individual decisions taken in the pursuit of self-interest.

The commonest, and probably best, economic explanation of the loss of dynamism in British industry is that it was the result 'ultimately of the early and long-sustained start as an industrial power'.[4] It illustrates the deficiencies of the private-enterprise mechanism in a number of ways. Pioneer industrialization naturally took place in special conditions which could not be maintained, with methods and techniques which, however advanced and efficient at the time, could not remain the most advanced and efficient, and it created a pattern of both production and markets which would not necessarily remain the one best fitted to sustain economic growth and technical change. Yet to change from an old and obsolescent pattern to a new one was both expensive and difficult. It was expensive because it involved both the scrapping of old investments still capable of yielding good profits, and new investments of even greater initial cost; for as a general rule newer technology is more expensive technology. It was difficult because it would almost certainly require agreement to rationalize between a large number of individual firms or industries, none of which could be certain precisely where the benefit of rationalization would go, or even whether in undertaking it they were not giving away their money to outsiders or competitors. So long as satisfactory profits were to be made in the old way, and so long as the decision to modernize had to emerge from the sum-total of decisions by individual firms, the incentive to do so would be weak. What is more, the general interest of the economy would very likely be lost sight of.

The British iron and steel industry is a good example of the first effect. British iron-masters were slow to adopt the Gilchrist-Thomas 'basic' process because they could import non-phosphoric ores easily and cheaply, and because a great deal of capital sunk in plant for the production of acid steel would lose its value. It is perhaps true that other nations had a very much greater incentive to switch to basic steel, since they would derive much greater benefits from it, whereas Britain might at most hope not to lose. And yet her slowness to exploit the new process – and her own resources of phosphoric ores – adequately is extremely striking. If Britain in the 1920s could produce almost five million tons of basic steel as against two and a half million of the old acid steel, then why could she not, some twenty years after a Briton had invented the process, have produced more than 800,000 tons of it (against over four million of the old steel)? Why were the phosphoric ore deposits of eastern England not seriously exploited until the 1930s? The answer is that the heavy investment in obsolete plant and obsolete industrial areas anchored the British industry to an obsolete technology.

Railways and coalmines are good examples of the second effect. Two illustrations may be given. In 1893, Sir George Elliott, frightened by the national coalminers' lockout then raging, suggested the formation of a coal trust to rationalize the industry, since the independent operations of its three thousand odd mines produced considerable inefficiencies in the exploitation of each coalfield, not to mention senseless competition. The response from the collieries was negative, chiefly because the inefficient ones did not wish their share of the trust to be valued – and as they felt, undervalued – by rational criteria. Nothing was done.

The second illustration comes from the railways. One of the many archaisms of the British railways – like the entire British economy – was that the freight cars transporting coal were not merely far too small for efficiency, but owned by the collieries and not the railway companies.* It was long known to all experts that the most efficient size of freight car was more than twice as large as the actual, and how great the economies of a change would be. Both railways and collieries, at all events before 1914, could certainly have found the money for it. Yet because it would have involved a joint decision of both rail and coal to invest money, nothing was done until both were nationalized in 1947. The collieries did not see why they should spend money to benefit, among other things, the general business operations of the railways; the railways did not see why they should take the entire risks of an investment which would also benefit the collieries. Both would have benefited substantially, but private enterprise provided no mechanism for achieving their visible advantage.

There are in a private-enterprise society some ways in which such problems can nevertheless be solved, though they operate as it were tangentially, and by no means always. We have seen

*Both were relics of the original assumption on which railways were constructed, namely that they were another form of road.

(pp. 109–14) how the problem of the construction of a British capital-goods industry was solved in the early railway age, but of course that situation was highly exceptional. Sheer catastrophe can sometimes come to the rescue of capitalism, as in Germany in two wars which destroyed and removed so much old plant that new and modern plant simply had to be installed. The threat of economic catastrophe can also produce a very strong incentive to spend money on modernization which would otherwise have not been spent. And, indeed, during the Great Depression (especially in the 1880s and 1890s) the obvious threat to British industry and its generally gloomy situation led to a good deal of talk about modernization, to a good deal of pressure by one industry for the modernization of others on which its profits depended, and actually to some modernization.

We have already noted Sir George Elliott's ambitious plan for the rationalization of the coalmines, stimulated by the rise of militant trade unions, which was also characteristic of this period of depression (see p. 189). Another industry, gas manufacture, was actually driven by trade-union pressure to turn itself into the most rapidly mechanizing in Europe. The railways were under heavy pressure from their industrial customers and from politicians to reduce their transport costs, especially between 1885 and 1894, and major – but still inadequate – changes were made; for example the Great Western finally installed a new track in 1892. Technical change in engineering speeded up very considerably, though in part under the pressure not of economic but of military competition; that is under the spur of the rapidly expanding and modernizing armaments industry and especially the Navy. This was also the period when industrial combination – cartels, trusts and the like – was widely discussed, and some such concentration actually took place.* However, by American and German standards these changes were comparatively modest, and the urge to undertake them soon

*The Salt Union in the chemical industry, the thread monopoly of J. & P. Coats and the Bradford Dyers Association in textiles, the International Rail Syndicate (of which Britain had a two thirds share) are among the best known examples of monopolist developments in this period, but the growth of large integrated units in armaments and shipbuilding (e.g. Armstrong, Whitworth and Vickers) and elsewhere was probably of greater importance.

slackened. The Great Depression was, alas, not great enough to frighten British industry into really fundamental change.

The reason for this was that the traditional methods of making profits had as yet not been exhausted, and provided a cheaper and more convenient alternative to modernization – for a while. To retreat into her satellite world of formal or informal colonies, to rely on her growing power as the hub of international lending, trade and settlements, seemed all the more obvious a solution because, as it were, it presented itself. The clouds of the 1880s and early 1890s lifted, and what lay before the eye were the shining pastures of cotton exports to Asia, steam-coal exports to the world's ships, Johannesburg gold-mines, Argentine tramways and the profits of City merchant banks. In essence, what happened, therefore, was that Britain exported her immense accumulated historic advantages in the underdeveloped world, as the greatest commercial power, and as the greatest source of international loan capital; and had, in reserve, the exploitation of the 'natural protection' of the home market and if need be the 'artificial protection' of political control over a large empire. When faced with a challenge, it was easier and cheaper to retreat into an as yet unexploited part of one of these favoured zones rather than to meet competition face to face. Thus the cotton industry merely continued its traditional policy when in trouble, of escaping from Europe and North America into Asia and Africa; leaving its former markets to the exporters of British textile-machinery, which made up a quarter of all the country's rapidly increasing machinery exports. In so far as they exported, British coal flowed rapidly in the wake of the British steamship and the vast merchant fleet. Iron and steel relied on the Empire and the underdeveloped world, like cotton: by 1913 Argentina and India alone bought more British iron and steel exports than the whole of Europe, Australia alone more than twice as much as the USA. In addition, the steel industry tended – like coal – to rely increasingly on the protection of the home market.

The British economy as a whole tended to retreat from industry into trade and finance, where our services reinforced our actual and future competitors, but made very satisfactory profits.

Britain's annual investments abroad began actually to *exceed* her net capital formation at home around 1870. What is more, increasingly the two became alternatives, until in the Edwardian era we see domestic investment falling almost without interruption as foreign investment rises. In the great boom (1911–13) which preceded the First World War, twice as much, or even more, was invested abroad than at home; and it has been argued – and is indeed not unlikely – that the amount of domestic capital formation in the twenty-five years before 1914, so far from being adequate for the modernization of the British productive apparatus, was not even quite sufficient to prevent it from slightly running down.

Britain, we may say, was becoming a parasitic rather than a competitive economy, living off the remains of world monopoly, the underdeveloped world, her past accumulations of wealth and the advance of her rivals. That, at all events, was the view of intelligent observers, only too keenly aware of the country's relative loss of momentum and decline, even though their analysis was often defective. And – especially in the Indian summer of Edwardian England – the contrast between the needs of modernization and the increasingly prosperous complacency of the rich grew ever more visible. As Britain ceased to be the workshop of the world, it became, as the disillusioned democrat and ex-Fabian William Clarke pointed out, the best country in the world to be rich and leisured in: a place for foreign millionaires to buy themselves estates:

> Situated as she is close to the historic lands of Europe . . . ships from all the world calling at her ports, with an old and well-ordered society, a secure government, an abundance of the personal service desired by the wealthy, a land of equable climate, pleasant if not grand scenery, a large and ample life organized to sport, amusement and the kind of enjoyments pleasing to the leisured classes – how can England help being attractive to the wealthy people who speak her own language?[5]

Chatsworth and Stratford-on-Avon, he predicted, not Sheffield and Manchester, would draw the foreigner to Britain. It had ceased to compete with the Germans and the Americans. But could it last? The prophets already – and not incorrectly – predicted the decline and fall of an economy symbolized now by the country house in the stockbrokers' belt of Surrey and Sussex and no longer by hard-faced men in smoke-filled provincial towns. 'Rome fell,' said the character in Bernard Shaw's *Misalliance* (1909); 'Carthage fell; Hindhead's turn will come.' Like most of Shaw's jokes, it was meant seriously.

And yet there was, especially in the last years before the First World War, an atmosphere of uneasiness, of disorientation, of tension, which contradicts the journalistic impression of a stable *belle époque* of ostrich-plumed ladies, country houses and music-hall stars. These were not only the years of the sudden emergence of Labour as an electoral force,* of radicalization on the socialist left, of flaring bushfires of labour 'unrest', but also years of political breakdown. Indeed, they were the only years when the stable and flexible mechanism of British political adjustment ceased to function, and when the naked bones of power emerged from the accumulations of tissue which normally concealed them. These were the years when the Lords defied the Commons, when an extreme right, not merely ultra-conservative but nationalist, vitriolic, demagogic and anti-semitic, looked like emerging into the open, when scandals of financial corruption racked governments, when – most serious of all – army officers with the backing of the Conservative Party mutinied against laws passed by Parliament. They were the years when wisps of violence hung in the English air, symptoms of a crisis in economy and society which the self-confident opulence of the architecture of Ritz hotels, pro-consular palaces, West End theatres, department stores and office blocks could not quite conceal. When the war came in 1914, it was not as a catastrophe which wrecked the stable bourgeois world, as the sudden death of the breadwinner wrecked the life of respectable families in Victorian novels. It came as a respite from crisis, a diversion, perhaps even as some sort of a solution. At all events, there is an element of hysteria in the welcome the poets gave to it.

---

* It was, as we know, due mainly to the decision of the Liberal Party not to oppose Labour candidates in a number of places, but, like the early grant of independence to colonial countries, this was not so much an act of grace as a recognition, or at most an intelligent anticipation, of realities.

NOTES

1. Clapham, Checkland, Landes, Ashworth (Further Reading 3). *C. Kindleberger, *Economic Growth in France and England 1850–1950*, (1964), and H. J. Habbakuk, *American and British Technology in the 19th Century* (1962), can serve as introductions to a complex discussion. M. H. Dobb, *Studies in the Development of Capitalism* (1946), for a marxist view. George Dangerfield, *The Strange Death of Liberal England*, remains an excellent survey of the pre-1914 uneasiness. D. H. Aldcroft, 'The Entrepreneur and the British Economy 1870–1914' (*Economic History Review*, 1964), contains references to the specialist literature. G. C. Allen, *Industrial Development of Birmingham and the Black Country* (1929), for a dynamic region. See also Figures 1, 13, 17, 18, 22, 26, 28, 32–4, 37, 51–2.

2. A. Ure, *Dictionary of Arts, Manufacturers and Mines* (1853), Vol. I, p. 626.

3. A. Ure, op. cit., Vol. II, p. 86.

4. H. J. Habbakuk, op. cit., p. 220.

5. *William Clarke*, ed. H. Burrows and J. A. Hobson (1899), pp. 53–4.

10

THE LAND
1850–1960[1]

AFTER the middle of the nineteenth century British agriculture
ceased to be the general framework of the entire economy, and
became merely a branch of production, something like an
'industry', though of course the biggest industry by far in
terms of employment. In 1851 it employed three times as many
as the textile industries – indeed, it employed a quarter of the
entire occupied population – and even in 1891 it still employed
more than any other industrial group, though by 1901 transport
and the metal industries complex had passed it. Still, between
1811 and 1851 its contribution to the gross national income fell
from one third to one fifth, and by 1891 it was merely one
thirteenth. By the 1930s it had become a very minor factor
indeed. Agriculture provided work for only about five per cent
of the occupied population and less than four per cent of the
national income.

However, it is worth special attention for two reasons (apart
from the fact that it always is given special attention in books of
economic history). First, because in the eyes of anyone except
an academic economist it was plainly not merely just another
industry. In terms of sheer area – and appearance – the great
bulk of Britain remained, and indeed still remains, a place where
plants grow and animals feed. In social terms, it was the
foundation and framework of an entire society, rooted in
remotest antiquity, which rested on the man who made the land
produce, and was governed by the man who owned land. While
the former was not of great political importance, once farming
ceased to be the occupation of the bulk of the population, the
latter was. The political and social structure of Britain was
controlled by landlords, and what is more by a rather small
group of perhaps four thousand people who between them
owned something like four sevenths of the cultivated land,

which they let to a quarter of a million farmers who in turn employed – I take 1851 as a convenient date – about a million and a quarter labourers, shepherds, and so on. Such a degree of concentrated landownership was unparalleled in other industrial countries. What is more, the richest individuals in Britain continued to be large landlords, deep into the nineteenth century.* This powerful landlord interest was naturally anxious to preserve both its economic and its social and political position, and its traditional influence as well as its political stranglehold over the nation made it the most formidable of vested interests. Until 1914 the 'counties' could easily outvote the 'boroughs' in Parliament, that is to say – though with increasingly numerous reservations – non-industrial Britain could outvote industrial Britain. Until 1885 landowners still formed the absolute majority in Parliament.

The second reason for taking a special look at agriculture is that its fortunes reflect, in an exaggerated and distorted form, those of the economy as a whole, or rather, the changes in national economic policy. This is partly because agriculture is more sensitive to the intervention or non-intervention of governments than other sectors, and partly because – for this reason as well as for the reasons mentioned above – farming is pretty steadily involved in politics. Agriculture under Free Trade reflected the triumph of the British economy in the world and anticipated its decline. Agriculture in the state-interventionist economy of the mid twentieth century demonstrated the possibilities of economic modernization more convincingly than industry.

*

British farming had risen and flourished with the Industrial Revolution, or more precisely with the limitless expansion of the urban and industrial sectors' demand for food. For practical purposes it enjoyed a natural monopoly of this market, for transport costs made more than marginal food imports impossible until the third quarter of the nineteenth century.

*Though some, like the Barings, Jones Lloyds and Guests, were capitalists who had bought themselves into landed status.

Conversely, if British farming could not feed the British population under normal circumstances, nobody could, and prices for farm products were therefore high, and the incentives as also the means to undertake agricultural improvement were considerable. The Corn Laws which the farming interest imposed upon the country in 1815 were not designed to save a tottering sector of the economy, but rather to preserve the abnormally high profits of the Napoleonic war-years, and to safeguard farmers from the consequences of their temporary wartime euphoria, when farms had changed hands at the fanciest prices, loans and mortgages had been accepted on impossible terms. Consequently as we have seen their abolition in 1846 did not in fact lead to any fall in wheat prices for another generation.*

The post-Napoleonic slump therefore concealed the strength of British farming, all the more so as it discouraged agrarian investment and technical progress. In the booming middle decades of the nineteenth century advance was correspondingly rapid and impressive. For a generation everything went the British farmer's way (though not the Irish peasant's). There was no shortage of capital, the new means of transport widened his markets and not yet those of his overseas competitors, new scientific knowledge (such as Liebig's researches into agricultural chemistry) was available, and the insatiable demand of industry for unskilled manpower thinned the ranks of his labour-force, and encouraged him – almost for the first time in many parts of England – both to pay higher wages and to look for labour-saving methods.† For the first time agriculture came to

*Annual average prices of agricultural and industrial products per decade (Rousseaux index)

Years	Agricultural	Industrial
1800–19	173	173
1820–9	128	112
1830–9	124	103
1840–9	120	100
1850–9	113	111
1860–9	118	117

†Between 1851 and 1861 seven English counties lost population absolutely: Wiltshire, Cambridge, Huntingdonshire, Norfolk, Rutland, Somerset and Suffolk; between 1871 and 1891 another five (Cornwall, Dorset, Hereford, Shropshire, Westmorland).

depend, not on devices for battering down the economic inflexibility of traditional peasant agriculture and the application of the common sense long learned by better farmers to the practice of worse ones, but on the use of industry, machinery, outside fertilizers and artificial feeding-stuffs.

Yet this golden age could not last. It was threatened by two powerful facts: the necessity of the British industrial economy to import heavily, so that its customers would be able to buy its exports, and the capacity of new lands to undersell British agriculture even in its home market. It took a generation of railroad and ship to create a sufficiently large agriculture in the virgin prairies of the temperate world: the American and Canadian Middle West, the pampas of the River Plate lands and the Russian steppes. When they were capable of full production, nothing could protect the high-cost domestic farmers against them except high tariffs, and while other European countries might be willing to impose these, Britain was not. The 1870s and 1880s were an age of universal catastrophe for agriculture: in Europe because of the flood of cheap food imports,* in the new overseas producing areas because of the glut in output and the rapid fall in prices. British farming was all the more vulnerable because it had expanded its traditional and least competitive products, the basic bread grains – and especially wheat.

The Great Depression therefore faced both British farming and the landed interest with an acute crisis. It could survive only by shutting out the competitive outside world or by adjusting itself to the loss of its natural monopoly. The first choice was no longer possible, and it is significant that it was a Conservative government – under Disraeli, who had won his leadership of the party by his opposition to Free Trade – which took the crucial decision *not* to protect British agriculture, in that period of turbulent and continent-wide farming discontent, 1878–80.

*Imports of wheat into the United Kingdom (thousands of cwt)

1840–4	39,700	1865–9	148,100
1845–9	49,400	1870–4	197,800
1850–4	82,200	1875–9	260,200
1855–9	79,800	1880–4	288,000
1860–4	144,100	1885–9	280,600

The fortunes of the economy, it was clear, depended on its industry, trade and finance which – so it was thought – required Free Trade. If farming went down, so much the worse for it. The large landowners were not prepared to do more than make a nominal protest, for if their income was not already diversified by forays into urban real-estate, mining, industry and finance, it could easily be so salvaged. The Earl of Verulam, for instance, in the 1870s had an annual income of about £17,000 (which he usually overspent), of which £14,500 came from rents and timber sales. His son the third earl extended his small share portfolio to some fifteen companies, mainly in the colonies and other overseas parts, and became a multiple director of companies, again mainly of African and American mines. By 1897 almost a third of his income came from such unbucolic sources. Moreover, though one would not think so from the tone of contemporary lamentations, not all British farming collapsed. Cereals and wool suffered; but livestock and dairy farming did not, and in general the sort of mixed farming which the Scots had, fortunately for themselves, had imposed on them by their implacable climate was in no trouble.

Nevertheless, in agriculture as in industry, the Great Depression was a moment of truth for Britain, and in both the truth, briefly glimpsed, was soon shut out again. Instead of facing its situation as one country among many in a competitive world, Britain retired behind the ramparts which still gave it some natural protection, abandoning cereal farming for the less vulnerable livestock and dairy production, low-quality meat (in which refrigeration broke down the immunity of the home producer after the 1880s) for high-quality produce, the farm for the orchard and market garden. By Edwardian times agriculture once again seemed moderately stable, though some of the profits were due to a decline in expenditures on maintenance and investment. The inter-war price-depression showed that this recovery was illusory. It was in any case bought at the cost of a major contraction of agriculture, and especially of tillage. In 1872, at the peak of the golden age, 9·6 million acres were under cereal crops, 17·1 million under pasture. In 1913 there were 6·5 million acres under cereals, and 21·5 million under pasture; in 1932 (at the bottom of the inter-war depression) the figures were 4·7 million and 20·3 million. In other words, the area under cereal crops had halved in sixty years, and after 1913 the entire area under both tillage and pasture diminished.

This sorry record contrasts with the fortunes of other European countries equally hit by the depression of the 1870s and 1880s, but which discovered ways of meeting its challenge other than that of evasion. Denmark, which began to supply the breakfast tables of Britain with bacon and eggs towards the end of the nineteenth century, is the obvious example. The strength of these lively and modern-minded farming communities lay not in any major technological transformations of production, but rather in revolutions of processing, storage, marketing and credit, and especially in the spread of cooperation for these purposes. Under the pressure of crisis such cooperative methods developed fast everywhere – except in Britain.* The truth was that, as in so many other fields of British activity, the economic structure of the pioneer, admirably suited for its purpose in the initial stages, had become a fetter on further development.

The strength of British farming in the eighteenth and nineteenth centuries was the concentration of landownership in the hands of a few very rich landlords, ready to encourage efficient tenants by the terms of their leases, capable of substantial investments and of taking at least some of the strain of bad times by reducing rent or allowing arrears to accumulate.† This certainly eased the pressure on farmers during the Great Depression, and kept their political temperature low – except, characteristically enough, in the few regions of small peasant tenants such as the highlands of Scotland and Wales, and of course Ireland, where the 1880s were a time of acute, and sometimes revolutionary, unrest. At the same time it made revolutionary new departures less essential for collective survival. Nor did the very individualist

---

* A contemporary observer describes the state of agricultural cooperation in Britain (excluding Ireland) round 1900 as 'a mere blank, darkened by a few failures'.[2]

† They frequently had no other choice, since any kind of tenant was better than none. Unlike peasant countries, Britain possessed no great reservoir of land-hungry small cultivators working smallholdings with family labour. The farm-labourers wanted good wages, not land.

structure of the relationship between landlord and commercially minded tenant, or farmer and trader, encourage collective action. In brief, the large capitalist landlord, who had once been a force pressing progress forward, was now a shock-absorber; the large commercially minded farmer, once immeasurably superior to the family-peasant – pioneer or otherwise – as a unit of efficient agriculture, was now too small for optimum efficiency, but too large and well-established to subordinate himself to a co-operative organization capable of operating on a larger scale. No alternative existed between the individual farm and the intervention and planning of the state.

Eventually the state stepped in. But before it did so the failure of British agriculture had brought about a fundamental change in British landed society, whose repercussions were felt far beyond the countryside. The old landed aristocracy and gentry abdicated. They sold their land, and under the temporary impact of the war and post-war boom after 1914, they found plenty of purchasers among tenant-farmers who bought their holdings and profiteers who bought themselves the country seat which was the badge of their social success. In the early 1870s perhaps ten per cent of the land of England was farmed by owner-occupiers, and in 1914 not much more, but by 1927 thirty-six per cent. (After that the agricultural crisis stopped further land transfers for some time.) 'Precisely one quarter of England and Wales', writes F. M. L. Thompson, 'had therefore passed from being tenanted land into the possession of its farmers in the thirteen years after 1914. . . . Such an enormous and rapid transfer of land had not been seen since the dissolution of the monasteries in the sixteenth century', perhaps not since the Norman Conquest.[3] Yet the curious thing about this virtual revolution in landownership is that hardly anyone noticed it at the time, except the tiny percentage of the population professionally concerned with agriculture and the real-estate market. And this in spite of the fact that radicals had campaigned against the evils of the aristocratic land-monopoly for generations – though with greater success in the towns than in the countryside – and that as recently as 1909–14 the Liberal government, and in particular its Welsh Chancellor of the Exchequer, Lloyd George, had made the campaign against the dukes the cornerstone of his demagogy.

No doubt the absence of fuss about the actual retreat of the landed aristocracy was largely due to the irrelevance of agrarian demands to the great bulk of the British working class, which had far more urgent concerns, especially during and after the First World War. Such demands were notoriously easy to pass resolutions about, notoriously slow to reach action.* Lloyd George's miscalculation was precisely the belief that an issue which raised genuine and concrete passions in the peasant society of North Wales could for long divert a movement of industrial workers. Yet there was more to the lack of interest in Britain's rural transformation than this. The landed classes as such were simply ceasing to be of national importance. The old-fashioned earl was becoming as much of a backwoodsman without automatic political power as the old-fashioned squire had long been. Those who lacked the share portfolio and the guinea-pig directorships of the adaptable aristocrat disappeared from sight; as often as not to Kenya or Rhodesia, where the colour of the lower orders' faces guaranteed another two generations of undisturbed gentlemanly life. They found a few mourners, like the brilliant and quixotic novelist Evelyn Waugh, but on the whole their funeral was private.

The truth is that the foundations of a British society dominated by the landed classes all collapsed together with and during the Great Depression. Landownership ceased, with some exceptions, to be the basis of great wealth, and became merely a status symbol. Trade and finance maintained its façade. In one of its strongholds, Ireland, it was actually challenged by a revolutionary movement of peasants in the 1880s – organized by Michael Davitt's Land League – and its political triumph could only be postponed at the price of the quiet liquidation of

---

*Land nationalization is the earliest of all demands of its kind, but no government, including those of Labour, has ever made any move to implement it; nor that hardy annual of Trade Union Congresses, the condemnation of tied cottages. The demand for the right of leaseholders to buy out their leases has periodically emerged in politics since the 1880s. It remained unsatisfied until the 1960s.

the landlord's economic power soon after.* Simultaneously landownership lost its perquisite of local political power in Britain, partly because of the democratization of the national franchise in 1884–5 and of county administration in 1889, partly because administration became too complicated to be left to part-time and unqualified squires. Democratization did not shake the Conservatism of the countryside, for the dissenting, radical-liberal impetus which made so many farm-labourers vote against squire and parson in their first free election (1885) was on the point of exhaustion, and the Labour Party inherited few purely rural strongholds outside the old radical and puritan bastion of East Anglia. But its quality had subtly changed.

The Conservative Party, which had been kept alive for a generation after Free Trade as a nobleman's and squires' rump, revived from the 1870s. But in reviving it ceased to be essentially the agrarian party. It was the Midland manufacturer and imperialist Joseph Chamberlain who reconverted it to protectionism in the early 1900s, though the passion with which it clung to tariffs thereafter owed something to the dumb resentment of its rural backwoodsmen, ready to die in the last ditch of the House of Lords against the damned radicals. So did the party's equally passionate imperialism, for the Empire provided investments, jobs and sometimes even estates, and the defence of landed property against revolution was an even more dramatic and certainly a more genuine problem in parts of it – for example Ireland – than in Britain. But though the Irish question in the 1880s brought virtually all important landed aristocrats into the Conservative fold, leaving the Liberals denuded of their traditional Whig nobles, even the Tory party was now a businessmen's party. It was no longer led by a Bentinck, a Derby, a Cecil or a Balfour, but – after 1911 – by a Glasgow Canadian iron-merchant (Bonar Law), and two Midland industrialists (Baldwin and Neville Chamberlain).†

* Under the land purchase laws of the Conservative governments in 1885, 1887, 1891, 1896 and 1903 almost thirteen million Irish acres in 390,000 holdings changed hands by 1909. The total number of holdings in Ireland in 1917 was about 570,000.

† The apparent revival of its aristocratic atmosphere after the Second World War was due partly to the rise of new and untypical leaders after

Meanwhile the acute and this time virtually universal farming crisis between the wars forced governments to take action after 1930, and thereby to save British agriculture. The essential devices were protection and the guarantee of farm prices, increasingly combined (as in potatoes, milk and, rather less successfully, pigs and bacon) with state-initiated Marketing Boards. These were half-hearted measures, since even the Conservative governments still accepted the nineteenth-century Liberal view that a large volume of food imports was essential to British prosperity, and that agriculture, like any other languishing industry, must contract until it found its modest level of profitability, or else go under. Since in the late 1930s about seventy per cent of the country's food (as measured in calories) was supplied from imports,* the traditional argument that farming deserves special treatment because it feeds the people hardly seemed to apply.

Yet when war broke out it evidently did. The blockade of Britain and the shortage of shipping made the expansion of food production essential. Fortunately the 1930s had already laid some sort of basis for systematic government planning, devoted primarily to the expansion of arable farming. In the course of the war arable acreage rose by fifty per cent, from twelve to eighteen million acres,† the number of sheep, pigs and poultry fell substantially, though the number of cattle – valuable for milk – rose by about ten per cent. The yields of this increased area of often marginal land increased substantially, thanks to what amounted to a major technological revolution. The quantities of fertilizer used increased twice or three times over (phosphates and nitrogens), but, above all, between 1939 and 1946 the machinery on British farms multiplied from two million to five million horsepower. The number of tractors

---

the bankruptcy of Chamberlainite Conservatism in 1940, partly to nostalgia for the *belle époque* of Britain's former greatness. It barely outlasted the 1950s.

*Eighty-four per cent of its sugar, oils and fats, eighty-eight per cent of its wheat and flour, ninety-one per cent of its butter.

†These figures are not comparable to those given on pp. 199–200.

multiplied almost fourfold, as did combine harvesters. Within five years British agriculture changed from one of the least to one of the most mechanized of farming systems in advanced countries. This was done by a combination of financial incentives and planned compulsion. The County 'War Agricultural Committees' could and did decide what was to be cultivated and where, allocate labour and machinery (often from collective machinery depots analogous to the Soviet 'Machine and Tractor Stations'), and replace inefficient by efficient farmers.

The immediate results were dramatic. The British people was adequately fed while its food imports were halved. Home output almost doubled (measured in calories) between 1938–9 and 1943–4, with an increase of only about ten per cent in the labour force – and that mainly of inexperienced women or casual workers. The long-term results were scarcely less impressive.* In 1960 output per head of the agricultural population was higher in Britain than in all West European countries except the Netherlands. The British farming population produced about its proportion of the gross domestic product, as did the Dutch. In all other West European countries, except some backward ones lacking industry, it produced less. In other words, British farming was no longer a way of life, but it had become, by international standards, an efficient industry.

*Agriculture in the European economies

	Agricultural labour force (millions)	millions acres (1961)	Gross domestic product from agriculture, forestry, fishing (£millions, 1960)
Britain	1	48·8	2·6
France	4	85·3	5·8
W. Germany	3·7	35·1	4·4
Italy	6·7	51·1	4·8
Denmark	0·4	7·8	0·8
Holland	0·4	7·5	1·1

NOTES

1. In addition to the works quoted in Chapter 5, Note 1, C. Orwin and E. Whetham, *History of British Agriculture 1846–1914* (1963), E. Whetham, *British Farming 1939–49* (1964), E. M. Ojala, *Agriculture and Economic Progress* (1952). On political changes, W. L. Guttsmann, *The British Political Elite* (1965). See also Figures 4, 13.
2. C. R. Fay, *Co-operation at Home and Abroad* (1908).
3. F. M. L. Thompson, *English Landed Society* (1963), p. 332.

11

BETWEEN THE WARS [1]

THE Victorian economy of Britain crashed in ruins between the two world wars. The sun, which, as every schoolboy knew, never set on British territory and British trade, went down below the horizon. The collapse of all that Britons had taken for granted since the days of Robert Peel was so sudden, catastrophic and irreversible that it stunned the incredulous contemporaries. At the very moment when Britain emerged on the victorious side in the first major war since Napoleon, when her chief continental rival Germany was on her knees, when the British Empire, sometimes lightly and unconvincingly disguised as 'mandates', 'protectorates' and satellite Middle Eastern states, covered a greater extent of the world map than ever before, the traditional economy of Britain not only ceased to grow, but contracted. Statistics which had advanced almost without a break for 150 years – not always at equal or satisfactory rates, but still advanced – now retreated. 'Economic decline', something that economists argued about before 1914, now became a palpable fact.

Between 1912 and 1938 the quantity of cotton cloth made in Britain fell from 8,000 million to barely 3,000 million square yards; the amount exported from 7,000 million to less than 1,500 million yards. Never since 1851 had Lancashire exported so little. Between 1854 and 1913 the output of British coal had grown from 65 to 287 million tons. By 1938 it was down to 227 million and still falling. In 1913 twelve million tons of British shipping had sailed the seas, in 1938 there was rather less than eleven million. British shipyards in 1870 built 343,000 tons of vessels for British owners, and in 1913 almost a million tons: in 1938 they built little more than half a million.

In human terms the ruin of the traditional industries of Britain was the ruin of millions of men and women through mass unemployment, and it was this which stamped the years between the wars indelibly with the mark of bitterness and poverty. Industrial areas with a variety of occupations were not wholly devastated. The labour force in cotton fell by more than half between 1912 and 1938 (from 621,000 to 288,000), but Lancashire had at least some other industries to absorb some of them: its unemployment rate was by no means the worst. The real tragedy was that of areas and towns relying on a single industry, prosperous in 1913, ruined between the wars. In 1913–14 about three per cent of the workers in Wales had been unemployed – rather less than the national average. In 1934 – after recovery had begun – thirty-seven per cent of the labour force in Glamorgan, thirty-six per cent of that in Monmouth, were out of work. Two thirds of the men of Ferndale, three quarters of those in Brynmawr, Dowlais and Blaina, seventy per cent of those in Merthyr, had nothing to do except stand at streetcorners and curse the system which put them there. The people of Jarrow, in Durham, lived by Palmers' shipyard. When it closed in 1933 Jarrow was derelict, with eight out of every ten of its workers jobless, and having as like as not lost all their savings in the crash of the yard, which had so long been their harsh and noisy universe. It was the concentration of permanent, hopeless unemployment in certain derelict areas, politely renamed 'special areas' by a mealy-mouthed government, which gave the depression its particular character. South Wales, central Scotland, the north-east, parts of Lancashire, parts of Northern Ireland and Cumberland, not to mention smaller enclaves elsewhere, resisted even the modest recovery of the later 1930s. The grimy, roaring, bleak industrial areas of the nineteenth century – in northern England, Scotland and Wales – had never been very beautiful or comfortable, but they had been active and prosperous. Now all that remained was the grime, the bleakness, and the terrible silence of the factories and mines which did not work, the shipyards which were closed.

At all times between 1921 and 1938 at least one out of every ten citizens of working age was out of a job. In seven out of these eighteen years at least three out of every twenty were unemployed, in the worst years one out of five. In absolute figures unemployment ranged from a minimum of rather over a million to a maximum (1932) of just under three million; at all events, according to the official figures, which for various reasons understated it. In particular industries and regions the record was even blacker. At its peak (1931–2) 34·5 per cent of coalminers, 36·3 per cent of pottery-workers, 43·2 per cent of cotton operatives, 43·8 per cent of pig-iron workers, 47·9 per cent of steelworkers, and 62 per cent – or almost two in three – of shipbuilders and ship-repairers were out of work. Not until 1941 was the back of the problem broken.

The years of slump followed those of world war, and everybody lived in the shadow of these cataclysms. Though their effect varied considerably from one region, industry or social group to another, they had very general consequences. The first was fear: of death or maiming in war, of helplessness and poverty in peace. Such fear does not necessarily correspond to the reality of the danger. In the Second World War the average citizen's chances of death were not in fact very high, and the majority of workers between the wars were not likely to be out of work for very long. Yet even those who knew this also knew themselves and their relations to be only a hair's breadth from the abyss. Even in peacetime a job lost meant more than a period of uncertainty or poverty. It might mean a family of lives destroyed. This acrid fog of anxiety was the atmosphere which men and women breathed during a generation. Its effect cannot be statistically measured, but, equally, it cannot be left out of any account of these years.

It was visibly reflected in the pattern of politics in Britain, which increasingly dominated the life of the citizen through the growing activities of the state. The war and the years of ferment which followed multiplied the electoral forces of the Labour Party, essentially the class party of the manual workers, over eightfold. Its votes grew from half a million in 1910 to 4½ million in 1922. For the first time in history, a proletarian party became and remained the major alternative government party, and the fear of working-class power and expropriation now haunted the middle classes, not so much because this is what the Labour leaders promised or performed, but because its mere existence as a mass party threw a faint red shadow of potential Soviet revolution across the country. The leaders of the trade unions and the Labour Party were far from revolutionaries. Few of them even trusted themselves in government, which they regarded as essentially, or anyway normally, the function of employers and upper classes, their own being to demand improvements and concessions. But they stood at the head of a vast movement united by the consciousness of class separation and exploitation, and capable of showing its force in such unparalleled acts of solidarity as the General Strike of 1926. Theirs was a movement which had lost confidence in the capacity, perhaps even in the willingness, of capitalism to give labour its modest rights, while at the same time it observed abroad – and perhaps somewhat idealized – the first, and at that time the only, working-class state and socialist economy, Soviet Russia.

The depression produced a further swing to Labour, though the later phase of it was delayed by a temporary stampede of frightened and disoriented citizens to the so-called 'National' government under the impact of the crisis of 1931 (see p. 241). The Second World War ended with the first effective Labour government of Britain, and by 1951 the party polled more votes than it had ever done in history. In the prosperous fifties it ceased to advance.

Only one part of the Victorian economy seemed briefly to resist collapse: the City of London, source of the world's capital, nerve-centre of its international trading and financial transactions. Britain was no longer the greatest international lender; indeed, she was now on balance in debt to the USA, which had taken her former place. However, by the middle of the 1920s, British overseas investments earned more than ever before and so, even more strikingly, did her other sources of invisible income – financial and insurance services and so on. But the interwar crisis was not merely a British phenomenon, the decline of a former industrial world champion, all the more sudden and sharp for having been delayed for decades. It was the crisis of the entire liberal world of the nineteenth century, and therefore British trade and finance could no longer regain what British industry lost. For the first time since industrialization began the growth of production in *all* the industrial powers faltered. The First World War reduced it by twenty per cent (1913–21), and hardly had it resumed its rise to new heights, when the slump of 1929–32 reduced it temporarily by about a third (largely due to the simultaneous collapse of all the major industrial powers except Japan and the USSR). What is more to the point, the three great international flows of capital, labour and goods, on which the liberal world economy was based, dried up. World trade in manufactured goods only just regained its 1913 level in 1929 and then plummeted by a third. It had not quite recovered by 1939; its value halved in the 1929 slump. World trade in primary products, which was so vital for Britain which sold largely to their producers, fell by considerably more than half after 1929. Though the primary producers desperately sold increased quantities at knock-down prices, they were in 1936–8 unable to buy more than two thirds of what they had been able to buy in 1913, or much more than a third of what had been within their reach in 1926–9. A network of walls rose along the world's frontiers to prevent the free entry of men and goods and the exit of gold. Britain, the international junction of a flourishing traffic-system, saw the traffic on which she depended disappear, while her investment income from the depressed industrial and the even more hard-hit primary producers fell. Between 1929 and 1932 her foreign dividends fell from £250 to £150 million, her other invisible earnings from £233 million to £86 million. Neither had recovered by the time the Second World War broke out, to reduce her foreign holdings by over a third. When in 1932 Free Trade was finally buried (see p. 244), the Victorian economy went with it. It was only just that the Liberal Party, which had been essentially the party of the liberal world economy, should have finally lost its political prospects with its traditional *raison d'être* in 1931.

Those responsible for the economy were shocked, numbed and profoundly puzzled by this collapse of all they had taken for granted. The failure of businessmen, politicians and economists to recognize the facts, let alone to know what to do about them, was overwhelming. We are now aware of the unorthodox minority which anticipated the thinking of our own generation, the marxists who actually predicted the great slump and gained prestige both from their prediction and from the immunity of the USSR to it, or J. M. Keynes whose critique of the prevailing economic orthodoxy has in turn become the orthodoxy of a later era. We tend to forget how small and uninfluential a minority they were, until after the economic catastrophe had become so overwhelming – in 1932–3 – as to seem to threaten the very existence of the British, and the world, capitalist system. The businessmen of the 1920s went into it with little more than the conviction that if wages and government spending could be cut savagely enough British industry would once again be all right, and with indiscriminate calls for protection from the economic hurricane. The politicians – both Conservative and Labour – went into it with little more than the almost equally futile slogans of Richard Cobden or Joseph Chamberlain. The bankers and the officials who were the guardians of 'Treasury orthodoxy' dreamed of a return to the liberal world of 1913, put their confidence in balanced budgets* and the Bank Rate and staked all on the impossible hope of maintaining the City of London as the world's financial centre. The economists, with what can only be described as a quiet heroism worthy of Don Quixote, nailed their flag to the mast of Say's Law which proved that slumps could not actually occur at all. Never did a ship founder with a captain and crew more ignorant of the reasons for its misfortune or more impotent to do anything about it.

*

Nevertheless, when we compare the inter-war depression with the period before 1914, we are inclined to judge it a little less severely. It is hard to find anything positive to say about the Indian summer of the Edwardians, that season of almost deliberately missed opportunities which made certain that the decline of the British economy would be a catastrophe. It had not even achieved that most modest of objectives, the stability of the standard of living of the poor, though it had made the rich

*Thus almost certainly making the slump worse by cutting government spending when it would have done most good.

a great deal richer (cf. pp. 166–7). On the other hand – perhaps just because economic catastrophe left very much less scope for complacency – the inter-war years were not entirely wasted. By 1939 Britain looked a great deal more like a twentieth-century economy than she had done – in comparison with other industrial states – in 1913. By the four criteria listed in Chapter 9 Britain was no longer a Victorian economy. The importance of scientific technology, of mass-production methods, of industry producing for the mass market, but above all of economic concentration, 'monopoly capitalism' and state intervention was very much greater. The inter-war years neither modernized the British economy nor made it internationally competitive. It remains old-fashioned and undynamic to this day. But at least certain foundations for modernization were laid, or rather certain major obstacles to it removed.

The reason why the inter-war catastrophe had not more fundamental consequences is threefold: the pressure on the economy was not desperate enough; the most efficient – and indeed indispensable – method of modernization, state planning, was used very sparingly, for political reasons; and virtually all economic changes initiated in this period were defensive and negative.

The pressure on the economy was inadequate, partly because the peculiar international position of Britain somewhat blunted the impact of the sharpest spur to action, the great slump of 1929–33. Since the traditional basic industries of Britain were already depressed after 1921, the effect of the slump was less dramatic: those who are already low do not fall so far.* Moreover, while the export industries were battered, the rest of the economy benefited abnormally from the disproportionate fall in the cost of primary products – food and raw material – from the colonial and semi-colonial world. Again, because the Victorian economy had relied so very little on production for the domestic mass market, the scope for a shift into home sales was considerably greater. Britain was in crisis, but she was not faced in the

*For instance, manufacturing production (1913 = 100) in the USA fell from 112·7 in 1929 to 58·4 in 1932; in Germany from 108 to 64·6; but in Britain merely from 109·9 to 90.

starkest and least avoidable form with the alternative: compete or die.

Second, the state refrained from adequate intervention. Its capacity to intervene effectively was demonstrated in both world wars, but especially the Second. When it did, its achievements were sometimes little short of sensational, as in British agriculture, which it transformed between 1940 and 1945. The necessity for its intervention was evident, for several of the basic industries – notably railways and coalmines – were so run down as to be quite beyond the scope of private restoration, and several others were clearly not capable of rationalizing themselves. Yet after both wars the apparatus of state control was dismantled with nervous speed, and the state's reluctance to interfere with private enterprise remained profound. Its interventions, like the gestures of industry itself in the direction of modernization, were essentially protective in a negative sense.

This is particularly obvious in the field of economic concentration, for in 1914 Britain was perhaps the least concentrated of the great industrial economies, and in 1939 one of the most. There was of course nothing new about economic concentration. The growth in the scale of productive units and units of ownership, the concentration of a growing share of output, employment, and so on in the hands of a declining number of giant firms, the formal or informal restriction of competition which may reach the point of monopoly or oligopoly:* all these are among the best-known tendencies of capitalism. Concentration first became noticeable during the Great Depression – in the 1880s and 1890s – but until 1914 its impact in Britain was strikingly smaller than in Germany and the USA. In its industrial structure Britain was wedded to the small or medium-sized, highly specialized, family-operated and family-financed, and competitive firm, just as in its economic policy it was wedded to Free Trade. There were exceptions, notably in the public utilities and heavy industries (iron and steel, heavy engineering, shipbuilding) which had long required higher initial capital investments than could be raised by individuals and partnerships, and where concentration was fostered by the

*See p. 177 n.

needs of war. But broadly speaking, the small and disintegrated industry in the open market prevailed, and as it continued to be prosperous, and generally lacked government protection or aid, there was no great reason for it to decline. The average size of plant increased. The public joint-stock company, which hardly existed outside banking and transport before the last quarter of the century, entered industry and multiplied after 1880, and this further increased the size of firms. There were already in 1914 some outstanding examples of great capitalist combinations, and a few which had reached the point of monopoly. The tendency to concentration undoubtedly existed, but it had certainly not transformed the economy.

However, between 1914 and 1939 it did so, accelerated partly by the First World War, partly by the depression (and especially, after 1930, the great slump), and almost invariably fostered by a benevolent government. Unfortunately, it cannot be easily measured, for the statisticians, like the academic economists, did not seriously investigate its quantitative importance or its theoretical implications until after 1930.* Yet there can be no doubt about the broad facts.

Before 1914 there were already a few monopolist products: sewing cotton, Portland cement, wallpaper, flat glass and some others; but in 1935 at an absolute minimum upwards of 170 products were produced substantially by one, two or three firms. In 1914 there had been 130 railway companies; after 1921 there were four giant non-competing monopolies. In 1914 there had been thirty-eight joint-stock banks; in 1924 there were twelve, of whom the 'Big Five' (Midland, National Provincial, Lloyds, Barclays, Westminster) completely dominated the field. In 1914 there had been perhaps fifty trade associations, mainly in iron and steel. By 1925 the Federation of British Industries (founded, like the National Association of Manufacturers, in the last years of the war) alone had 250 such associations affiliated to it;† after the Second World War there were perhaps a

---

*This is itself a symptom of its growing importance.

†Out of a sample of a hundred trade associations existing during the Second World War twenty-six had been formed before 1914, thirty-three in 1915–20 and thirty-seven between the wars.

thousand. In 1907 an expert inquirer could still write: 'Great as is the extent to which industry has passed into the hands of large combinations, greater still is the domain still subject to the individual trader.'[2] By 1939, an expert observer had to note that 'As a feature of industrial and commercial organization free competition has nearly disappeared from the British scene.'[3]

In terms of employment, economic concentration was fairly marked by the middle 1930s. Broadly speaking, there were then a little over 140,000 'factories' in Britain. There were then in Britain only 519 plants employing more than a thousand workers, out of a total of a little over 140,000 'factories', of which all but some 30,000 were very small establishments of less than twenty-five workers. Yet these few plants then employed about one in five of all workers covered by the Census of Production, and in several industries (electrical machinery, motor and cycle manufacture, iron and steel rolling and smelting, silk and artificial silk, newspaper production, shipbuilding, sugar and confectionery) more than forty per cent. In other words, one third of one per cent of all factories employed 21·5 per cent of all workers. But since increasingly a single firm owned several plants in the same industry – not to mention in other industries – the actual concentration of employment was even higher. There were thirty-three trades in Britain in which the three largest firms employed seventy per cent or more of all workers.

We cannot compare this precisely with the situation before 1914, but we have some guide in the structure of typical old-fashioned industries, which, as one might expect, were less affected than the technologically new ones characteristic of the twentieth century. In 1914 the average coalmine – an unusually large undertaking by contemporary standards – employed some three hundred men; and as late as 1930 the typical cotton-weaving firm was one which employed one to three hundred workers, and almost forty per cent worked in plants of less than two hundred. In the 'average' British industry in 1935, a little more than a quarter of workers were employed by the top three firms. In the most highly concentrated industries (chemicals, engineering and vehicles, iron and steel) forty per cent or more were employed by the top three; in the least concentrated –

mines, building, timber – ten per cent or less. It is fairly certain that before 1914 most of British industry was much more like the last than either of the two others.

But the most striking change was not so much the conversion of Britain into a country of giant corporations, oligopolies, trade associations, and so forth, but the positive approval of business and government for a change which would have horrified J. S. Mill. It is true that opposition to economic concentration had always been much weaker in practice than in theory. Britain possessed no powerful movement of radical-democratic 'little men' such as that which time and again imposed the (quite ineffective) anti-trust legislation on the USA; and the socialists, though hostile in theory to concentration, were opposed to it because it served private ends rather than at all costs. (In practice, the labour movement was not opposed to it at all.) Nevertheless, the belief in competitive capitalism was almost as firm and dogmatic as that in Free Trade. But what we see between the wars is the systematic effort of governments to *reduce* competition, to foster giant cartels, mergers, combinations and monopolies. The iron and steel industry had been riddled with price-fixing arrangements even before 1914; but it was not, as it became after 1932, a giant restrictionist cartel in open partnership (through the Import Duties Advisory Committee) with the government. The belief in free competition died quickly and painlessly before the belief in Free Trade.

Now economic concentration is not in itself undesirable. Often it is essential, especially in the extreme form of nationalization, to ensure adequate industrial progress. The belief that 'monopoly capitalism' is *ipso facto* less dynamic or technologically progressive than unrestricted competitive enterprise is a myth. Yet the economic concentration which took place between the wars cannot be primarily justified on grounds of efficiency and progress. It was overwhelmingly restrictive, defensive, and protective. It was a blind response to depression, which aimed at maintaining profits high by eliminating competition, or at accumulating great clusters of miscellaneous capital which were in no sense productively more rational than their original independent components, but which provided financiers with investments for surplus capital or with the profits of company promotion. Britain became a non-competing country at home as well as abroad.

In a sense, the strong domestic orientation of British business in this period was also a defensive response to the economy's crisis. Industries like iron and steel frankly fled from the bleak international scene into the protected home market,* though such flights could not save the old, export-oriented industries like cotton from disaster. The government after 1931 systematically protected the home market, and certain industries – notably motor manufacturing – rested entirely on the protection, which in this instance had existed since the First World War. However, it was not mere escapism which made British business turn inwards. It was to a great extent the discovery that the mass consumption of the British working class held unsuspected sales opportunities. The contrast between those branches of the economy which had always looked outwards, and those which flourished because they had not, was bound to strike the most superficial observer.

The most startling example of expansion during this depression period was retail distribution (see also pp. 162–3). The number of tobacconist's shops rose by almost two thirds between 1911 and 1939, the number of confectionery outlets multiplied two and a half times (1913–38), the number of shops selling medical preparations multiplied more than three times; and shops selling such things as furniture, electrical goods, hardware, grew even faster. And this, while the small shopkeeper lost ground and the large enterprises – cooperative, department store, but above all the multiple shop – gained ground rapidly. The discovery of the mass market was not new. Certain industries and industrial areas – notably the Midlands – had always concentrated on the domestic consumer, and had done well by this policy. What was new was the visible contrast

---

*Output and domestic consumption of steel (annual average, million tons)

	1910–14	1927–31	1935–8
Output	7·0	7·9	11·3
Domestic consumption	5·0	7·6	10·6

between the flourishing home market industries and the despairing exporters, symbolized in the contrast between an expanding Midlands and south-east, and a depressed north and west. In a broad belt stretching between the Birmingham and London regions, industry grew: the new motor manufacture was virtually confined to this zone. The new consumer-goods factories multiplied along the Great West Road out of London, while emigrants from Wales and the north moved to Coventry and Slough. Industrially, Britain was turning into two nations.

The turn to the home market has some connexions with the striking expansion of technologically new industries, organized in a new way (mass-production). Though some of the 'new' inter-war industries had good export sales, fundamentally – and unlike the nineteenth-century staples – they relied on domestic demand, and indeed often on natural or government protection from outside competition. Several – and normally those which relied on a more complex and scientific technology – relied even more directly on government support or backing. The aircraft industry would not have existed otherwise, and the entire buoyant complex of electrical industries benefited more than is measurable from the government monopoly of the wholesaling of power and the construction of the national 'Grid' – a system of power distribution unparalleled at this time anywhere else.

The other side of this picture was, of course, a distinct, and in spite of some patchiness very widespread, improvement in the standard of living of the working classes, which benefited both by the cheapening and widening of the range of goods available, and by their being more efficiently sold. By 1914 only the food market had been seriously transformed in this manner. The rise of the mass market was somewhat delayed after 1914 both by the effect of the two wars (the first rather more than the efficiently and equitably administered second)* and by the insistence of government and employers that the solution to depression lay in cutting wages and social security payments. Nevertheless, and even allowing for mass unemployment, there was probably

---

*For instance, food consumption fell by about ten per cent between 1939 and 1941. Thereafter, thanks to efficient planning, it actually increased a little. In the First World War, food expenditure dropped continuously.

some over-all improvement. The least sanguine estimates, which spread the losses of unemployment (somewhat unrealistically) over the whole population, still suggest a modest average rise of five per cent in real wages, and the more rosy ones (which do not allow for unemployment) of anything up to forty per cent, though this is very implausible. And there is little doubt that between the wars the new mass-production economy really triumphed.

It is true that the mass goods which now came on the market or were decisively cheapened were not yet the expensive 'consumer durables' which few could afford, except perhaps for the bicycle. While by 1939 the USA already provided 150 new refrigerators per year for every 10,000 of its population and Canada fifty, Britain in 1935 got only eight. Even the middle class had only begun to buy motor-cars at the modest rate of four per 1,000 consumers (1938). Vacuum cleaners and electric irons were perhaps the only pieces of domestic machinery, apart from the already ubiquitous radio set, which were bought in quantity by the end of the 1930s. The new goods which made the greatest impact were cheap articles of domestic and personal use, of the kind sold in the rapidly multiplying variety stores of the 'Woolworth' type, the expanding and diversifying 'chemists' (the number of Boots stores rose from 200 in 1900 to 1,180 in 1938) and similar emporia. Cheap cosmetics, for instance, came into use in this period, and so did fountain pens. Both, incidentally, belonged to the short list of most heavily advertised commodities, with cigarettes, drinks and manufactured foods. For advertising also came of age between the wars and with it the modern national multi-million circulating press, which depended on it.

In one field, however, technological revolution already created an entirely new dimension of life between the wars. In addition to the traditional and declining music-hall and the equally old-fashioned but expanding 'palais-de-danse', two technologically original forms of entertainment triumphed after 1918: radio and cinema. Of these the first was more revolutionary than the second, for it brought round-the-clock entertainment ready-made into people's actual homes for the first time in history, though this was not the primary purpose of the uncommercially minded public corporation which controlled it, the BBC. The cinema took the place of both gin-palace and music-hall as the poor man's dream substitute for luxury. The gigantic and baroque Granadas, Trocaderos and Odeons, their names hinting at exotic languor and luxury hotels, their cushioned seats opening vistas of million-dollar spectacles and huge organs rising to blow out heavy sentiment amid changing coloured lights, rose in the working-class districts with the rate of unemployment. They were probably the most effective dream-producers ever devised, for a visit to them not only cost less and lasted longer than a drink or variety show, but could be – and was – more readily combined with the cheapest of all enjoyments, sex.

The rise in the standard of living remained modest and limited. Much of it was due (at least for those in employment) to the fortunate fact that years of slump also tended to be years of falling costs of living. One pound in 1933 bought four shillings more than it had in 1924, and a man earning £3 a week – the average of employed male workers in 1924 – was still about five shillings better off in 1938.* The improvements which came with full employment in the 1940s and with prosperity in the 1950s would not have seemed so remarkable if those of the inter-war years had not been so unimpressive. Nevertheless, the paradox that depression, mass unemployment and – at least for very many members of the working class – a rising standard of life went together reflects the changes in the British economy between the wars.

For a country with Britain's international position, the turn to the internal market was not to be welcomed without qualification. After the Second World War, when governments attempted to encourage the new industries to export, their now established preference for the much easier domestic market was only too obvious. More serious, even the new British industries remained less technologically dynamic than the best of the foreign ones, and where new innovations came from Britain – as they often did – British industry often proved incapable of developing

* In other words, some of the burden of depression in Britain was transferred to the primary-exporting underdeveloped countries.

them commercially, or unwilling to do so. In the pure sciences, Britain's position was eminent, and became even more distinguished after 1933 with the exodus of Germany's best scientific brains; though it depended dangerously on a very small number of men in one or two universities. Britain's place in the development of nuclear physics, of the theory of computers, and in industrially as yet less important branches of science like biochemistry and physiology was assured. But it is fair to say that between the wars few looked to Britain for the development of new techniques (except in the state-sponsored field of armaments – for example radar and the jet engine) and even fewer for a model of what modern industry should be like. Among the very few typical products of our century which were actually developed practically in Britain was television, which was first broadcast here in 1936; but even this – characteristically – owed its advance not merely to a go-ahead private firm (Electrical and Musical Industries), but to the dynamism of the state-owned BBC. It is perhaps significant that Britain remained far ahead of all countries except the USA in its use of television; a rare situation.*

To some extent this sluggishness was due to the failure of British business to undertake the systematic and expensive research and development which was increasingly essential for the advance of industries based on scientific technology. The Balfour Committee on Industry and Trade in 1927 bitterly contrasted the 'slow progress made in respect of scientific research generally' with the record of German and American industry.[4] This failure was not so much one of research – for even in the USA, as in Britain, the really major expansion in this field occurred during and after the Second World War under government auspices, and mainly for military purposes – as in 'development', that is in the expensive nursing of discovery or invention towards commercial practicability. Few inventions could be *developed* except by some giant: the Calico Printers Association's researchers, who happened on a most valuable artificial fibre (Terylene), simply passed it on to Imperial

---

*In 1950, Britain had almost 600,000 sets and the rest of Europe none. Even in 1960 well over half all European TV sets were in Britain.

Chemicals in Britain, Dupont in the USA. But the British giants were on the whole less interested in innovation than their opposite numbers abroad.

Nevertheless, when all reservations have been made, the record of British industry between the wars was not unimpressive. The output of *all* British manufacturing industry (including, that is, the declining ones) grew considerably faster between 1924 and 1935 than between 1907 and 1924; and this at a time of depression and mass unemployment. Total industrial output per head may have just about doubled between 1850 and 1913, or a little more. It hardly changed between 1913 and 1924. But from then until 1937 it rose by about one third, considerably faster than in the heyday of the Victorians. Naturally, this was achieved mainly by the new growth industries. The output of electrical goods almost doubled between 1924 and 1935, that of motor-cars more than doubled, as did the supply of electricity. The output of aircraft and silk and rayon (mainly the latter) multiplied five times over in the same brief period. In 1907 the 'growth industries' had produced a mere 6·5 per cent of total output; in 1935 they produced almost one fifth.

*

At the outbreak of the Second World War Britain was therefore a very different country economically from 1914. It was a country in which there were fewer agriculturalists but many more government employees; fewer miners but very many more road transport workers; fewer industrial workers but many more shop assistants and office workers; fewer domestic servants but many more entertainers; and within manufacturing industry, fewer textile workers but more in metals and electricity. (See Figures 7–9.) It was a country with a different industrial geography. Even in 1924 the traditional industrial regions (Lancashire and Cheshire, west Yorkshire, the north-east, South Wales, Central Scotland) had produced half the total net output of industry. In 1935 they produced only 37·6 per cent, barely more than the new industrial regions which had grown rapidly since then: Greater London and the Midlands. And this was natural: South Wales had, even in 1937, forty-one per cent of its workers in the declining industries, but the Midlands only seven per cent; the north-east thirty-five per cent but London only one per cent.

It was a country of two divergent sectors of the economy, the falling and the rising, linked only by three factors: the great accumulations of capital which grasped both, the increasing intervention of government, which spread over both, and the archaism, born of Britain's unusually successful 'fit' into the pattern of nineteenth-century world liberal capitalism, which surrounded both. The liberal world economy was dead by 1939. It died – if we can assign its death a precise date – in 1929–33, and has never revived since. But if its ghost stalked any country, it was Britain which had learned the job of workshop to the world, of its trader, shipper, and financial centre, but did not quite know what to do now that this occupation became re-dundant. We still do not quite know what to do. But whatever it was, it implied a change in the functions of government which the nineteenth century would have regarded as inconceivable. To this we must now turn.

NOTES

1. See the works of Mowat, Ashworth, Pollard in Further Reading. G. C. Allen, *The Structure of Industry in Britain* (1961), D. L. Burn, *The Economic History of Steelmaking* (1940). For the international setting, I. Svenilsson, *Growth and Stagnation in the European Economy* (1954), and Arthur Lewis, *Economic Survey 1918–1939* (1949). See also Figures 1, 3, 7, 10–11, 13, 15, 17–18, 22, 26, 28, 37, 41, 46, 49–52.

2. H. W. Macrosty, *The Trust Movement in British Industry* (1907), p. 330.

3. Quoted in Pollard, *Development* (1962), p. 168.

4. Committee on Industry and Trade, *Factors in Industrial and Commercial Efficiency* (1927), pp. 38–9.

12

GOVERNMENT AND ECONOMY[1]

The characteristic attitude of British or other governments towards the economy before the Industrial Revolution was that they had a duty to do something about it. This is also the almost universal attitude of governments towards the economy today. But between these two eras, which represent what might be called the norm of history, and indeed of reason, there occurred an age in which the fundamental attitude of the government and the economists was the opposite: the less it could manage to intervene in the economy, the better. Broadly speaking this era of abstention coincided with the rise, triumph and domination of industrial Britain, and it was indeed uniquely suited to the situation of this country, and perhaps one or two more like it. The history of government economic policy and theory since the Industrial Revolution is essentially that of the rise and fall of *laissez-faire*.

Policy is of course based on theory, though not always on the best theory. It might therefore appear logical to begin this chapter with a brief consideration of economic theory, all the more so since this subject of inquiry was, for a large part of the period with which this book deals, dominated by the British, though never to quite the extent that patriots have suggested. However, there are two reasons for not spending much space on the development of British economic theory, which is in any case very adequately treated in a large specialist literature. In the first place economics, an essentially applied subject, is inevitably much influenced by the prevailing climate of practical discussion and reflects the situation of the economy. When its prospects appeared bleak, it was more likely than not to become the 'gloomy science', as in the first third of the nineteenth century; when problems of wage-payment began to preoccupy industrialists, economists, who had hitherto not thought much about them, began to do so; when during the inter-war depression mass unemployment dominated the horizon, the most characteristic modification of economics, Keynesianism, had the provision of full employment at its core. Moreover, a good deal of economics has the function not so much of telling government or business what they ought to do, as of telling them that what they are doing (or not doing) is right. In the second place government policy tends to reflect not so much the best contemporary economics (even allowing for the time-lag between the control of policy by middle-aged men who have learned their theory in their youth and the rise to influence of younger men) as the politically most acceptable economics, and often the simplified and vulgarized version of the science which is what actually tends to penetrate outside the ranks of the experts. In a country like Britain, in which few professional economists have ever been Cabinet ministers and none permanent secretary of the Treasury, this filtering process has – except in the two world wars and to some extent since the Second World War – always been very effective. Policy is normally 'orthodox', that is it is theory hardened to some extent into uncritical dogma. Of course over a period of time even orthodoxies sometimes change.

Total government *laissez-faire* is of course a contradiction in terms. No modern government can *not* influence economic life, because the mere existence of government must do so: the 'public sector', however modest, is nearly always a very large 'industry' in terms of sheer employment, and public revenue and expenditure form a significant proportion of the national total. Even at the peak of British *laissez-faire*, around 1860, government expenditure amounted to several per cent of the national income. And of course any government activity – any system of public laws and regulations – must affect economic life, quite apart from the fact that the least interfering government rarely finds it possible to abstain from controlling certain obviously economic matters such as the currency. What is at stake is not the fact of government intervention, or even (within certain limits) its weight, but its character. In the classical liberal economy its object is to create and maintain the best conditions for capitalism, which is regarded as an essentially self-regulating and self-expanding system which tends to maximize the 'wealth of the nation'.

At the outset of the British Industrial Revolution the major problem was to create these conditions; from about 1846 (the abolition of the Corn Laws) it was to maintain them. From the last quarter of the century it became increasingly clear that they could not be maintained without growing government intervention in matters which, according to pure theory, were best left untouched, but until 1931 (the abolition of Free Trade) the attempt to maintain the liberal economy was not abandoned. After 1931 it was. This, in a nutshell (and all nutshells are bound to constrict their contents), is the history of government policy in the age of British industrial glory.

To create the best conditions for the smooth operation of private enterprise meant, in the first place, to eliminate the numerous forms of existing government interference which could not be justified by the prevailing economic orthodoxy. These, in the early nineteenth century, were of four kinds. First, there were the remains of the traditional economic policy now commonly called *mercantilism*, which had as its object the exact opposite of economic liberalism, namely the systematic fostering of national wealth through state power (or state power through national wealth, which often amounted to the same thing). Second, there were the remains of the traditional social policy, which assumed that government had a duty to maintain a stable society in which every man had the right to live in the (generally low) station to which the Almighty had called him. Even after this view had lost ground at the highest levels of policy, it was persistently held not only by the labouring poor, but also by the more traditionally-minded of their betters. For instance, as late as 1830 the gentry and magistrates in the several counties affected by the great farm-labourers' riots insisted, against higher advice, on recommending the fixing of minimum wages and the abolition of machines which created unemployment. They were rapped on the knuckles for it from Westminster. Third, there were the vested interests of such social groups as stood in the way of rapid industrial progress – notably the landed classes. Lastly, there was the sheer accumulated lumber of tradition, the huge, heterogeneous, inefficient and expensive pile of institutions and institutional gaps which clogged the road of progress.

Of these the first posed the most serious problem in theory, the third (and in so far as vested interests protected it the fourth) in practice. The second had, essentially, only the poor on its side. Except for the Poor Law, the social code established in the Tudor era had long fallen into obsolescence, though here and there in the eighteenth century strong – that is normally very riotous – bodies of workers had still sometimes secured the legal fixing of prices or wages or the legal control of other conditions of labour. By the end of the eighteenth century it was assumed that labour was a commodity to be bought and sold at the free market price, and when in the hard years of the Napoleonic Wars the early working-class movement attempted to revive the legal protection of the old code, its relics were abolished by Parliament without fuss in 1813. Thenceforth, until the early twentieth century, the legal fixing of wages – though not the legal control of hours and some other labour conditions – was officially regarded as the certain prelude to ruin. As late as 1912 Asquith, an unemotional man, wept as he proposed the (inoperative) Miners' Minimum Wage Bill, which a national coal strike had forced down the throats of the government.

The Poor Law could not be abolished for political reasons, for it was supported both by the natural and profound conviction of the poor that a man has a right to life, if not actually to liberty and the pursuit of happiness, and the powerful prejudice of the agricultural community in favour of a stable social order, that is to say against the ruthless conversion of both men and land into mere commodities. Only in Scotland had Calvinist logic abolished the *right* of the poor to maintenance, putting their relief entirely into the hands of the charity of their social betters in the kirk, though of course it was in a sense morally obligatory. Moreover, it has lately been argued that a fairly indiscriminate Poor Law may have been useful in the early stages of industrialization in absorbing the large amount of concealed unemployment, especially in the countryside, at a time when the rate of industrial expansion was as yet unable to provide sufficient employment for the growing population.

There is indeed evidence that the eighteenth-century Poor Law, in spite of bourgeois theory, became more generous, and when poverty became catastrophic, during the hard years of the middle 1790s, the country gentry went dead against the grain of economic theory in the 'Speenhamland System'. In its most ambitious versions this set out to establish a minimum wage based on the cost of bread, if necessary subsidized out of the rates. 'Speenhamland' did not arrest the pauperization of the farm-labourers, and in any case was not widely or lastingly applied in its full form, but it horrified the theorists, for it took the Poor Law further away from their ideal. This was (*a*) to make the Poor Law as cheap as possible; (*b*) to use it as an engine, not of relief for concealed or overt unemployment, but for driving unemployed labour resources on to the free labour market, and (*c*) to discourage the growth of population which, as was then widely believed, must lead to growing pauperization. It was regrettably impossible not to provide *any* relief to the destitute, but it must be deterrent and in any case 'less eligible' than the lowest-paid and least attractive jobs on the market. A 'New' Poor Law with these inhuman characteristics was pushed through Parliament in 1834, by a combination of political pressure and lies disguised as statistics. It created more embittered unhappiness than any other statute of modern British history, even though the revolt of the not entirely helpless workers prevented its full application (no relief outside the workhouse, separation of families within it, and so on) in the industrial north. Oddly enough nobody has seriously investigated whether it actually made labour supply more flexible. It is improbable that it did.

The argument for carting away the institutional rubbish-heap was more convincing, if only because this visibly saved a lot of money. The power of the older vested interests – notably crown, church and aristocracy, but also the impenetrable jungle-barricade of the lawyers – limited the scope of such rationalization. The more wholehearted, though also some of the more elementary reforms – such as, for instance, the application of reason to spelling, weights and measures – generally require a social revolution to push them through, and there was none. Nevertheless, though the monarchy, the established church, the old universities, the war office, the foreign office, the law-courts and some other ancient monuments survived the era of radical reform fairly unscathed, a good deal was achieved, mainly in the course of three bouts of political and administrative spring-cleaning: in the 1780s, in the 1820s and 30s, and again from 1867 to 1874. (The gaps in reforming activity between these bouts were due chiefly to the fear of social revolution in the Jacobin and Chartist periods.) 'Economical reform' – the attack on the practice of using the central state apparatus as a warehouse of financial favours for private distribution by great political patrons – began in the 1780s, though it did not get very far. The principle of a salaried public service (instead of one living on the fees and profits of office), of the separation of private and public funds, and of systematic accounting for such funds was at least enunciated. The 'Budget' – the word came into use in the late eighteenth century – probably owed more to the needs of war-time finance after 1793, but it reflects these preoccupations. A considerable clean-up of the criminal law and the fiscal system took place under middle-class ministers in the 1820s, and the newly reformed Parliament after 1832 launched a major attack on old abuses. It succeeded where the older vested interests saw no harm in it – notably in the Poor Law and urban administration (Municipal Reform Act, 1835) – but ran into the sands elsewhere. However, after 1860 some of the earlier proposals were at least partly realized with the substantial transformation of the Civil Service, the partial reform of the ancient schools and universities, the institution of a public system of primary education, and even some modest trimming of the thickets of the law.

The reason for this refusal to be more than half rational was not the mythical taste of the British for continuity and their equally mythical distaste for logic. Few countries have ever been more totally dominated by an *a priori* doctrine than Britain was by *laissez-faire* economics in the period when institutional reforms were left incomplete, and few countries' institutions were more radically and ruthlessly reconstructed than those of India, in this very same period, and by precisely the kind of Briton whom this myth tends to idealize. The continuity of British institutions in this era was the result of a political compromise between older vested interests, which could not be broken without the risk of revolution, and the new industrialists, who were unprepared to run such a risk except in matters they regarded as absolutely vital, that is to say in economic policy. Over the issue of protectionism or free trade they were prepared to fight to the death, if necessary at the cost of a hunger insurrection which the most militant of them were prepared to provoke. And the 'landed interest', realizing this, gave way quietly over the abolition of the Corn Laws in 1846 fortified by the much reduced vulnerability of their rents by 1846. But nothing else was worth this risk. The cost of institutional inefficiency, high though it was, was little more than petty cash to the most dynamic industrial economy of the world. An economy which, to take an obvious example, could raise all the investment capital it needed and more, under an obsolete legislation which virtually precluded normal joint-stock enterprise, was not going to cavil at little extras. True, institutional inefficiency – for example the need to pass special Acts of Parliament at extortionate cost for every railway line – helped to make the British railways much more expensive per mile than all others. There is no evidence that British railway building was in the least inhibited by this.

The removal of all these obstacles to *laissez-faire* was simply a matter of how much pressure the new industrialists could, or wanted to, exert against the social groups which stood in their way. The dismantling of the old 'mercantilist' policies alone raised issues of theoretical principle also. It is true that to some extent it was simply a matter of vested interest. But it was easy to show that the 'West India interest', which stood for slave-owning and a monopoly sale of colonial sugar, or the old woollen cloth interest, which stood for the systematic supervision and protection of what had always been England's staple industry, were – even fiscally – less important than cotton, especially as they had far less political backing than the 'landed interest'. It was not so easy to show that the interests of British capitalism would be best served by a total withdrawal of all government support and protection for manufacture and trade. All the more so, since the triumph of the British economy had been achieved in the past very largely because of the unswerving readiness of British governments to back their businessmen by ruthless and aggressive economic discrimination and open war against all possible rivals.

But that very triumph made complete *laissez-faire* possible, indeed desirable. By the end of the Napoleonic Wars Britain's position was unassailable. As the only industrial power, she could undersell anyone else, and the less discrimination there was, the more she could undersell. As the only naval power in the world she controlled access to the non-European world, on which her prosperity rested. With one major exception (India) she did not, economically speaking, need even colonies, for the entire underdeveloped world was her colony, and would remain so if, under Free Trade, they bought in the cheapest market and sold in the dearest, which meant, if they bought and sold in the only big market there was, Britain. This, at all events, is how matters looked to men who readily confused the historic accident of Britain's early industrial start with the fortunate dispensation of a providence that had, apparently, fitted the British to be the workshop of the world and the rest to produce cotton, timber or tea. All that British industry needed was peace: and there was peace.

The two main pillars of mercantilism had therefore crumbled. They were the desirability of protecting British trade by economic means (including the maintenance of a private reservation for it in the colonies) and the need to defend it by force of arms. The first had already been abandoned by Adam Smith; the second still – and very reasonably – preoccupied him. After 1815 even this lost its force. And so, mainly in the 1820s, the surviving parts of the mercantilist code were abandoned. The Navigation Laws were relaxed, though not formally repealed until 1849, the system of colonial preferences in the 1850s, the prohibition on the export of British machinery and technical experts lifted (it had long been a farce). The remainder of the system went with the Corn Laws after 1846 (see Chapter 5).

*

Government and Economy

By the middle of the nineteenth century government policy in Britain came as near *laissez-faire* as has ever been practicable in a modern state. Government was small and comparatively cheap, and as time went on it became even cheaper by comparison with other states. Between 1830 and the 1880s the annual public expenditure per head of population trebled in Europe, and rose even faster (but from a ridiculously low base) in the countries of European stock abroad, but in Britain it remained substantially stable. Except for the mint, some armaments establishments and – inevitably – some building, government kept out of direct production. It even succeeded in avoiding direct responsibility for some things normally regarded as obvious functions of government, such as (until 1870) education. Where it intervened – and the complexity of national affairs was bound to multiply *ad hoc* government administrative incursions – it was, like the traffic policeman, to regulate but not to encourage or discourage. It was not widely accepted that the one implies the others. Two examples will illustrate the degree of government abstention. Britain was the only country which systematically refused any fiscal protection to its industries, and the only country in which the government neither built, nor helped to finance (directly or indirectly), or even planned any part of the railway system.

Yet there were two ways in which government had to intervene in the economy under all circumstances, and such economic policy as it had therefore concentrated on these: taxation and currency.

The traditional eighteenth-century bases of revenue had been three: impositions on consumption (of imported products by *customs duties*, of home products by the *excise*), on property (that is mainly land and buildings) and on various legal transactions (that is stamp duties). In 1750 – as indeed during most of the eighteenth century – something like two thirds had come from the first, the excise normally producing about twice as much as the customs, and most of the rest from direct taxes, though stamp duties tended to rise. Then there was also borrowing, mainly for special purposes. The modern fiscal system has retained the first of these pillars and replaced the second by the death duties, which are a levy on property, but above all it added a third: the progressive tax on incomes. By 1939 customs and excise provided only one third of revenue, direct taxes on income or profits provided about forty per cent, death duties about eight per cent. The balance came mainly from the much-swollen activities of government enterprise, namely the post office, and from the novel tax on motor-cars and lesser sources. Income taxes were first introduced as a temporary measure during the revolutionary and Napoleonic Wars (1799–1816), but, in spite of the obvious distaste of the citizenry and the economists, they were reintroduced for good – though still thought of for a long time as a temporary expedient – in 1842. As late as 1874 Gladstone proposed to abolish income tax – it was then running at the ruinous rate of 2d. in the £* – and had he won he might have done so. It began to rise steeply after 1900, especially after 1909. Death duties, which would fall mainly on the large accumulations of the landed aristocracy, were never so unpopular in business circles, but until the end of the century, when they were faced by the combined new demands of social expenditure and armaments, the landed interest held them successfully at bay. They became a serious source of revenue just before the First World War, but still a minor one compared with income taxes.

Until the twentieth century this pattern of taxation developed not out of any systematic or rational view of the most effective or socially equitable methods of raising revenue or even out of any consideration of the economic effects of different kinds of taxation. Fiscal policy was dominated by three considerations: how to interfere least with businessmen, how to put the least burden on the rich, and how nevertheless to raise the necessary minimum for meeting public expenditure without going more heavily into debt. Primitive political economy had favoured indirect taxes (such as customs and excise) on the ground that they were socially unfair: the poor paid a larger share of their income in them, leaving the rich more capital to accumulate for the benefit of the entire economy. *Laissez-faire* fiscal theory, though more sophisticated, was also more superficial. It did not

*During the Crimean War it reached a peak of 1s. 4d. in the £.

like indirect taxes because they interfered with the free flow of trade, and partly also because, in so far as they raised the cost of living of the poor, they might also raise the minimum wage necessary to keep them from starving. Between 1825 and 1856 a bonfire of older duties reduced indirect taxes to the minimum needed to get revenue, and their load on the citizen lightened perceptibly. The doctrine of Free Trade prevented it being raised. Since Britain also lacked any profitable government enterprises beyond the post office, such as those which supplied the new German Empire with over half its revenue,* in the long run direct taxes on income and property had to carry a growing burden.

The fundamental object of public finance was to keep expenditure low and the budget balanced. This policy, which makes little sense when in the modern guided or managed economy, was much less irrational under *laissez-faire*, and so was the equally firm conviction that the public indebtedness ought to be reduced. It had grown steadily throughout the eighteenth century and steeply during its last and greatest war against France (1793–1815), and indeed wars were the chief reasons for borrowing, though after 1900 there was a significant amount of borrowing for investment for the growing state sector of the economy. The century of peace after 1815 reduced the debt gradually to about three quarters of its peak (1819), but after 1914 it rapidly multiplied ten times over. As with the income tax, the hope that this source of funds would be temporary, disappeared.

The second unavoidable economic activity of government, the control of the currency, brought it much more directly into the path of business. The initial problem was how to keep the pound sterling stable, mainly in the interests of British international trade and finance. The case for what often looked like a permanent deflationary bias is by no means as evident as nineteenth-century orthodox economists assumed, brushing away the occasional proponents of controlled inflation, such as the Birmingham banker Attwood, but for a country which was the fulcrum of the international trading and financial system it was

* For example railways.

not unreasonable. Since the early eighteenth century the basis of this stability had been the 'gold standard', a fixed and rigid relationship between the unit of the currency and a fixed quantity of gold. Before 1931 it broke down only twice, in the course of the two great wars – 1797–1821 and 1914–25; the slump killed it for good.

The gold standard raised two problems. First, how to control the issue of coin or banknotes and to avoid debasement or over-issue; second, and more difficult, how to influence the flow of gold into, out of and within the country, without resorting to exchange controls or the suspension of convertibility, both of which were regarded as profoundly undesirable except by the inflationist minority. The logical alternative, to adjust issue to the supply of bullion, might work when gold flowed in, but might create an impossible stringency when it flowed out very rapidly; it was indeed in the latter situation that the gold standard had from time to time to be suspended (as in the crises of 1847, 1857 and 1866) or abolished (as in 1797, 1914 and 1931). The solution to the first problem was the centralization of note issue in the Bank of England; coinage had long been mono-polized by the mint. This was for practical purposes achieved, after decades of passionate discussion, by the Bank Charter Act of 1844, and was by then quite beside the point, because non-monetary means of payment (bills of exchange, cheques, and so on) were increasingly used for all except petty cash transactions. They were quite unaffected by the control of bank-note issue.

The second problem was solved, or so it was believed, by the manipulation of 'Bank Rate' – the rate at which the Bank of England was prepared to discount bills of exchange, that is to advance money against them. The Bank was supposed to act as the 'lender of last resort'. Bank Rate was supposed to indicate what assistance it was prepared to give the other banks, while at the same time (so it was argued) protecting its crucial reserve of bullion by drawing gold to London with a sufficiently attractive, that is high, rate. Since the City of London was the financial centre of the country, and indeed increasingly of the world, Bank Rate came to set the general rate of short-term loans throughout the world, and in doing so it would, so the theory ran, smooth the fluctuations of credit: encouraging or discouraging as the economic situation suggested. This type of manipulation began seriously in the middle of the 1840s.

All this assumed two things, first that the Bank of England would act as a central bank and nothing else, and second, that there were no economic fluctuations which could not be teased out by such short-term hints. The first condition was gradually realized in the half-century after the Bank Charter Act, as the Bank slowly and reluctantly abandoned its ordinary banking business and profit motives and learned its obligations as a state bank. After the 'Baring crisis' of 1890 it had probably done both. The second remained a pious myth. The stability of the British currency rested on the international hegemony of the British economy, and when it ceased no amount of bank-rate manipulation did much good. And there is no evidence that Bank Rate, or any other government method of intervening on the market as a lender or borrower, diminished the sharpness of the booms and slumps which punctuated the movements of the economy every few years.

*

The foundations of *laissez-faire* crumbled in the 1860s and 1870s. As other countries industrialized it became evident that Free Trade was not enough to maintain Britain as the only, or even the chief, workshop of the world; and if she was so no longer, the basis of her international economic policy needed to be revised. As the 'Great Depression' hit her, it became less evident than it had seemed before that the only thing the British economy needed from government apart from low taxes and a stable currency was to be left alone. As the working classes got the vote – in 1867, but especially in 1884–5 – it became only too obvious that they would demand – and receive – substantial public intervention for greater welfare. As a great power emerged in Europe with Germany, and two new ones abroad with the USA and Japan, world peace (with its corollary of low budgets) could no longer be taken for granted. Furthermore – though this was not yet obvious – one might already begin to suspect that the logical consequence of unrestricted private enterprise would not be a modest state apparatus in an un-observed corner of the competitive economy of smallish masters. It might well be an increasingly large and bureaucratic state amid increasingly large, bureaucratic, and very incompletely competitive big corporations.

It was not to be expected that business opinion and government policy adjusted themselves to this new situation. During the Great Depression small groups of ideologists emerged who demanded a clean break with *laissez-faire* 'individualism', which was so identified with British capitalism that the two terms were often confused, just as its opposite, state interference, was widely identified with 'socialism'. The genuine Socialists, who reappeared in Britain in the 1880s, saw things mainly from the point of view of the working class, the proponents of various anti-*laissez-faire* policies of 'national efficiency', and 'imperialism' from the point of view of the international competitive position of the British economy, or more generally (and dangerously) from the point of view of some vast national or racial destiny which had called Britannia to rule both waves and far-flung shores. But the Socialists remained small minority groups even within the labour movement, though they rapidly provided it with an unusually large number of leaders. Not until 1918 did the Labour Party commit itself even in theory to a programme of the socialization of the means of production, distribution and exchange. The systematic imperialists – to give a name to a trend which is difficult to define clearly – occupied a similar position within the ruling classes, and therefore had a much more direct impact on policy. But they were – as the career of Lord Milner shows – if anything less typical of prevalent political opinion in the upper classes, and fortunately so for their thought pointed uncomfortably towards what later came to be known as fascism. The bulk of labour and – to a much greater extent, naturally, of the business classes – drifted from what the ideologists called 'individualism' towards 'collectivism' in little spurts and eddies, pushed by the pressure of events.

Events, of course, were always pushing, yet at five times more sharply and irresistibly than at others: during the 'Great Depression' (especially in the late 1880s and 1890s), after 1906, during and immediately after the First World War, under the impact of the 1929 slump, and during the Second World War.

The first period produced no real change in economic policy, for (to the lasting misfortune of Britain) the depression eventually passed before business and politics had been sufficiently frightened. It merely raised the question whether traditional orthodoxy, and especially its quasi-religious symbol Free Trade, should be abandoned. Nor – and for analogous reasons – did it produce any serious change in social policy. On the other hand 'imperialism' and war – considered by their champions as solutions to both the economic and social problem – revolutionized British foreign policy. If the state had to adjust its approach it was largely because of the administrative and above all the financial burdens of flag- and sabre-rattling. Naval expenditure increased from an annual average of about £10 million in 1875–84 to well over £20 million per year in the second half of the 1890s and well over £40 million in the last pre-war years. Government loans for direct enterprise largely connected with armament and communications rose from zero before 1870 to around £50 million just before the First World War. It was this rather than the negligible expenditure on social welfare (other than education) which made the old policy of cheap and inactive government impossible.

The emergence of a Labour Party, and behind it of radical strike movements, did not affect policy much before it produced forty working-class MPs in 1906, but led to the construction of an ambitious framework of social welfare legislation by 1912. It costs were still small, but it marked two major departures from the principles of the old *laissez-faire* state. The Poor Law, though it resisted attempts to abolish it until 1929, was no longer assumed to exhaust public responsibility for the poor, and, more important, the necessity for direct government intervention in the labour market – if need be by actually fixing wage-rates – was recognized. So – an equally novel departure which can be traced back to the national coal lock-out of 1893 – was the necessity for government to intervene in labour disputes which might damage the entire economy; a contingency which nobody had considered in the happy days when Britain had no effective foreign competitors. These changes implied two others: the official recognition that trade unions were not simply bodies just tolerable by the law, but bodies involved in government action, and the use of taxation, at least potentially, as a method of damping down social discontents by reducing excessive inequality of income.

The political radicalization brought about by the First World War translated several of these changes from theory into expensive practice, and faced governments with the even more awful prospect of a labour movement actually committed to the nationalization of industries. In 1919 the nationalization of the mines had actually to be promised, for one disingenuous moment, to the embattled miners. But the major effect of the war was to destroy temporarily, but almost totally, the entire Victorian system. A world war could simply not be combined with 'business as usual'. By 1918 the government had taken over the running of several industries, controlled others by requisitioning their output or licensing, organized its own bulk purchase abroad, restricted capital expenditure and foreign trade, fixed prices and controlled the distribution of consumer goods. Fiscal policy was used – clumsily – to divert more resources to the war effort than the people were willing to forgo, largely by indirectly induced inflation. One part of this fiscal war-effort, the so-called McKenna duties of 1915 (on the import of cars, cycles, watches, clocks, musical instruments and film), made the first *de facto* breach in the wall of Free Trade; they were later retained – to the lasting benefit of the British motor industry – as protective duties. In fact between 1916 and 1918 Britain was forced to evolve a first incomplete and reluctant sketch of that powerful state-economy of the Second World War.

It was dismantled with unseemly haste after 1918. Little of it remained by 1922, and in 1926 one last nostalgic effort actually restored the gold standard and with it, it was hoped, all the happy self-regulating freedom of 1913. Nevertheless, nothing could be quite the same again. The apparatus of government remained larger and more comprehensive than before. The protection of 'key' industries was no longer a theoretical issue.

The compulsory rationalization and amalgamation of industries by government, or even their nationalization, was now a matter of practical policy. Above all, the possibilities of government action had been tested. It would henceforth be possible to hate state intervention, but no longer to claim reasonably that it could not work.

Curiously enough the inter-war depression encouraged the state's interventions in business much more than did its welfare activities. Labour political pressure slackened after the early 1920s. The immediate reaction of government opinion to the vast swelling of welfare expenditure under the pre-1914 schemes – there were no substantial new ones – was a feverish effort to reduce them to 'actuarial soundness', that is to cut them to the bone. The automatic reaction of financial orthodoxy to the 1929 slump was to cut expenditure generally. The 1931 cuts in the salaries of public employees produced the first mutiny of the British Navy since 1797. The cut in unemployment benefits and beneficiaries and above all the imposition of the 'Means Test' produced hunger marches and unrest. The resentment accumulated in consequence of these desperate measures to keep welfare expenditures under control was one of the main reasons for the delayed electoral triumph of Labour in 1945. But in the short run the depression did not lead governments towards the welfare state; it led them into desperate efforts to prevent its extension.

On the other hand the needs of the crisis-stricken industries cried out for government action, and the short period of de-control was therefore followed by an unprecedented era of state intervention in business, which was palatable only because it was so obviously in favour of business. The government's own sector of the economy was not revolutionized, though private enterprise was supplemented or replaced in some industries, either novel or (more likely) of military importance, or both. Even before 1914 the Navy had broken through *laissez-faire* by making the British government a part-owner or subsidizer of the Suez Canal, the Anglo-Persian Oil Company (1914), the Cunard steam ship company (1904) and – at the cost of a notorious corruption scandal involving high figures in the government – the Marconi

Radio Telegraph Company (1913), while the Post Office (1912) had bought out the main telephone company, thus virtually nationalizing the service, though the word was still taboo. After the war public support for such industries was extended – notably air-transport and radio-communications – and broadcasting was built up as a public monopoly, mainly for political reasons. However, the main interventions of government, its inhibitions lifted by the wartime experience, were still aimed at making private industry more efficient rather than at replacing it. In practice this meant breaking down its traditional competitive and dispersed pattern. Between the wars, and especially during the 1930s, Britain, as we saw, turned from one of the least into one of the most trustified or controlled economies, and largely through direct government action. It achieved the amalgamation of the railways (1921), the concentration – indeed the partial nationalization – of electricity supply (1926), the creation of a government-sponsored monopoly in iron and steel (1932) and a national coal cartel (1936), though success was less in cotton. Equally unthinkable in terms of Victorian capitalism, the government set about regulating prices and output by legal compulsion, notably in agriculture, about one third of whose output was brought into state-sponsored marketing schemes in the early thirties (pigs, bacon, milk, potatoes and hops). By the end of the 1930s some of these schemes had reached the verge of nationalization – for example of coal royalties (1938) and of British airlines (1939) – while the collapse of industry in the depressed areas had produced at least the principle of a policy for the direct and subsidized fostering of industry by government planning. Politically the expansion of state activity during and after the Second World War was still shocking. Economically and administratively it merely continued along well-explored paths.

But the most dramatic consequence of the slump was the death of Free Trade. And since Free Trade was the almost religious symbol of the old competitive capitalist society, its end not merely demonstrated as it were publicly that a new era had begun, but encouraged the vast extension of government management. While it lasted, government action was an exception, an individual and regrettable departure from the ideal, which had to be carefully scrutinized and strictly limited. After it had gone, what was the point of measuring it in the homoeopathic doses of the past?

That Free Trade was swept away with the gold standard in 1931 was natural. It is much more surprising that it did not go earlier. It had come under fire as early as the 1880s when the 'Fair Traders' suggested retaliation as a bargaining weapon against the other countries which were then putting up tariffs on all sides. At one moment (1886) even the Vatican of Cobdenite orthodoxy, the Manchester Chamber of Commerce, was in two minds about this. After 1902 Joseph Chamberlain's Tariff Reform Campaign made it into a major issue of domestic politics and converted the Conservative Party to it. The rather defensive assumption behind it was that, as British industry could no longer dominate the whole world, it might as well concentrate on the quarter of it which was in a British Empire fenced off against the aggressive foreigners. The case against Free Trade was indeed powerful, especially when British industry was no longer either the largest or the most efficient in the world, and when the country was notably lagging in the technologically new industries of the twentieth century. The classic Manchester argument that an industry which could not produce more cheaply than any other on the world market ought to go out of business might bear the sacrifice of a few small occupations, or even of British agriculture, but hardly of a large chunk of Britain's basic industries and prospects. Moreover, while it was reasonable in 1860 to neglect the contingency of major war, it was so no longer from the 1890s. And, as Adam Smith had recognized, the needs of national defence overrode even freedom of trade.

There were three reasons which nevertheless maintained Free Trade against all its critics. First, the Great Depression of 1873–96 lifted before it had frightened government and business sufficiently (see pp. 190–91). Second, and more important, the vast sector of the British economy which depended on international trade had nothing to gain by protection (unless the mere threat of it was enough to tear down foreign tariffs, which was unlikely). Tariffs protected the domestic market. They could do little to protect the export market, and in so far as they cut down the exports of other countries to Britain, with which they paid for their purchases of British goods, they made the situation worse. Not until the basic and export-oriented industries of the late nineteenth century collapsed after the First World War, and the domestically oriented industries became decisively important, was the road to protection clear. Last, and most important, British finance triumphed even as British industries flagged. The world domination of the City of London became, if anything, more complete than ever before in 1870–1913, and its role in the balance of payments more vital. The City could function only in a single untrammelled world economy, at all events one in which free flows of capital were unimpeded. Governments – themselves closer to the City than to industry – knew it. Even during the First World War heroic efforts were made to safeguard it against disturbance. Given the choice between industry and finance, industry would have to suffer. It was not until the slump of 1931 finally destroyed the single web of world trading and financial transactions whose centre was London and the £ sterling that Free Trade went. Even then it was not Britain that abandoned it. It was the world that abandoned London.

*

By the middle 1930s *laissez-faire* was therefore dead even as an ideal, except for the usual financial journalists, spokesmen for small business, and the economists; and even the economists were fighting a rearguard action. J. M. Keynes, the typical 'unsound' writer of the 1920s, became the basis of a new economic orthodoxy thanks to the *General Theory* (1936), which did not say much that had not been adumbrated before, but said it when his readers lived in the shadow of the 1931 crisis. Two economic policies therefore faced each other, both equally remote from John Stuart Mill. On the one hand there was socialism, based essentially on the aspirations of the working-class movement, but greatly strengthened by the experience of the USSR, which impressed even non-socialist observers by its apparent immunity to the great slump. It contained little by way of precise policy except the ancient demand for the nationalization of the means of production, distribution and exchange and the slogan of 'planning' which the Soviet Five-year Plans made extremely fashionable. On the other hand there were those – mainly economists who came from Liberalism (like J. A. Hobson) or who still remained Liberals (like Keynes and Beveridge) – who wished to save the essentials of a capitalist system, but realized that this could now be done only within the framework of a strong and systematically interventionist state; or even through a 'mixed economy'. In practice the difference between these two trends was sometimes hard to discern, especially as some Keynesians abandoned the Liberalism of their inspirer for socialism, and as the Labour Party tended to adopt the Keynesian policies as its own, in preference to the more traditional socialist slogans. Still, broadly speaking the socialists favoured their proposals because they were for social equality and justice, the non-socialists theirs, because they were for the efficiency of the British economy and against social disruption. Both agreed that only systematic state action (whatever its nature) could get rid of and avoid slumps and mass unemployment.

The Second World War by-passed these discussions after 1940 by forcing Britain, in the interests of survival, into the most state-planned and state-managed economy ever introduced outside a frankly socialist country. Its construction owed something to the experiences of 1916–18, which it developed systematically, something to the experiences of the 1930s, and something to the new Keynesian economics which rapidly infiltrated government through the massive recruitment of academic and other outsiders into the civil service. But it also owed much to the implicit political pressure of the working classes, which injected a deliberate element of social equity into public policy, such as had been notably absent during the First World War. The government was not only closer to the working classes (if only because the war, unlike the first, was and remained deeply *popular*). It not only applied a systematic policy of 'fair shares'. It also anticipated a vast extension of welfare legislation (for example by the Beveridge Report of 1942), and – a revolutionary departure – committed itself to the maintenance of 'a high level of employment' as a primary object of government (1944). By the end of the war it was clear that the road back to 1913 was pretty effectively barred. The apparatus of economic management and control was dismantled rapidly after 1945, as after 1918. From the middle 1950s there was a very obvious return to policies favouring private enterprise and the free market. Nevertheless, the scope left to unrestricted business was even then far smaller than it had ever been before 1941, and those who demanded 'flexible employment' – a higher percentage of unemployment than one or two per cent – were not politically influential.

The Labour governments of 1945–51 were, in a sense, the delayed results of the bitter experiences between the wars. Yet in terms of government policy their achievement was not revolutionary. They nationalized some industries which had been *de facto* under public control for a long time (the Bank of England, Cable & Wireless, the airlines and public utilities such as gas and electricity), some others which had been so run down as to be beyond private salvage (notably the coalmines and railways), and two which were not actually bankrupt, iron and steel and road haulage. These were denationalized in the early 1950s. The state sector of the economy which thus emerged was somewhat, but not significantly, larger than that which emerged at the same time in several continental countries. No serious attempt was made to operate it coherently. The standard form of nationalization was one developed *ad hoc* between the wars (for broadcasting, electricity supply and London transport), namely the 'public corporation' operating as an autonomous and in theory profit-making entity, if necessary against other public corporations. The concept of 'social profitability' (the argument that an enterprise which is unprofitable by itself may in fact save the rest of the economy far greater sums than it loses) came into practical politics only at the end of the 1950s, mainly in connexion with investments in public transport. Nor did the government (having dismantled most of the wartime mechanism for this purpose) make a serious attempt to 'plan' the economy except by *ad hoc* and mainly negative interventions. Such mechanisms for coordinating and controlling the joint development of the public and private sectors as were tentatively devised – and not until the end of the 1950s (NEDC) – owed little to Labour inspiration, but a great deal to the planning experiments in France, whose rapid economic advance increasingly impressed observers.

On the other hand the welfare planning of the Labour era was – thanks to the comprehensive National Insurance system (1946) and above all to the National Health Service (1948) – far more ambitious than anything which had preceded it. The actual level of expenditure – either *per capita* or as a proportion of the national income – was not outstandingly high, at all events after a decade or so of inflation. In 1964 it lay very much below *all* Common Market countries as a percentage of national income. However, thanks to the Labour reforms the UK acquired a greater variety of social security services and a more complete coverage than any nation in Europe.

What John Stuart Mill or Gladstone would have thought of the government-dominated economy of Britain in 1960 makes for entertaining speculation: government expenditure amounting to almost thirty per cent of the gross national product or even forty per cent if we include local government, public enterprises investing thirty-two per cent of gross fixed investment, the public sector as a whole forty-two per cent. In fact, however, these developments were not peculiar to Britain, or indeed to countries of any particular political orientation. By 1960 eleven West European countries (and the USA) had government expenditures in excess of twenty-five per cent of the GNP, and five characteristic sectors of the economy (railways, airlines, electric power, central banks and coal) were substantially under government control in France, Italy and the Netherlands – and but for coal, West Germany – as well as in Britain. Austria had a larger public sector than Britain, France spent a higher proportion of its GNP on government outlays. Indeed, in many respects other countries had made more serious public inroads into the traditional territory of private enterprise: France and West Germany with the public ownership of large sections of the automobile industry, France and Italy in oil, France in aircraft, Austria in iron and steel, Italy and Austria in engineering. None of these countries claimed to be socialist. All of them reflected the transformation of the traditional capitalist economy into a mixed economy of government and large corporations, the operations of each sector becoming increasingly difficult to distinguish. The major question of policy was no longer whether or to what extent the state ought to enter the economy. It was how it should control the economy, how far it should refrain from taking over hitherto unoccupied 'commanding heights' of the economy because it wished to make a present of their profits to private enterprise, and what the objectives of its control should be.

NOTES

1. See Further Reading, especially Mowat, Pollard, Clapham. For some activities of the state, U. K. Hicks, *British Public Finance 1880–1952* (1954), F. Shehab, *Progressive Taxation* (1953), M. K. Bowley, *Housing and the State 1910–1944* (1945), W. Hancock and M. Gowing, *British War Economy* (1949). For the 'City' and government, W. Bagehot, *Lombard Street* – the classic Victorian statement – L. Feavearyear, *The Pound Sterling* (1934), E. V. Morgan, *The Theory and Practice of Central Banking* (1943). For views about the state's functions, E. Halévy, *The Growth of Philosophic Radicalism*, B. Semmel, *Imperialism and Social Reform* (1960), R. F. Harrod, *The Life of John Maynard Keynes* (1951), E. Eldon Barry, *Nationalisation in British Politics* (1965). For social reform and security, E. H. Phelps Brown, *The Growth of British Industrial Relations* (1959). For the Labour era after 1945, A. Rogow, *The Labour Government and British Industry* (1955). For the history of economic thought, E. Roll, *A History of Economic Thought* (3rd edn, 1954). See also Figures 38–42.

13

THE LONG BOOM[1]

THE British economy of the 1960s contained very little of importance that could be traced back to the days of Queen Victoria, some elements which emerged in the days of Edwardian imperialism, more which belong to the era of King George V (1910–35), and not very much that was not already in existence or predictable on the eve of the Second World War.

If we look at the twenty great industrial units of 1965, we shall find only one which would have meant much to the contemporary of Benjamin Disraeli (the P & O Steam Navigation Company). A number (such as Shell, the British-American Tobacco Company, the Imperial Tobacco Company or Courtaulds) would have been familiar to the Edwardians, though not on their modern scale or in their modern diversification. Others, though familiar as expanding combines to the student of economic concentration at that time, took their modern form only between the wars: Imperial Chemical Industries was formed in 1926, Unilever (like Shell and Anglo-Dutch enterprise) in 1927–30, Vickers merged with Armstrong in 1928–9, Guest, Keen & Nettlefold, though its basic merger dates back to 1902, also took its modern form in the late 1920s. Some would have been familiar enough between the wars (Ford, A E I, Bowater, Hawker Siddeley) but not before. None represents a development belonging essentially to the last thirty years.* The great units of banking and insurance date back to the inter-war years, when the 1921 merger created the 'Big Five' banks (Barclays, Lloyds, Midland, National Provincial, Westminster), and the great insurance and building societies acquired their dominant position as investors on the open capital market. ('Small' savings, channelled through such institutions, had

---

*Of the hundred largest industrial companies periodically surveyed in *The Times*, the largest of the real newcomers would seem to be Great Universal Stores (26th), and the Rank Organization (47th).

amounted to only £32 million or thirteen per cent of net accumulation in 1901–13, but to £110 million or half of total investment in 1924–35; almost all controlled by insurance and building societies.)

On the other side of the picture, the trade-union movement is recognizably the incompletely reformed and rationalized giant that emerged between the great 'labour unrest' of 1911 and the aftermath of the General Strike. The Trade Union Congress has not been reformed since 1920 (four years after the setting-up of the Federation of British Industries, which under one name or another has been the national employers' organization ever since). Its giants are the Transport and General Workers' Union (the result of mergers in 1924 and 1929), the General and Municipal Workers (which finally emerged in 1928), the Amalgamated Engineering Union (born as such in 1921), the older Miners' Federation (converted into a National Union of Mineworkers in 1944) and the National Union of Railwaymen (1913). Except for the merger of distributive unions (1947) there has been no major rationalization of union structure since the Second World War, though a tendency for smaller craft unions (for example in printing and shipbuilding) to merge made itself felt in the early 1960s, and there were signs of further and much-needed rationalization in the engineering industry.*

Only in the field of government action has there been a major change, though not perhaps a greater one than could already be foreshadowed in the 1930s.

As we have seen, the British economy reacted in four main ways to the collapse of its traditional foundations between the wars:

1. The traditional basic industries, and all that pertained to them, declined with their export markets.

2. The commercial and financial sector, though disoriented

---

*This has ceased to be true. Since the middle 1960s the pace of amalgamation, both among trade unions and more especially, among big firms, has speeded up dramatically; the latter with the active support of government. Indeed, future historians may well record that the one major achievement for which the Labour administrations since 1964 can claim genuine responsibility was to initiate and foster the most rapid and drastic period of economic concentration since the 1920s. (December 1968).

by the collapse of the liberal economy, maintained sufficient strength, especially in the formal and informal empire, and sufficient international relations, not to collapse in the same manner. It had certain alternative possibilities, which it continued to exploit, backed by the unwavering support of governments which regarded the City and the pound sterling as vital economic assets.

3. The technologically new mass-production industries, based essentially on the home market, expanded and flourished all the more, because Britain had a long way to catch up in the development of a mass-consumption economy. On the other hand, just because such expansion was easy, it did not produce industries capable of very effective international competition, and because the internal market was the main preoccupation of the dynamic sector of industry, a fairly consistent friction developed between its interests and those of the nation's international dealings, as reflected in the balance of payments.

4. There was a striking development both of concentration in the private sector and of state action in the economy; and indeed the two processes were closely connected.

All in all the British economy has continued to evolve along these lines, and attempts to influence its motion (mainly by government action) have served to regulate these tendencies rather than to change their direction. The traditional basic industries have continued to decline, and so, in spite of almost unbroken and desperate efforts to the contrary, has the export-orientation of these industries. *Coal* has retreated. On the eve of the Second World War production was twenty per cent below what it had been on the eve of the First World War. After the disruption of the Second World War it recovered, but even at its peak in the early 1950s never quite reached the 1939 output, and since then it has declined again, to a level about one third below that of 1913.* Coal exports fell from 98 million tons in 1913 to 46 million in 1939, and since the war have never reached

*Coal output in million tons

1913	287	1954	224
1939	231	1960	194
1945	183	1964–5	193

20 million. In spite of the optimistic plans to reach 25–35 million by 1961–5, in the early sixties they ran at the derisory level of about 5 million. *Textiles* have continued to fade away. In 1937 only about half the quantity of woven cloth was produced as in 1913, in the 1950s peak production barely reached two thirds of 1937, and the average for the decade (1951–60) was little more than half that figure.* *Shipbuilding* appeared to hold up rather better, mainly owing to the increased size of ships (especially tankers).† Yet the best year of the 1950s (measured by the tonnage commenced in that year) was below the best year of the 1920s, before the slump virtually destroyed the industry, just as the best of the 1920s had been a little worse than 1913.

Since the 1930s, or at any rate since the Second World War, most serious observers have been reconciled to this decline. Whatever the foundations of British prosperity were going to be, they would no longer be coal and cotton, pig-iron, steel girders or shipyards.‡ The real problem, it was increasingly obvious, was how to plan the double contraction of the old and obsolescent sectors of the economy in such a way as to minimize the profound human suffering it entailed. The spontaneous collapse of Britain's traditional economy between the wars showed what human catastrophes it could bring about: industries and regions left empty and helpless, their industry dead, their housing and social equipment slowly decaying for want of maintenance and investment, their men seeping away to more prosperous parts of the country or, much more probably, frozen to their old street-corners, demoralized, ageing, increasingly difficult to employ,

---

*Woven cloth in million yards

1913	8050	1951	1961
1937	4103	1951–60	2100
1945	1847	1962	2612

† Shipbuilding (ships commenced in tons gross)

1913	1,866,000
1927–9	1,570,000
1951–60	1,300,000

‡ It may be argued that they exaggerated the darkness of these prospects, at least so far as shipyards went.

waiting for the improbable return of even the old times, when life was hard but a man could work at the only trade he knew. The shipbuilding industry might minimize its financial losses by simply shutting down 'uneconomic' yards, but only at the cost of the unintended assassination of communities of craftsmen and labourers, like Jarrow. Special measures to encourage employment and industrial diversification in such distressed areas (notably Scotland, South Wales and the north-east), for example by letting factories at attractive terms in newly set up 'trading estates', were pioneered in the 1930s. The war helped even more by successfully mobilizing the civilian population for the war-effort, that is by providing plenty of work everywhere. Regional development was encouraged after 1945, and especially in the later 1950s, when it became clear that the general prosperity and economic expansion did not automatically reduce the gap or even the growing divergence between the prosperous south and south-east and the relatively prosperous, but also relatively backward north and Wales.

Regional development thus goes back to the 1930s. On the other hand the planned rationalization of contracting industries as a social process hardly began until the Second World War. It implied systematic thought about the effect of such contractions on the workers within the industry, and in the 1930s the bodies mainly concerned with their defence, the trade unions, were rather weak and politically out of favour. The Second World War gave them strength through labour shortage and the need to mobilize active support for the war effort, and the Labour government of 1945–51 reinforced their position. Moreover, it brought some of the most obsolescent and declining industries (mines and railways) under nationalized ownership, and therefore under greater trade-union pressure than they would have been in private hands.* As a result a remarkably difficult, and potentially tragic, situation was handled both successfully and fairly.[2] In coalmining, employment was cut down by about one sixth between 1949 and 1960

---

*The miners also had the advantage at this time of being led by the most brilliant and capable trade-union leader of twentieth-century Britain, the Communist Arthur Horner.

with a minimum of actual dismissals and redundancy; the number of coalmines was reduced by almost a third; the output per manshift at the coal face raised by almost a third; and mechanization strikingly increased.* A glance at the human wreckage in such areas as the Appalachians in the USA gives a measure of both the humanity and the success of the British experience. On the railways this success was less marked, partly because the terms on which they were nationalized were far more onerous – they cost the nation about seven times the price of the mines – partly because the railwaymen, unlike the miners, failed to establish adequate wages for themselves when they could still have done so, partly because of uncertainties about what exactly transport rationalization meant.

But as the old declined, the new rose. Manufacturing multiplied about two and a half times (in value) between the middle 1920s (1924) and 1957. Yet within industry, how striking the disparities between the branches which actually declined (like mining), those which rose much less than the average (such as textiles, leather, clothing), those which more or less kept pace with the average (such as food, drink and tobacco, paper and printing), and those which leaped ahead. The great complex of *engineering and electrical* goods, even though it included the sluggish shipbuilding, rose by 343 per cent, *chemicals* quadrupled its output, 'vehicles' – mainly motor cars and aircraft – and the 'other manufactures' which represent so many of the new consumer goods industries, almost quintupled it. Being based on modern science and technology, which are indispensable for warfare, the two world wars – the second even more than the first – fostered these new industries. The number of coalminers fell from about 770,000 in 1939 to about 710,000 in 1945. But the number of workers in the new electronics industry virtually doubled (from 53,000 at the peak of the pre-war boom to 98,000 in 1944). War helped to tilt the British economy away

*Coal, 1949–62.

	1949	1962
Employment (men)	720,000	556,000
Number of NCB mines	901 (1951)	669
Output per manshift at face (cwt)	66	91

from the nineteenth and towards the twentieth century.* The thirties dug the foundations; the war laid them. After the adjustment from war to peace, the building could rise into the air.

If we take the motor and electronics industries as typical of the new twentieth-century orientation, we can illustrate this process by their example.[3] The motor industry was preserved from destruction after the First World War by the McKenna duties, which safeguarded it from the overwhelmingly greater American industry, at that time virtually the only exporter in the world and undoubtedly capable of swamping all other mass-production car manufacture. (In 1929 the USA exported about three times as many as Britain, France, Germany and Italy put together, and almost twice as many cars as were *manufactured* in Britain.) British output rose to about 180,000 cars and 60,000 commercial vehicles before the Great Slump, more than doubled in the 1930s, and more or less recovered its pre-war level – the war economy needed few private cars – by 1948-9. (Commercial vehicles came out of the war with a much greater output than before; the new line of tractors emerged with almost double their pre-war production.) By 1955 car output had doubled once again, by the end of the 1950s it had passed the million mark, by the mid-sixties it was around two million, while the production of commercial vehicles reached double the pre-war output in 1949, and doubled again by the later 1950s. In *electronics*, as we have already seen, the war almost doubled pre-war employment, though post-war adjustment took longer, largely because the major domestic market of the 1930s, radio sets, had ceased to expand – most people by then had radios – and the major domestic market of the 1950s, television sets, had not yet established itself. Still, between 1950 and 1955 employment in

*Production and the Second World War

	1938	1944
Coal	227 m. tons	193 m. tons
Woven cloth	4103 m. yards (1937)	1939 m. yards
Ships commenced	1,057,000 tons gross (1937)	959,000 tons gross
Crude steel	10·4 m. tons	12·1 m. tons
Electricity	24,600 kw	38,800 kw
Chemicals (1958 = 100)	35·8	53·7 (1946)
Tractors	10,000	28,000 (1946)

the industry doubled again, and now stood at about 200,000. That is to say, whereas in 1939 there had been about fifteen coalminers for every man or woman employed in electronics, by the middle 1950s there were only about three.

One welcome consequence of this shift from old to new was that it looked like providing some sort of answer to the prize question of the British economy: exports. Between the wars these had struggled along as well as they could with the products with which Britain had dominated the world markets before 1914 (which, by that time, already included a fair amount of machinery). Even in 1938 almost thirty per cent of our exports still consisted of textiles and coal, though about twenty per cent were already made up of machinery, vehicles and electrical goods. Since the markets for the old staples were gone for good, there was not much hope here. But by the middle 1950s the situation had already changed quite fundamentally. The 'old' exports were down to less than ten per cent of the total (coal had virtually disappeared), whereas the engineering-electrical-vehicle-building complex alone now provided thirty-six per cent of our foreign sales. At last, it seemed, Britain had something to sell to the twentieth-century as distinct from the nineteenth-century world. And there can be no doubt that the unbroken decline of British exports was halted, perhaps even modestly reversed, in the 1950s. In 1900 our exports had amounted to about thirty-six per cent of our total domestic consumer expenditure, in 1913 to over forty per cent; that is for every £1 spent for all purposes on goods and services in Britain, eight shillings' worth were exported abroad. In the best years between the wars (1935–9) exports amounted to twenty-seven per cent of domestic consumer expenditure, but in the 1950s, on average, to just over thirty per cent. In other words, whereas British production between the wars veered sharply away from overseas markets to the home market, after the Second World War it began to turn its face back to the sea and what lay beyond.

It was a change welcomed, indeed desperately advocated, by all post-war governments, which have filled the air since 1945 with a permanent buzz of (probably ineffective) exhortation to export or die, and the files of their departments with an endless series of plans and devices to encourage exports and from time to time to discourage domestic consumption. And the export performance of the British economy has indeed been remarkable. The volume of exports has been raised by about two and a half times since 1938, that of imports by less than half. Whereas in the 1930s less than two thirds of our imports were paid for by exports of merchandise, by the end of the 1950s well over ninety per cent of them were. Amid the persistent cries of alarm about the British export performance, this achievement deserves more attention than it has received outside the ranks of the specialists.

Nevertheless, it must be qualified by two observations. It has not, for reasons we shall discuss shortly, solved the problem of the British balance of payments, and by international standards the export drive has been somewhat half-hearted and not conspicuously impressive.[4] By insular standards, the 'modern' industries have done unexpectedly well; by world standards they have not. Once again the motor industry may illustrate these weaknesses. It began to export – mainly to the Empire – in the 1930s, but its real opportunity came after the Second World War, when for a few years it had the field virtually to itself, partly because of the decline of American car exports, partly because of the disruption of the continental car industries thanks to the war, partly because the policy of keeping down domestic consumer demand which the Labour governments favoured deprived the industry of the easy option of selling at home. (Simultaneously, of course, it received considerable assistance with its export drive.) In the three great years of post-war re-stocking, 1949–51, the British motor industry exported over one million cars, more than twice as much as the USA, and more than twice as much as France, Italy and Germany put together. In those years (1948–52) something like two thirds of British motor output went abroad. Yet with the end of domestic austerity, the industry naturally turned to the home market and its relative export effort slackened. Meanwhile the other European motor industries, though themselves supplying even more buoyant home markets, exported with tremendous zest. By the middle 1950s Germany sold more cars abroad than Britain, and the three main continental producers between them exported about twice as much as this country, though they did not produce twice as many cars. By 1963 Germany produced considerably more cars than Britain, and both France and Italy almost as many: in 1955 Britain had still outproduced Germany by a good margin, and turned out almost twice as many vehicles as France, four times as many as Italy.*

While Britain acquired new sources of visible exports, the invisible ones, which had once more than balanced our international payments, languished. Britain was simply no longer the centre of the world's commercial and financial system, nor its major maritime carrier.† On the other hand British investments abroad apparently held their own rather well. They had taken a bad beating after 1914. Wars forced their liquidation, slump devalued and discouraged them, and from the 1930s a new cloud darkened the foreign investor's horizon: the nationalization of industries, which was threatened not only by certified Bolshevik governments, but by all independently minded regimes in the underdeveloped world. Inevitably this hit such traditional outlets for British capital as railways and public utilities, and threatened even mines and oilfields. Nevertheless, the outward flow of British capital resumed after 1945 on a vast scale. Perhaps something like £4,000 million were exported between 1946 and 1959, at an annual rate of between a third and a

---

*Relative position of British motor industry. Output in thousands of cars.

	1929	1937	1950	1955	1963
USA	4,587	3,916	6,666	7,920	9,100
Germany	117	264	216	706	2,700
France	211	177	257	560	1,700
Italy	54	61	101	231	1,800
UK	182	390	523	898	2,000
UK percentage of total	3·5	8	7	8·5	11
UK percentage of Europe	32	44	48	37·5	24

†Even in 1939 the Commonwealth owned over thirty per cent of the merchant tonnage of the world, Britain alone about twenty-five per cent. In 1964 the Commonwealth percentage had fallen to eighteen, the British alone, to fourteen.

quarter of net investments in fixed capital at home. This was well below the best Edwardian years (1909–13), but probably up to the late-nineteenth-century level. It was offset, however, by a rather large import of foreign (mainly American) capital, particularly from the 1950s. By 1950 it could be guessed that foreigners drew from their British investments perhaps two thirds of what Britons drew from their foreign ones.

In some respects this new bout of foreign investment was similar to the old capital export. It went increasingly into developed rather than genuinely underdeveloped regions, and maintained a fondness for the old Empire (now persisting economically as the 'Sterling Area').* In other respects, however, it changed. Much less of it now came from individuals investing privately, or in such things as government stocks. Far more of it now came directly from large corporations developing overseas subsidiaries and getting a stake in foreign companies. The sun of the old-fashioned rentier was setting. The sun of the giant international corporation was at its zenith. The oil companies were the most familiar example of such corporations, and indeed but for oil investment our capital exports to the ex-colonial and semi-colonial countries would have been little more than half their actual size. They were in any case no longer very impressive, and neither was British official aid to such countries. In absolute figures (1962) it was less than half of French aid and smaller than German, as a percentage of central government expenditure it was lower than the USA's, France's, Germany's, Belgium's and Japan's, and even as a percentage of the national income it was lower than all of these except Japan.

At first sight much – in the underdeveloped countries perhaps half or even more – of this investment came from the profits retained by British businesses overseas. Yet a net outflow of capital is difficult to maintain for any length of time without a surplus in the country's balance of payments, and Britain's balance was notoriously in constant difficulties. Certainly it produced nothing like the size of our capital export. It would seem that a good deal

* In 1962 one third of British direct investment abroad went to what was euphemistically called the 'developing' countries, not counting oil and insurance.

of this came from various forms of short- and long-term borrowing: from the dollar loans and grants of the first ten post-war years, from the colonial 'sterling balances' accumulated in London until the middle 1950s, and the balances of oil-rich sheiks which continued to accumulate there, as well as from the gold production of the Sterling Area (that is South Africa) and the surplus on dollar trade of part of the Sterling Area. Increasingly it has been also based on the foreign investment in Britain and especially the very large sums of 'hot money' attracted to London for short periods by high interest rates. For the City of London tried more and more to compensate for the decline of its older functions, by making sterling attractive to foreign speculators (which implied, among other things, the maintenance of the pound at a stable, and overvalued level). This was a dangerous situation, not only because of the inherent risk of borrowing short to invest long, and the large burden of payments to creditors and investors abroad, but because of the constant risk of massive and rapid withdrawals of capital from Britain. What is more, it could be increasingly argued that it imposed an intolerable burden on both industry and government.

Dangerous runs on the pound occurred from time to time since 1931, and were sadly familiar during the Labour governments after 1964. Because of the government commitment to maintain sterling at an arbitrarily high and stable exchange rate, they tended to blow up into politico-economic typhoons within a matter of weeks or even days, as they drained the gold and foreign exchange held by the British government, and thrown on to the market to buy sterling in order to maintain the price of sterling against the rush of sales. Since British governments now owned far less in the way of such readily mobilizable assets than foreigners owned by way of equally readily saleable liabilities, every such crisis was potentially disastrous.* Time and again, as in 1931 and 1964–6, such crises took governments by surprise, and forced them to seek support for the pound abroad, at the

---

*In 1937 the government disposed of about £6 in gold and foreign exchange for every £5 of 'sterling balances' which volatile foreigners might wish to sell. In December 1962, for instance, they only disposed of £1 in reserves for every £4 in the foreigners' sterling balances.

cost of adjusting their domestic policies to the wishes of our supporters and creditors.

The case for maintaining sterling as a world currency, in spite of these hazards, was that the British balance of payments derived greater advantages from attracting the foreigner to sterling than were readily or quickly available in other ways, given the diminishing importance of the traditional 'invisible' income. The case against it was that the foreigners no longer found sterling attractive because behind it there stood a great and flourishing economy, but only because they were being given special inducements to hold it, and even with these they were sufficiently nervous to withdraw at the slightest sign of trouble, real or imaginary. What was more, the special inducements (high interest rates, an overvalued pound, the domestic deflation which was supposed to maintain the foreigner's confidence) might harm the growth of the British economy as a whole. Once again factories might be sacrificed to banks, but no longer, as before 1913, to encourage the vast and certain profits of the City on which the balance of payments depended heavily, but on the increasingly risky gamble that the occasional high profits which came to London would turn out larger than the substantial losses from the recurrent and predictable exchange crises. Such crises occurred in 1947, 1949, 1951, 1955–7, 1960–61, 1964–6, and 1967, when the pound had to be devalued for the second time since the war, and it became clear that the days of sterling as a world currency were numbered. However, by then the entire international monetary system, of which sterling formed a part, was in such disarray that crisis had become endemic, affecting various countries in turn – including the USA itself – and thereby perpetuating the vulnerability of the pound.[5]

Observers incidentally noted the ironic fact that the actual payments deficits which made Britain so vulnerable were normally quite negligible. At most times they amounted to little more than a fraction of the very large military expenditures which Britain incurred in order to maintain a waning global role in politics. A reduction of this spending from the seven per cent or so of the national income to what, say, the French and

Germans were spending for analogous purposes, would have wiped out our deficits on current account in most years.*

However, the imbalance of payments was the symptom of a more profound problem rather than the problem itself. It could be righted. But could this be done without jeopardizing the growth of the economy, which was already lagging by world standards?† Experience seemed to show that it could not, for time and again exchange crises were solved by throttling down domestic demand, and developed again as soon as the economy advanced, increasing imports more rapidly than exports and thus once again producing a deficit. The choice seemed to be between an economy of free enterprise which was solvent because it stagnated, or lurched between alternative bouts of acceleration and hard braking, and a planned economy in which imports and capital exports were controlled by government in order to prevent economic expansion from unbalancing payments. The 1945 Labour government chose essentially the second course, making itself unpopular by the consequent 'austerity' at home. The Conservative and Labour governments after 1951 chose the first.

Such questions did not much preoccupy the bulk of Britons, who benefited from the longest and most continuous boom in the nation's modern history. Unemployment virtually disappeared during the Second World War and remained negligible

*Britain spent a higher proportion of its income on defence than any state except the USA and USSR, and a few others which, like Egypt and Israel, believed themselves to be permanently on the verge of local wars.

†Average annual growth rates of real product (*Source:* UN Statistical Yearbook)

	Period	Total %	per capita %
USA	1954–62	2·9	1·2
Belgium	,,	3·5	2·5
France	,,	4·9	3·7
West Germany	,,	6·4	5·1
Italy	,,	6·1	5·5
Netherlands	,,	4·3	2·9
Norway	,,	3·7	2·8
Sweden	,,	3·7	3·1
UK	1953–61	2·7	2·1
USSR	,,	9·4	7·5
Czechoslovakia	1954–62	6·2	5·3

thereafter, except in a few areas. It averaged 1·7 per cent for the United Kingdom during the 1950s. Share prices virtually trebled during that decade, consumer expenditure almost doubled, rising rather faster than prices. The trading profits of companies occasionally faltered – in 1952, in 1957 and again in the early 1960s – but in general rose steadily, doubling between 1946 and 1955, rising by about a third again in the next five years. The echoes of the trade cycle of boom and slump were faint. In the post-war years of Labour government business felt itself hampered by government controls, but when the Conservative governments deliberately relaxed these, few of them had any serious complaints. The sun of Conservatism shone brightly on private enterprise and private consumer expenditure. 'It was like getting a licence to print money,' said a Canadian millionaire of one of the most striking innovations of this era, the introduction of commercial television. Others might have said the same, had they been equally frank; including some who would probably have been unfit to flourish in a climate less gentle for even the inefficient big businessman.

The persistent worry of economists and civil servants about the critical state of the economy therefore made little impact on the British people, except in so far as travellers observed the notably higher standards of life in North America, the notably more rapid economic advance in some continental countries. For a generation to whom 'crisis' had meant unemployment and poverty, financial stringency, production cuts and no profits, it seemed incomprehensible to use the term of a period when ninety-one per cent of British households had acquired electric irons, eighty-two per cent television sets, seventy-two per cent vacuum cleaners, forty-five per cent washing machines and thirty per cent refrigerators, and when the workers' bicycle rapidly gave way to the adult's motor car, the youth's motor-scooter or motor-bicycle. (Almost half the washing machines, more than half the refrigerators, and more than a third of the TV sets had been bought for the first time between 1958 and 1963.) It was an unquestionable fact that most people 'had never had it so good' in material terms, and if this was due not only to technological revolution and higher incomes but to the increasing spread of hire purchase, it was still a fact. Instalment buying had become general between the wars and was already then developing its own financial institutions. It burst the bounds of traditional caution and moral reprobation of debt after the Second World War, though ancient habits were still reflected in a partly irrational dislike of Hire Purchase Finance Houses. By 1957 the British people owed a collective instalment debt of £369 million, by 1964 of some £900 million, not to mention a collective overdraft of more than £4,500 million. The British standard of living now rested largely on debt, and was therefore particularly vulnerable to restrictions of credit as well as of income, as the British motor industry discovered in the summer of 1966.

Under these circumstances the spontaneous impetus to modernize the British economy was weak. Hence perhaps the surprising feebleness of structural change in its private sector. Even economic concentration does not seem to have advanced very much between the 1930s and the early 1960s, though comparisons are difficult, and in some fields fairly substantial mergers took place in the 1950s. What made the forces of change even weaker was the shelter which government now provided for one and all. There was no reason in principle why this should have been so. In other countries, socialist or non-socialist, government proved that it could act as both the pacemaker of change and the force driving the economy forward. But in Britain this was not so.

The role of the government and other public authorities had increased notably since the 1930s, as we have seen, particularly in consequence of the Second World War. So far as the ordinary citizen was concerned, it took two main forms: legal regulations and compulsion, direct and indirect social payments and subsidies (collectively called 'the welfare state'). The ordinary workers' lot was not greatly changed by the two other extensions of public action, which affected business rather more, namely the extension of the public sector, which by the 1950s employed twenty-five per cent of all working Britons (as against three per cent in 1914), and the extension of the practice of managing the economy. The latter normally committed government to something like full employment; but it is not clear how far the full employment since the war was due to this laudable object.* The conditions of people in public employment differed from those of the rest chiefly by their greater inflexibility, sometimes for the better, sometimes for the worse; and in the older kinds of public service, by greater security and pension rights.

The main forms of social security payments, pensions, health insurance and unemployment insurance, introduced on a modest scale before 1914, had multiplied unexpectedly after the First World War.† The Second World War and the subsequent Labour government achieved a remarkable extension of this social security system, unifying the various social benefits, creating a comprehensive health service, and adding new payments, such as family allowances for second and subsequent children. In one year (1956), to take an example, about fifteen million claims were made for various benefit payments in England and Wales, which is about one for every three inhabitants.‡ 3¼ million families also received allowances for 8·4 million children, and an even larger number received the indirect subsidy of tax remission for their children, not to mention various gifts in kind such as school meals and welfare milk. One

*However, the government's policy of rigid restrictions on immigration, inherited from the inter-war period, probably did help, in so far as it was not offset by the accident that its attachment to the 'Commonwealth' allowed large numbers of people from the former colonies and dependencies to enter the country freely; until – once again without anyone considering the economic consequences of this act – the immigration of coloured people was sharply restricted in 1963.

†Beneficiaries of social payments (in millions)

	1914	1938
Old Age Pensions	0·8	2·5
Unemployed Insurance	2·25	15
Health Insurance	13	20

‡This was the approximate breakdown:

Unemployment	2·2 million claims
Sickness	6·9
Pensions	4·2
Widows	0·4
Death grants	0·2
Maternity grants	1·1

and a half million received National Assistance from the rather more humanized successor of the old Poor Law. Virtually all benefited from the National Health Service of 1948, and ninety to ninety-five per cent of children attended schools maintained wholly or partly out of public funds. Never before had so few citizens entirely escaped the net of public welfare.

How much this system contributed to the income of the average citizen is another and more complex question. Actual grants to people were virtually negligible before 1914, except for the Poor Law and the five shillings a week old-age pension for those over seventy. By 1938 they may have amounted to about five to six per cent of total personal incomes (before tax). Since then, surprisingly, they have not gone up much: in 1956 they were estimated at only about seven per cent. This is because the rise in prices has made the present social security benefits less valuable in real terms than those before the war, and also because of the fall in unemployment. The apparatus of social security had become much more all-embracing, but its benefits to all the destitute citizens were still marginal. Moreover, by 1960 they no longer compared favourably with those available in many other West European countries (except for the health service and National Assistance). This inadequacy is specially marked in the cash payments the citizen receives when unable to earn wages. Today, as before 1914 and between the wars, the man or woman who depends *exclusively* on unemployment pay, pensions, national assistance, and so on is a very impoverished citizen indeed.

On the other hand, government intervention has played a major role in housing, education and, since 1948, in health. In addition to rent control, the first war and post-war initiated systematic public house-building, mainly by local councils. Between the wars about 1·9 million dwellings were built directly or with public subsidies, as against about 2·7 million by unsubsidized private builders. After the Second World War the great majority of all dwellings were built by councils, though in the 1950s there was a considerable rise in the proportion which came from private builders, encouraged by the official return to a modified free-market economy. Before this change, out of the

13½ million dwellings in England and Wales, three million were publicly owned and another four million rent-controlled, so the importance of public intervention is obvious. Of course, it also operated in reverse, for example by pushing up the rents of uncontrolled tenancies.

Curiously enough, however, the basic source of most people's income, their wage or salary, remained largely unaffected by the expansion of public control, except for a few interventions – mostly before 1945 – to provide a legal minimum wage in industries with weak trade unions, or to encourage conditions of labour such as paid holidays. (Before the Holidays with Pay Act of 1938 between 4½ and 7½ million people were said to enjoy paid vacations; within five years fifteen million, and since the war almost every employed Briton.) But what determined wages was essentially free bargaining between employers and trade unions, and the state's interventions, except in times of crisis, were mainly designed to foster this. Since the period 1890–1914 such bargains had tended to become basically national agreements between national unions and, increasingly, associated bodies of employers within a given 'industry', though common economic conditions, common movements of the cost of living, and the tendency of each type of worker to try to keep pace with comparable workers in other industries tended to make the whole wage-structure lumber in the same direction. In practice such agreements became more imprecise as they became more national. Moreover the national trade unions and the employers' organizations, the latter by far the most conservative bodies on the industrial scene between the First World War and the early 1960s, each in their own way favoured the maintenance of formal systems of for example wage-payment which were increasingly remote from reality, so that the gap between negotiated minimum wage-rates and actual take-home pay widened considerably. In consequence the *real* negotiations which determined what employers were *really* prepared to concede to their workers increasingly took the form of an unofficial and quite unsystematic web of bargaining between the representatives of individual firms, largely at plant level, and a growing number of 'shop stewards' or similar grass-roots negotiators.

It was typical of the *laissez-faire* character of industrial relations that virtually nothing was known about them – estimates of their total number in 1959–60 ranged between 90,000 and 200,000 – except that their numbers were increasing rapidly. In the Amalgamated Engineering Union they increased by perhaps sixty per cent between 1947 and 1961, half of this increase occurring between 1957 and 1961.[6]

What government intervention did was thus to stabilize the *status quo* such as it was. It supplemented the workers' income without (except for the very poorest) determining it. It provided a base from which each man or group could negotiate and gave recognition (and therefore permanence) to such unions or employers' associations as were in existence, but without seriously influencing – except in brief forays at times of crisis – the results of the bargains or the structure of the wages system. At bottom it left matters to the free play of negotiation and tradition. The result was a complex process of muddling through, which gradually caused the actual wage-level and the actual way in which it was determined to diverge increasingly both from the theory and from the realities of industrial structure. Full employment, the general rise in living standards, and the capacity of booming industries to pass wage-increases on to the consumer (at the cost of legitimizing further increases to meet the rising cost of life) obscured the disadvantages of this state of affairs, except to economists and those underpaid groups of workers whose low wages and status it tended to perpetuate. By the early 1960s criticism of it was mounting, but much of it took the negative form of opposition to trade-union bargaining as such,* which in turn reflected the traditional and erroneous view that the unsatisfactory condition of the economy was due to the workers. It was not. The economic irrationalities of workers and management were the two sides of the same coin. Indeed it might be argued that the attempt to limit the pressure of unions deprived the economy of at least one powerful incentive for industrial modernization.

* As usual in such cases, the lawyers launched an attack on the legal status of trade unions, and in 1966 a panic-stricken government reinforced them by temporarily abrogating freely negotiated collective agreements.

The Long Boom

Government had equally little planned effect on the structure of business. After 1945 Britain acquired a substantial public sector and retained the capacity to determine the general movements of the economy. However, with the dismantling of the very successful mechanism of wartime planning and post-war reconstruction, it lost interest in what to do with its powers until about 1960, when the spectacle of French economic success revived it again. The nationalized industries (coal, railways and some other forms of transport and communications, and the nationalized, denationalized and eventually renationalized steel) were the result of a combination of circumstances,* but each was operated quite separately, uncertain whether its purpose was to provide a service to the rest of the economy (and if so what and at what cost), or to make a profit like any other business, or to order goods from other British industries such as aircraft, or simply to keep its deficit low enough to avoid awkward debates in Parliament and the Press. Its relation to competing private businesses, run on ordinary principles of making the highest profit, was left obscure. Its policies as purchaser of products – and the size of public sector orders made it dominate several industries – were left undefined. Naturally it played a much smaller role in the economy than it might have done.† This is true not only of the nationalized industries themselves, but of the even more important body of investment controlled by the public authorities.

What happened was that, except in time of war, the prevalent theory of public enterprise did not consider it as a means of

*For instance, of the industries supplying power, electricity and gas had long been partly public, coal was nationalized because it was bankrupt under private enterprise and both miners and public opinion insisted on public ownership, and oil was not nationalized at all, presumably because Britain did not wish to encourage other countries to nationalize the oilfields from which (via the handful of huge corporations with which the government kept excellent relations) we derived valuable foreign exchange.

†Except perhaps for the BBC, there are no examples of technological, or economic pace-making which can compare with continental public enterprise (for example Renault and Volkswagen in the motor industry, the French and some other state railways, or the Italian oil and natural gas industry).

assuring economic growth. Britain, the first of all 'developed' economies, found it hard to think in the terms which came so naturally to backward nations trying to catch up advanced ones, to poor ones trying to become rich, to ruined ones trying to rebuild, or even to those with a continuous tradition of technological pioneering. British socialists thought of the public sector as an engine for achieving a redistribution of incomes and a measure of social justice, or more vaguely (and in contrast to profit-making capitalism) a 'public service'. (In fact this meant producing the cheapest possible goods and services for 'the public'; but since the main consumers of nationalized industries are private businesses, it meant subsidizing private business, incidentally diminishing its incentive to modernize itself.) Businessmen thought of it in much the same way, if they thought about it at all, though in different terminology. Their ideal of public enterprise was one which (*a*) did not interfere in private business, (*b*) cost the tax-payer no money, (*c*) supplied goods and services below market rates, (*d*) ordered goods and services at monopoly prices and (*e*) subsidized or bore the costs of research and development.* These objectives were incompatible. Government, finally, saw the public sector, like public expenditure, by tradition primarily as a stabilizer of the economy – a smoother-down of short-term fluctuations. Once it found itself in possession of a very large chunk of the economy, it could not merely encourage or discourage private business by fiscal and financial measures, but also throw its own huge weight this way and that (that is, in practice, cut down public civilian investment from time to time). But it still did not think of itself, at least for most of the period after the Second World War, as the major engine of the economy, though very slowly it became convinced that it ought to do something to ensure a more rapid rate of its growth.

One reason for this failure was that government hardly thought of itself as very distinct from private industry, from the handful of economically decisive giant corporations, often

*Between 1949 and 1958 nationalized industries purchased about £12,000 million of goods and services from the private sector, the government probably about as much again.

constructed like public bureaucracies, whose chiefs slipped into public service in times of crisis readily, as retired senior civil servants slipped into the economy-controlling giants.* It seemed unimportant that one sector operated on normal business principles, the other not, or indeed whether a sector was nominally private or nominally public, so long as the men who ran both thought in similar ways, and followed the general indications of the government economists (who in turn were not notably different from any other economists). Except for the left wing of the Labour Party and other socialists, nationalization was widely regarded as irrelevant, the existing nationalized industries as historic accidents. At one point the leadership of the Labour Party even suggested that the best way for the public to control the non-nationalized sector might be to buy government shares in the leading private companies. Outsiders might find it paradoxical that, during the financial crises of 1964–6, the Governor of the nationalized Bank of England, theoretically the spokesman of government, in practice acted as the spokesman of City opinion against the government, but this was a paradox which emerged naturally from the fusion of the two sectors, and the belief that the economy was really directed by the consensus of the sort of people who ran any kind of large enterprise.

The British economy in the early 1960s therefore still relied largely on the forces of 'natural' and spontaneous evolution, though nudged along by public policy. It did so all the more because, after 1951, government deliberately abstained from administrative controls, except (theoretically) as short-term crisis measures. By then this state of affairs came under increasingly heavy criticism, and it was clear that much more systematic measures of planning, of rationalization, of destroying irrationalities and inefficiencies, would soon be needed. By international standards, British performance was poor. The fundamental problem of Britain's position in the international economy had clearly not been solved. It was by no means clear that an economy of Britain's size could meet the challenge and

---

*Thus the chief of Imperial Chemical Industries in 1966 was a former civil servant, whereas the expert appointed to rationalize the nationalized railways was an executive of Imperial Chemicals.

the rivalry of the much larger super-economies such as the USA, the USSR and the European Economic Community. But it seemed reasonably certain that it had not yet found its way.

NOTES

1. Peter Donaldson, *Guide to the British Economy* (Pelican, 1965), and G. C. Allen, *The Structure of Industry in Britain* (1961), are useful introductions. A. R. Prest, ed., *The UK Economy, A Manual of Applied Economics* (1966), is less elementary. For the wider setting, M. M. Postan, *An Economic History of Western Europe 1945–1964* (1967). See also Figures 1, 6–7, 10–11, 13, 15, 18–19, 22, 25–30, 32–7, 39, 50–2.

2. However, the increasingly precipitate decline of coal faced all West European countries, including Britain, with much more acute problems in the middle 1960s.

3. See G. Maxcey and A. Silberston, *The Motor Industry* (1959).

4. Exports as percentage of GNP and Export Index of various countries in 1965 (*Source: Guardian,* 22 November 1967)

Country	Exports as % GNP	Index (1958 = 100)
USA	3·9	153
Japan	10·1	294
France	10·8	196
Italy	12·7	278
UK	13·7	148
W. Germany	15·9	203
Sweden	20·2	190
Belgium/Luxemburg	36·4	210

5. The pound had finally to be devalued – with consequences which could not yet be foreseen at the time of writing – in November 1967.

6. R. C. on Trade Unions, Research Paper 1: *The Role of the Shop Stewards in British Industrial Relations* (1966), p. 5. For further information about the role and nature of shop stewards see the same Commission's Research Paper 10 (1968) on the same subject.

14

SOCIETY SINCE
1914[1]

IN economic terms this was a century of striking net improve-
in the standards of living. In social terms it was one of equally
striking and disorienting change. The wars and inter-war depressions kept Britons' minds largely off these secular changes –
they had more urgent preoccupations – but by the early 1960s,
after a series of peaceful years in which the material conditions
and habits of the people altered more profoundly and rapidly
than ever before, a mood of puzzled introspection and self-
criticism seized the literate parts of the population. What had
happened, what was happening to the country?

At first sight the most obvious phenomenon was its international decline. After 1931 Britain ceased to be the hub of the
international economy, after 1945 it ceased to be even a formal
Empire of substantial size, and comparisons with other industrial
countries became increasingly unfavourable. In fact, as we have
seen, the change in Britain's international position hardly
affected life within the country. The lives of businessmen depended on profits, and whatever the sources of these profits,
they were remarkably healthy. The lives of workers depended
on their employment and wages, and both were far higher than
before. The lives of the professional classes and intellectuals
depended on their employment and scope, and both expanded
immeasurably compared to the days before the Second World
War. The malaise which became so obvious from the late 1950s
was certainly not due to material discontent, still less to hardship
identifiable with Britain's decline. It was due to the apparent
dismantling of landmarks which past generations had, without
much thought, taken as permanent. The proverbial country of
puritanical morals appeared to have become, at least as far as
large sections of its younger citizens went, a country of unusually
permissive sexuality. The nation which prided itself on abiding

by an incorrupt law became celebrated for the daring and impunity of its robbers, and began to suspect the integrity of its policemen. The nation whose working-class citizens had hardly ever crossed the Channel except in uniform sent millions to Mediterranean beaches and Alpine ski-runs each year, received (with considerable reluctance) a modest but only too visible influx of coloured citizens, and took to consuming scampi, chop suey and, in quantities hitherto unprecedented, wine. Or so it seemed.

The most acute 'malaise' was that of the 'middle classes', by now (as we have seen) mainly composed of salary-earners. The rich had little cause for complaint, though (as always) they saw themselves taxed and oppressed out of existence. Certainly there was no major equalization of property between the wars and no substantial redistribution since. Before the First World War (1911–13) the top five per cent of the population owned eighty-seven per cent of personal wealth, the bottom ninety per cent, eight per cent; just before the Second (1936–8) seventy-nine per cent and twelve per cent, and in 1960 seventy-five per cent and seventeen per cent.[2] As for *investment* income, in 1954 the top one per cent still received about fifty-eight per cent of all of it. Britain remained very far from a 'property-owning democracy'. At the very top of the scale the exceedingly rich became slightly more numerous, slightly richer per head, but formed a some-what smaller percentage both of the number of owners and the total value of property. In 1936–8 15,000 individuals owned some twenty-two per cent of all property; after the war 19,000 owned almost fifteen per cent, and since 1948 concentration once again resumed.

What had happened was a modification in the bases of in-equality in the context of a changing, and increasingly state-influenced economy. Those who failed to adjust to this suffered, those who seized the new opportunities prospered. Between the wars, when the ideal of a return to 1913 still haunted the rich and those in charge of the state, this was not yet as obvious as it became after the Second World War. This is most evident in the field of taxation. Officially direct progressive taxes and levies on wealth such as death duties rose to ever dizzier levels, so that the very rich were theoretically stripped of the great bulk of their excess income. In fact, and under the benevolent eye of the state, a variety of legal devices for tax evasion were perfected which largely exempted those whose incomes did not take the form of wages and salaries and were taxed at source. The most important of these loopholes was probably the absence of any capital gains tax until 1962, which brought vast and untaxed windfalls to the owners of security and negotiable real estate in the long post-war years of uninterrupted capital appreciation. The most striking new fortunes of this period (for example those of real-estate speculators) were based on this. 'Gifts' of property to relatives side-stepped death duties. And so on.

The very rich, therefore, remained pretty well as affluent as before, though their composition was somewhat altered. The First World War, a paradise for profiteers, made them richer, though it also (with the help of Lloyd George's sale of peerages) reduced *ad absurdum* their traditional social reward, adoption into the landed aristocracy. The inter-war depression troubled them a little, though not enough to create even a local legend comparable to the American myth of millionaires hurtling from Wall Street windows after the Great Crash of 1929. The Second World War and the subsequent Labour era discouraged free spending and frightened them. Not until the Conservative era of the middle 1950s did the confidence which flaunts its wealth in public return, while the official policy of relative austerity ended. As we have seen, in these years the rich undoubtedly grew much richer. They were also now joined by a comparatively new group, those whose expenditure (paid for in one way or another by firms as 'business expenses') was that of the wealthy, though their income and capital resources were not. Men shot grouse on moors bought by companies nominally for the sake of business contacts which could be made on them, made the fortunes of nightclubs and luxury car producers, and drank Château Mouton Rothschild 1921 in what formally masqueraded as 'works canteens' for directors.

Most of the 'middle class' lived below this level and were troubled (as were some of the rich themselves) by a state of affairs in which the highest material rewards went not to a traditional nobility or to the virtues of enterprise and hard work, but depended on what by nineteenth-century standards were lies and immorality. Their situation had, as they felt, changed considerably for the worse. By 1960 perhaps a quarter of the population belonged to this group of white-collar workers, salaried and professional classes, which had expanded continuously during the twentieth century, increasingly replacing the typical Victorian 'middle' and 'lower middle' classes which had consisted essentially of shopkeepers, small entrepreneurs and men living off 'fees and profits' (to quote the income tax classification) and not wages or salaries. Both financially and socially they lived up to their name. A relatively modest income (though one, two or three times as high as the average employed worker's) already ensured a degree of comfort inconceivable among the proletariat.* A thousand a year would get a man very far.

Modest ease was the ceiling of middle-class aspirations. In the hierarchic society of Britain the landed aristocracy was beyond their reach anyway, and even the millions of the plutocracy were rarely a temptation to the respectable. In Edwardian times an occasional romantic, like H. G. Wells' Uncle Ponderevo, or an occasional son of the manse, like John Buchan, dreamed of hitting the jackpot of wealth and social recognition by business or professional activities – mainly the law – and a great many young entrepreneurs from the colonies certainly hoped to make their pile and capture London. Some, like Lord Beaverbrook, did. But the path to the social peaks was narrow: Oxford, the Bar, Parliament or Johannesburg and the Stock Exchange. Neither Sir Thomas Lipton (groceries and yachts) nor Lord Birkenhead (law, politics and free spending) provided the dynamic for the average middle-class citizen. What he wanted was rather a position securely, and with luck increasingly, above the 'lower orders', ample supplies of domestic comfort, educa-

---

*Thus in 1937–8 a salaried family earning, say, £400 a year would spend twice as much as the average family of employed workers on clothes and (much superior) housing, a third more on heating and light, a fifth more on food. It would still have half its income left over for other items, on which it spent three times as much as the worker's family.

tion for his sons, a sense of being the 'backbone of the country', and perhaps an adequate provision of religious and cultural activities. But chiefly the first of these.

In economic terms a great many white-collar workers never had this secure superiority over the proletariat, for they might earn no more than the aristocracy of manual labour. It was their style of life, their social status, which differed from labour's, and they were therefore always extremely sensitive to any improvements below which might diminish these distinctions. Between the wars the thought that council houses might provide the workers with water-closets caused them gloom, and the widespread belief that the rehoused toilers would use their baths only to store coal expressed their hope rather than reality. It is possible that these marginal strata sometimes lost ground – for instance during periods of inflation. They possessed no unions (except in the public services) and, to tell the truth, no skill beyond the range of their shorthand-typing daughters. Throughout the past fifty years such men remained, pinching and resentful, a sullen army of the suburbs and massive supporters of right-wing and anti-labour newspapers and politicians.

In purely financial terms there is no evidence that the situation of the less marginal middle strata changed for the worse. If we take the elementary school teacher as a far from unduly privileged example of the lower middle class, his average annual salary probably lagged behind the cost of living during the First World War, shot well ahead immediately after it, and remained fairly stable until the Second World War, when its real value increased.* Pre- and post-Second World War are more easily compared from the income tax statistics, as in the table [3] appearing overleaf.

The post-war figures must be divided by about 3·5 to allow for the fall in the value of money, but it is still clear that more people were earning the pre-war equivalent of a middle-class income, and that the average income in the middle ranges of this

---

*Average annual pay of male certificated teachers ($£$)

1914	147	1928	334
1918	180	1933	296
1923	346	1938	331

class had probably risen. This was due not so much to improvements in the actual rate of salaries, but rather to a great deal of promotion into the expanding number of more highly-paid jobs.

NUMBER OF EARNERS ASSESSED FOR INCOME TAX

1938–9		1963	
Range of gross incomes (£)	*Number*	*Range of gross incomes (£)*	*Number*
200–400	3,030,000	700–1500	11,500,000
400–600	570,000	1500–2250	1,000,000
600–1500	459,000	2250–5000	510,000
Over 1500	158,000	Over 5000	100,000

And yet even among these 'middle' middle strata, the complaints about their plight never ceased; and indeed they were loud even in 1914. There were several reasons for this. The rising rate of taxation, which a salaried person could hardly escape, was one. For a family of two adults and three children earning about £1,000 it (roughly) doubled in monetary terms between 1913 and 1938, and again between 1938 and 1960. The pattern of middle-class expenditure was another. It always carried a comparatively heavy burden of insurance, payments for schools, house purchase, and so on, which inevitably cut down on other things except among the rather affluent; at least for a large part of life. And until the middle class learned to use the post-1945 social services, and turned out to benefit relatively more from them than the workers, the cost of corresponding private outlays – on medical services and education – became extremely heavy.

But the main reason was certainly that it became increasingly difficult or expensive to maintain that visible and *qualitative* superiority over the 'lower orders' which was the real badge of middle-class status. Servants went first. Before 1914 their employment had virtually defined those with, at least, middle-class aspirations, but by 1931 only five per cent of British households had resident servants and by 1951 only one per cent.[4] Except for the part-time cleaner domestic service disappeared, until in the 1950s it emerged again on a limited scale in the disguise of foreign 'au pair' girls. The middle-class monopoly of domestic comforts crumbled. By 1960 not even the telephone and the motor car, and certainly not the holiday abroad, remained as secure status symbols. This did not mean more money for other things, because the obligation to keep up with the neighbouring Jones's, in a society in which status was increasingly measured by money, kept up the pressure for conspicuous spending. Certain forms of it, for instance entertainment, became notably more ruinous. What is more, a mass-consumption society left only the very rich the hope of marking themselves off from the rest by the obvious quality of their possessions. The gap between the woman who owned a refrigerator and the one who didn't was vast, but the gap between the owner of the cheapest and most expensive refrigerator on the market was merely a few score of pounds, easily obscured by hire purchase. What was worse, this was true even of clothes, especially of that great social equalizer, leisure-time wear.

To some extent the middle classes reacted after the Second World War by that last resource of snobbery, when people seek distinction in superior dowdiness (as the landed gentry had long done from the parvenus of trade by its aggressively shabby tweeds), or by actually abstaining from mass-produced consumption. That the middle class ever bought television sets less freely than the workers was a myth, but – characteristically – a widespread one in the early days of this entertainment. Conversely, many of the characteristic middle-class ways of spending money became disproportionately expensive, some of its life unnecessarily laborious. Dreaming of servants, the middle-class housewife was slower than the working-class woman to adopt genuine labour-saving devices like washing-machines when she could afford them; and certainly to welcome the ready-to-eat pre-packaged foods which ease the lives of the masses.* Dreaming of privacy, they hesitated to benefit by the revolution in group-travel which transformed mass holidays, and attempted

---

*There was a marked reaction in the 1950s and 1960s against 'eating' and towards 'gastronomy' (especially, to begin with, of continental and exotic cooking), and later against 'manufactured' and towards 'natural' foods. Eating habits became one of the most reliable middle-class indicators, until the affluent proletarians began to catch up.

to cling to the old individualist form of travel, which was both more expensive and more uncomfortable. In brief, an entire mode of life became obsolete, and the most reliable way of maintaining a separate style of existence, namely intellectual and cultural activity, was not to the taste of the middle-class majority. Still, a marked emphasis on 'culture' was probably the most important innovation in the newspapers which appealed to the middle class in the post-war period, and which now fed their readers with book reviews, and pages on the theatre and the arts to an extent unusual before the Second World War.

The older, established middle classes also found their monopoly of social position undermined by the entry of the sons of the lower orders (including in this instance the lower middle class) into the increasingly large and important professions. The passing of examinations and professional expertise rather than parentage and 'character', knowledge rather than 'all-round ability' were hardly the test of success before the Second World War. After it, they became very much more important, and the old 'public schools' found themselves raising money to build not war-memorials and pavilions, but the unfamiliar structures of laboratories to compete with the grammar schools as nurseries of scientists and technologists. Established middle-class status no longer automatically bought positions of potential command, and when it did, they might have to be shared with newcomers from below. The deeply entrenched vested interests of the old elite – City, top industrial management, the law, medicine and other corporate professions and the Conservative Party – resisted as best they could, which was rather effectively. In the late 1950s there were even signs of deliberate reaction. But the threat was there, and it grew stronger.

The malaise of the middle classes was not therefore due to pauperization. Nor was it even due to any diminution in the distinction between classes, except in the superficial sense that they could not always be told apart so easily in public, especially when young. It was due rather to a shift in the structure and function of the middle groups in British society. It was the double malaise of those who did not adjust readily to it, and of those who found no adequate place for their talents because it was not changing fast enough: of the old 'gentlemen' and the new 'players'. Both united to blame the working classes.

*

Though few workers in the early 1960s were 'affluent' in any meaningful sense of the word, and perhaps one in ten were actually in want, the malaise of the working class was certainly not due to economic hardship. Most British workers were very much better off than ever before in their history and certainly much better off than they would have ever expected to be in 1939. For the first time a majority of them were, broadly speaking, free of the struggle for elementary daily necessities and the fear of unemployment. Only the fear of old age remained to haunt them, with its combination of poverty and emptiness. Yet two factors were in the process of changing the social situation as profoundly – indeed more profoundly – than that of the middle class.

The first and perhaps the less important was the mass-produced economy of mass consumption which rested on their now not quite so meagre wage-packets. A good deal of the pattern of life, the 'traditional working-class culture' which, as we have seen, developed towards the end of the nineteenth century, reflected their social isolation. They had been the pariahs of both economics and politics. The mere presence of a man wearing the worker's cap and speaking with the worker's intonation in Parliament – Keir Hardie in 1892 – was enough to create a shock which is still recalled in the history books. If they were no longer totally neglected by big business, the industry and commerce which supplied their wants was entirely distinct from that which catered to the middle classes, let alone the 'nobility and gentry', unless of course they deliberately bought middle-class goods. The contacts between working-class and upper-class life (apart from servants) were hardly closer than those between white and Negro life in the inter-war USA, the upper-class or intellectual fashion for patronizing boxers, jockeys, prostitutes and the music-hall hardly more than the passion of some whites for jazz. The 'proletarian world' was not entirely an underworld. It had its own social structure, culminating in that mixed elite of skilled workers, small shopkeepers, small entrepreneurs, publicans, elementary school teachers and so on, in the industrial areas, which the late Victorians knew as a 'lower middle class'. (It is not to be confused with the *new* 'lower middle class' of white-collar workers, nor with the small shopkeepers etc., in non-industrial areas, who neither interchanged nor identified with the aristocracy of labour.) Nevertheless, for all the average middle-class citizen knew of the working-class world, or it of him, the 'two nations' might have been living in different continents.*

Virtually all the institutions of the working-class world were therefore separate and created within it. They had to be. The proletarian market and shops (including the pawnbroker), the working-class sections of the hierarchically stratified pubs, their characteristic newspapers, combining racing tips, radicalism and reports of crime,† their music-halls, football teams and labour movement coexisted with the middle-class world but were not part of it and barely overlapped. If anything, between 1880 and 1914 this separation grew as the size of the 'works' increased, contact with employers diminished (or was made more difficult by the expansion of the new white-collar office-staff), and non-proletarians moved from mixed streets into single-class suburbs.

Nothing much changed between the wars. Woolworth, Boots and the Fifty Shilling Tailor were hardly yet enough to assimilate working-class to middle- or even lower-middle-class consumption, and housing developments (the rise of the 'council estate') if anything intensified residential class divisions. Over a large part of Britain depression welded all those who lived in its immediate shadow together into a grim bloc. A new class consciousness and sense of exploitation on one side, fear on the

---

* I remember as late as 1940 making the transition from one to the other over a distance of barely one mile in Cambridge: called up from college, billeted in a working-class street.

† The old *News of the World* was its most successful exemplar; *not* the much younger *Daily Mail* of Northcliffe (1896). The first modern mass-circulation newspaper which appealed to the workers because they were the largest 'market' was the *Daily Mirror* – and not before about 1940.

other, widened the gap between the two nations. A rigid educational system, a shaking economy, confined workers and their children to their own world. The able young proletarian still found the best opportunities for his talents within the labour movement – like Aneurin Bevan – or in schoolteaching. A secondary education for his son was not out of the question, though the Fisher Education Act of 1918 did not seriously widen the educational ladder.* A university education – there were, in 1938, only something like fifty thousand university students, twenty per cent of them in Oxford and Cambridge – was hardly a possibility.

Hence when the change became evident a few years after the Second World War, there had been little to prepare it. It was not due simply to the 'affluence' of the new durable consumer goods. In fact, compared to other countries, they were not bought in unusual quantity, except for television sets. (Thus in 1964 there were thirty-seven cars per hundred of the British population, but fifty in Germany and forty-seven in France.) It was not merely that more money, more comfort at home, and later more house-ownership tended to shift the centre of working-class life from the public and collective (the pub or football match) towards the private and individual, and therefore towards a model of life previously associated with the lower middle class. In the 1950s 'Andy Capp', the traditional home-fleeing, pub-seeking and wife-oppressing proletarian of a celebrated strip-cartoon, became a figure of fun (though also of a certain nostalgia).

The truth was that a mass-consumption society is dominated by its biggest market, which in Britain was that of the working class. As production and styles of life were therefore democratized, not to say proletarianized, much of the workers' former isolation melted away; or rather, the pattern of isolationism was reversed. No longer did the workers have to accept goods or enjoyments essentially produced for other people; for an idealized petty-bourgeois 'little man' (as in the most successful mass-circulation daily between the wars, the *Daily Express*), for a degenerate version of the middle-class matinee-going (as in

*Fees in maintained secondary schools were not abolished until 1945.

most of popular music),* or by a moralizing teacher (as in the BBC).

Henceforth, it was *their* demand which dominated commercially, even their taste and style which pressed upward into the culture of the non-working classes; triumphantly in the Liverpool-accented tones of an entirely new pop music, indirectly in the vogue for authentic working-class themes and backgrounds which swept not only TV but even that bourgeois stronghold the theatre, comically in the fashion for plebeian accents and behaviour which became *de rigueur* in such improbable environments as those of actors and fashion-photographers.† On the contrary, it was the 'A and B' market‡ which now developed its separatist mass media and commercial or cultural institutions; most visibly in the 'class' newspapers and periodicals.

Business therefore took over the task of filling the proletarian world. It did so at a time when poverty slackened its grip and diminished the need for constant collective battle against unemployment and want, and when politics absorbed the strongest organ of working-class separatism, the labour movement, into its routine. The Second World War and the Labour governments of 1945–51 demonstrated that 'labour' was no longer an outsider, even in theory. Its party was the permanent alternative government, whereas between the wars its periods of office had been freakish and episodic. Its trade unions were so tightly enmeshed in the web of big business and government that so traditional an activity as the strike became, at most times, associated almost entirely with unofficial action, or rank-and-file revolt. Wage changes became the almost automatic consequences of price-changes or regular periodic reviews by mechanisms which operated far above the heads of union members,

* A very high proportion of the popular song-hits until the middle 1950s had originally appeared in, or been written for, musical comedies – a very unproletarian genre.

† It went, at least for a time, with a marked recession in these quarters of the fashion for homosexuality.

‡ Of the five broad income classifications, which became the bible of advertisers, the first two corresponded, roughly, to the upper and middle classes.

whose membership was now often virtually automatic. Consequently, and contrary to middle-class mythology, Britain did not suffer greatly from strikes, and indeed suffered rather less than many other more dynamic industrial economies.* Nor did strikes tend to increase. On the contrary, since the peak just before and after the First World War, they have tended to diminish very substantially.

As a result there was a marked sagging in all the institutions of the traditional separatist working-class world. The secular progress of the Labour Party in national elections stopped in 1951 and did not resume. Trade-union membership stagnated. The older militants complained – correctly – that the fires of passion in the movement were flickering out. Even so nonpolitical a phenomenon as the enthusiasm for football declined. Like cinema attendances, it reached its peak shortly after the Second World War, and thereafter drifted steadily downwards. The 'traditional' Sunday newspaper of the urban masses, the *News of the World*, lost its pre-eminence; the mass-circulation daily built and maintained by the labour movement died. Young intellectuals, discovering 'traditional working-class culture' in its decline during the 1950s, idealized it – unduly – but their elegies did not revive it.

What was perhaps more serious, economic change eroded the very foundations of the working class as traditionally understood, that is the men and women who got their hands dirty at work, mainly in mines, factories, or working with, or around, some kind of engines. Three tendencies continued inexorably throughout the twentieth century, only temporarily halted during the two wars: (1) the relative decline of 'industry' as compared with tertiary employments like distribution, transport and various services; (2) the relative decline of manual as compared with 'white-collar' or 'clean-handed' labour within each industry;

*In 1959 about one tenth of one per cent of working days were lost by strikes. In 1950–4 the loss of working days per 1,000 workers was about fifteen per cent less in West Germany, about four times as great in Belgium, about five times as great in Canada and France, about six times as great in Japan, Australia and Italy, and almost ten times as great in the USA. Only Scandinavia and the Netherlands were much more peaceful in industry than Britain. (*International Labour Review*, Vol. 72 (1955), p. 87.)

(3) the decline of the characteristic nineteenth-century industries with their unusually high demand for old-fashioned manual work.* Admittedly the non-manual workers were also workers. By 1931 only about five per cent of the occupied population were employers and managers (in 1951 only two per cent were actual employers), and another five per cent or so worked on their own account. Ninety per cent were classified as 'operatives'. Moreover, and particularly after the Second World War, the non-manuals increasingly accepted their status and their community of interest with the manuals by joining trade unions, which in the later 1950s showed a marked tendency actually to enter, or to cooperate with, that fortress of horny-handed toil, the Trades Union Congress. Nevertheless, the difference between 'office' and 'workshop' was a substantial one. In working hours, and often out of them, it remained the most visible distinction between citizens.

Technology introduced another and increasingly ominous distinction: unlike the nineteenth-century type of industry, which had an almost unlimited demand for men and women without any qualifications except strength and willingness, the technology of the mid twentieth century has less and less use for them. For a while the tertiary activities became a refuge for unqualified labour, but by the 1950s organization had begun to economize it (as in self-service stores and supermarkets) or to replace it by machines (as in the automation of routine office

*Percentage of administrative, technical and clerical workers per 100 productive operatives in some industries (*Source:* J. Bonner in *Manchester School*, 1961, p. 75)

	1907	1935	1951
Textiles	3·5	6·7	10·6
Treatment of non-metalliferous mining products	6·4	9·9	14·7
Metal manufactures	5·9	10·8	19·0
Vehicles	7·6	13·8	22·1
Engineering and shipbuilding	8·1	20·1	27·3
Wood and cork	10·8	12·7	15·6
Clothing	11·5	10·7	11·2
Leather	12·7	13·0	17·0
Paper, printing	13·4	21·7	27·8
Food, drink, tobacco	15·8	26·1	24·1
Chemicals and allied products	16·2	32·4	41·0

work), perhaps even faster than in manufacturing industry. The demand for skill increased sharply; not necessarily the flexible all-round skill or adaptability of the nineteenth-century ideal – of workers as well as administrative – but nevertheless high specialization requiring a certain amount of training, intelligence, and above all, prior formal *education*. Manual dexterity was no longer enough. This was very obvious in the complex of occupations which, contrary to the general tendency for the labour force in manufacturing industry to stagnate, expanded by leaps and bounds throughout the century: engineering, metal-work and electrical work. In 1911 5·5 per cent of the male workers had been in this field; by 1950 18·5 per cent; by 1964 almost one in five of *all* occupied Britons (men and women).* These industries required both more skilled and more white-collar workers than most others.

Unfortunately the traditional working class, and especially the skilled and semi-skilled who in 1964 formed rather over a third of it, were at a considerable disadvantage in these intellectual or semi-intellectual regions. This was partly due to the marked anti-egalitarian bias of the British educational system, which the Education Act of 1944 had not greatly diminished, partly to the vicious circle which automatically gave the children of the uneducated and poor a worse chance of education, and indeed progressively cut down their capacities to benefit from what education was available. In 1956 some 134,000 children sat for the General Certificate of Education (the gateway to further schooling) in the grammar schools, some 52,000 from the 'public schools' which represented at a maximum 7·5 per cent of the population. But only 8,571 came from the 'modern' schools which contained sixty-five per cent of pupils in their early teens. Since examinations and certificates of formal education increasingly determined the access to most highly-paid wage-work (that is salaried posts), and indeed to most positions of social respect and authority, a large part of Britain's

---

*Conversely, in the early twentieth century almost one out of every five employed men had been miners and farm labourers; by 1964 all persons employed in mining formed less than three per cent of the labour force, and all in agriculture (including the farmers and fishermen) four per cent.

citizens, and most workers, increasingly found themselves apparently debarred from ambition, and a considerable minority had no hopes that even their children would do better than they. Their fate was decided before they reached puberty. They could expect better wages than their fathers, and good wages with low living-costs almost as soon as they left school – at least until marriages and children reduced their standard of living again. In the short run they might be better off than those whose education continued. But they reached the ceiling soon, and it was not high. Small wonder that the teenagers of this period became proportionately the highest luxury spenders of any part of the working class. Immediate enjoyment was the best that society offered them in return for the badge of permanent inferiority.

Two opposed tendencies therefore developed within the old working class. On the one hand some of it – in particular the skilled sector – was drawing closer in its functions, its style of life, its (or rather its children's) possibilities of social mobility, to the white-collar, technical and salaried strata, while large sections of these in turn were (as their increasing trade-union activity showed) drawing closer to the working class. All workers except the most destitute or isolated were rapidly adopting a style of life based on mass-production – on production geared to their own desires; but that production reflected only certain aspects – and those which least distinguished workers as a class – of their aspirations: notably the desire for a higher material standard of life and more material possessions for individuals and families. When the sociologists of the 1950s talked of *embourgeoisement* these were the changes they had in mind, though journalists tended to misinterpret their political significance. For, as in the 'affluent' era after Chartism, the improvement of living standards and the adoption of some habits hitherto confined to the middle class may have made labour movements less radical, but did not turn workers into small-scale models of middle-class citizens. On the contrary, whereas in Victorian Britain cultural assimilation had been entirely a one-way current (flowing, as it were, socially downwards), in the second Elizabethan Britain it flowed both ways.

But simultaneously the gap between the workers – especially the unskilled and unqualified – and the rest of society tended to widen. The difference between manual and non-manual work did not, on the whole, grow less. It was all the more obtrusive, because the clean-handed worker was no longer a freak, or a simple extension of 'management', but a large part of the labour force. The bigger the 'office', the less easy it was to overlook its substantial differences from the 'workshop'.

The old aristocracy of labour found its new situation particularly galling though made more tolerable by the improvements of its own, and especially its children's, prospects. It had probably reached the peak of its pride and position at the end of the nineteenth century, when it represented the undisputed top of the 'working-class world', its wages far above the 'labourers', its position not yet seriously challenged either by the alternative labour aristocracy of the while collar, nor by its demotion to the status of semi-skilled operators of specialized machines, many of them recruited from the unapprenticed ranks below or even from women. These positions of privilege it now lost. The dynamic and growing complex of engineering and electrical industries reflected its troubles with particular clarity because here the demands and the structure of the twentieth century clashed head-on with the entrenched strength of nineteenth-century craft pride and privilege: all-round manual skill with the semi-skilled operation of specialized machines, traditional time-wages with the spread of payment by results, artisan independence with mass-production discipline or 'scientific management', and the supremacy of the working-class 'engineer' with the rising tide of 'office' and technicians. From the start of the new technological era in the 1890s, metal manufacture was a front-line of class battle (as in the great national Engineers Lock-Out of 1897–8); at moments of unusual technological change, as during the world wars with their major advance in the mass production of armaments, it was *the* front line.* The

---

*The anti-war movements in all belligerent countries in 1914–18 had their trade-unionist base in the discontent of skilled metal-workers in armaments industries, and their industrial cadres in the 'shop stewards' of engineering works.

wage differential between the skilled and the unskilled narrowed
ineluctably after 1914. Where the skilled man was unable or
unwilling to adapt himself to the new structure of work and
wages, he might actually find himself earning less than the less
skilled 'process worker'. It was not surprising that the embattled
labour aristocrat turned sharply to the left. Even in the 1950s
the characteristic working-class communist cadre was a metal-
worker – at least a quarter of all delegates at party congresses
were normally engineers – and the chief spokesmen of the left
in the Trade Union Congress represented such formerly conservative bodies as the Boilermakers, Electricians, Foundrymen
and Amalgamated Engineers.* It is possible that by the end of
our period the new industrial structure was accepted, but for
most of the twentieth century this radicalism of the threatened
labour aristocrat was a major factor in industrial relations.

Conversely, the unskilled and unqualified benefited from
such changes, and their unions, mostly formed towards the end
of the nineteenth century by the new socialists and with
extremely radical policies, moved rapidly to the right as they
were officially recognized and realized that this recognition gave
them greater advantages than their feeble bargaining power
might have gained unaided.† In flourishing industries they
might even earn well, though in declining or ill-organized ones
their conditions were often very poor. Nevertheless, they were
oppressed more than others by the vicious circle of modern
industrial society in which the underprivileged found their lack
of privilege reinforced, the uneducated their lack of education a
permanent barrier, the stupid their stupidity fatal, the weak
their weakness doubled. Just because social mobility was now
rather easier, at least for boys good at passing examinations,
those who could not take this 'meritocratic' road upwards found
themselves permanently doomed to stay at the bottom, unless

---

*But also traditionally radical groups from declining industries like the
miners and dockers. An interesting 'new left', however, began to emerge
among the rising unions of technicians.

†The relapse into left-wing sympathies of the biggest of them, the
Transport and General Workers' Union, in the late 1950s, was due far
more to the Transport than the General component of their membership.

they won the football pools, took to crime or – the most likely prospect among the young – won the equivalent of the pools in show business or pop music, fields which now ceased to require any preliminary qualification. Sometime in the prosperous 1950s the conviction developed among a mass of citizens in the working class that their inferiority was officially ratified at the age of eleven, when they were excluded from further education; perhaps even that this reflected their own inferiority.* In a way this sense of exclusion affected most manual workers, except the new super-skilled and technical elite. More dramatically, it shackled a large minority of the bottom dogs, though the fact that they were and looked like remaining a minority frustrated them still further. Their resentment found no effective political expression, and was often sub-political, though among the young it sometimes flowed into vague temporary movements of mass protest against the *status quo*, such as the Campaign for Nuclear Disarmament. Nevertheless, there was a marked rise in a sort of bottom-dog consciousness, perhaps expressed best in the pop music in which the proletarian young discovered themselves in this decade, and which soon became the general idiom of all the young. Its two sources – the Negro blues and the protest tradition of folksong – spoke for the excluded and the rebellious. Its stars, working-class boys and, later, girls, preferably from the least middle-class-assimilated backgrounds (such as Bermondsey or Liverpool waterside), allowed the public to identify with the uneducated, the un-accepting, the unrespectable, who had nevertheless won money and an evanescent fame.

*

A simple division into two classes was widely accepted as the basic pattern of Britain. Yet in fact affluence and technological change produced new social groups and strata whose behaviour showed that they could not be simply identified with either: the 'intellectuals' and the young. Both were in this sense new

* The crucial role which the demand for egalitarian secondary schools played in this period in the otherwise not very active labour movement reflected this concern.

phenomena, though the origin of the 'intellectuals' as a special social group can be traced back to the period before 1914. The sheer increase in the numbers of brain-workers – overwhelmingly salaried, or the non-manual equivalent of casual labour – emphasized their collective problems. Their relative lack of involvement in management and government, their lack of traditional status, made them less conservative than others in their income bracket.*

They could no longer be recruited merely from the existing upper and middle classes, and the mass emergence of intellectuals from lower middle- and working-class backgrounds in the 1950s produced tensions which were reflected in the, sometimes rather superficial, cultural 'leftism' of the later years of this decade. The rapidly growing universities focused their political dissidence. For the first time in British history 'students' became both a political force and a fairly predictably left-wing group, though this had been anticipated on a small and localized scale – smaller and more localized than historical mythology allows – from the middle 1930s.

'Youth' as a recognizable group, and not merely as a period of transition, to be got through as quickly as possible, between childhood and adult life, also emerged in the 1950s; both commercially as the 'teenage market', and in habits and behaviour, and politically in such movements as the campaign against nuclear weapons. However, its overt political activities were mainly confined to middle-class and intellectual youths. Both the 'affluence' of the unmarried worker and the expansion of the educational system provided the material base for this phenomenon, but it was probably the remarkably rapid and unprepared change in the general social pattern which widened the chasm between the generations so abnormally in this period. Some writers, a few *ad hoc* and often temporary campaigning organizations, and of course businessmen – often rising with the new market which they had first discovered – observed and accommodated these changes. Official British society and politics was

*This is doubtless why such faculties as engineering, medicine and law provided far fewer politically dissident students than the natural sciences, and these in turn than the humanities and social sciences.

taken aback both by the rise of the intellectuals and of the young. Most of their activities therefore took place, at least initially, outside the existing institutions of both, and certainly outside politics, unless a revulsion against established parties, movements and politicians is regarded as a version of political commitment. If the emergence of youth as a self-conscious social group did nothing else, it brought some unexpected fire and gaiety, much silliness, and an atmosphere of intellectual and cultural excitement – not always followed by achievements – into the life of Britain in the early 1960s.

NOTES

1. See Further Reading, especially Mowat, Pollard, Taylor, Carr-Saunders etc., Abrams, G. D. H. Cole, Studies. For the entire period, A. Marwick, *The Explosion of British Society 1914–1962* (1963); for the inter-war years, Pilgrim Trust, *Men Without Work* (1939), G. Orwell, *The Road to Wigan Pier* (1937) (impact of the slump), R. Graves and A. Hodge, *The Long Weekend* (1940) for miscellaneous but not insignificant information; Allen Hutt, *The Postwar History of the British Working Class* (1937). On the *Impact of the War on Civilian Consumption*, the HMSO publication of that name (1945). On some more recent aspects of British society, D. Wedderburn, 'Facts and Theories of the Welfare State' in R. Miliband and J. Saville, ed., *The Socialist Register 1965*, J. Westergard, 'The Withering Away of Class: a Contemporary Myth' in P. Anderson and R. Blackburn, ed., *Towards Socialism*, and in general the weekly *New Society*, convenient introduction to a good deal of descriptive research on modern Britain. See also Figures 2–3, 7–14, 37, 41, 44–52.
2. From an unpublished paper by J. S. Revell, 'Changes in the Social Distribution of Property in Britain in the 20th Century' (Cambridge, Department of Applied Economics, 1965).
3. *Economist*, 23 May 1965.
4. The number of female domestic servants per 1,000 families had been 218 in 1881 and 170 in 1911. However, it ought to be noted that the inter-war unemployment had the effect of notably slowing down the decline in domestic service. In absolute figures it actually increased in the fifteen years after 1921.

15

THE OTHER BRITAIN[1]

WE have so far treated the economic history of Britain as a whole, devoting no special attention to Scotland and Wales, and none to Ireland, which is not, of course, part of Great Britain.* Except for marginal and thinly populated areas like the Scottish highlands, there has been only one economic history of Britain since the Industrial Revolution, though one with regional variations and specializations. On the other hand Scotland and Wales are socially, and by their history, traditions and sometimes institutions, entirely distinct from England, and cannot therefore be simply subsumed under English history or (as is more common) neglected. The present chapter will not discuss them to the satisfaction of Welsh or Scots readers, but it can at least serve as a reminder to English ones that Britain is a multinational society, or a combination of different national societies. It will also deal briefly with mass migrations into and within Britain, but not with Ireland, from which the most massive of these migrations came. For while economically Scotland and Wales have long been part of Britain, Ireland has not. It was a colonial economy and remains a separate one.

Wales had been officially assimilated to England in 1536, but this had little effect on the relations of the two countries, which were tenuous, and on its importance in the English economy, which was negligible. Below the crust of English institutions and an English (or anglicized) class of landlords, the Welsh lived the life of a backward subsistence peasantry in a poor and largely

* Its political union with Britain from 1801 to 1922 no more makes it a part of the British economy than the union of Algeria with France made that country part of France. However, the omission of Ireland implies the omission of the six counties which have, since 1922, chosen to maintain their links with Britain. This is inevitable, if regrettable. The economic history of Ireland cannot be included in this book, and the economic history of Northern Ireland since 1922 cannot get extended treatment in it. However, a few words will be said about the Irish in Britain.

inaccessible country; officially conforming to whatever religion or government there was, because all were equally remote from their language and way of life. Union with England deprived them of what little they had in the way of an upper class, and produced the characteristic populism of Welsh society, in which incomes ranged merely from the poor to the very poor, and classes from the peasant and small shopkeeper to the labourer. In a sense this remained the pattern of Welsh economic development, and explains the unquenchable radicalism of its politics. Industrialization, or any other economic change, was something done to Welshmen rather than by Welshmen; and in so far as it was done by Welsh enterprise, the first step of the rising Cambrian businessman tended to be to assimilate to the only pattern of an upper class there was, namely the English. The Powells, barons of iron and coal, became anglicized as the Williams-Wynns on their estates had done before them. Industrialism merely meant that the Welsh added a few towns to what had previously been an entirely non-urban society,* and a large class of proletarians to a declining class of peasants and petty-bourgeois.

By 1750 the threads which tied the Welsh hills to the rest of Britain had begun to tighten and grow stronger; mainly because of the development of livestock for foreign sale (farmers tended to pay their rents with the proceeds), but also because of the modest exploitation of the mineral deposits which are the Principality's major source of wealth. From the British point of view these developments were not yet of great moment, except perhaps for copper and lead, but for Wales the change was noticeable. It brought about something like the birth of a self-conscious Welsh nation out of a traditional Welsh-speaking peasantry. Its most obvious symptom was the mass conversion of the Welsh to unofficial religions – various branches of protestant nonconformity, some of them, like the Calvinistic Methodism of North Wales, strikingly national in spirit, and a self-conscious interest in Welsh culture and antiquities. The decentralized, democratic nonconformity which became the

*Before the Industrial Revolution, Swansea, the largest city, had 10,000 inhabitants (1801); Cardiff 2,000.

religion of the majority of Welshmen after 1800 brought three extremely important consequences: a marked development of education, of Welsh literature, and the creation of a cadre of native social and political leadership into which the scattered elements of the Welsh petty-bourgeoisie could be absorbed – the preachers and ministers of religion. It also brought an alternative set of social ambitions to the economic. Thenceforth the characteristic hope of the young Welshman would not be to become rich, but to become educated and eloquent. Unlike the Scots, the Welsh provided the industrial English economy with few captains of industry and finance – and the most eminent of them, Robert Owen of Newtown (1771–1858) was a highly untypical capitalist – but with plenty of preachers, journalists and eventually teachers and officials. The Welsh labour movement eventually provided a comparable cadre of leadership from the industrial working class, and another significant human contribution to English society, but its main impact outside the Principality was not made until the twentieth century.

Into this poor, remote and backward region the Industrial Revolution erupted in the general form of a greater involvement in the national and international economy, and the specific form of heavy industry – iron, copper, and eventually above all coal. Curiously enough it impoverished, but did not disrupt, agrarian society. Wales remained overwhelmingly a country of small family farms, though one of peasant-tenants rather than peasant-owners. No large class of agricultural labourers emerged, those who existed were not that much poorer than the peasantry, and the peasants themselves as often as not went as seasonal migrant labour to the new industries or sought some other supplementary income. Such agrarian movements as existed – and notably the great 'Rebecca Riots' of 1843 – were general movements of all rural groups (under the leadership of small farmers) against an alien or alienated, and often absentee, class of landlords which adopted little of capitalist economy except the discovery that rents ought to be periodically raised. On the other hand, the infertile mountains saved Welsh agriculture from the major fluctuations of English farming. It could neither expand grain production much in times of a boom in cereal prices, nor had it to contract them in times of slump. Its characteristic mixed farming, with the emphasis on livestock and dairying, happened to be a fairly stable basis for the rural economy, and the 'great depressions' of nineteenth-century agriculture were therefore felt much less, and then mainly in the form of pressure upon rents. However, the Welsh suffered the equivalent and more constant pressure of the small peasant economy: poverty, over-population and land hunger, which was palliated but not removed by emigration. Central Wales began actually to lose population in the 1840s, and all rural Wales in the 1880s.

Agriculture, however, was ceasing to be the characteristic occupation of the Welsh. The development of the Principality was overshadowed by the growth of industry in the three counties of Carmarthen, Glamorgan, and Monmouth, and especially the last two. From 1801 to 1911 the population of Wales multiplied between three and four times (from rather under 600,000 to over two million), but almost the whole of this increase benefited the industrial counties, which, by the First World War, contained well over three quarters of the total population.* This vast influx of population rested not only upon migration within Wales and local demographic increase, but also largely upon the immigration of English and to a lesser extent Irish workers. One of the consequences of industrialization was the decline of the Welsh language. Welsh-speaking Wales increasingly became little more than a mountainous agricultural annexe to the industrial South; peasant and petty-bourgeois Wales to a giant proletarian (and above all coalmining) block. Nor did the systematic support for the Welsh language by means of the state educational system in the twentieth century halt this decline. Until the middle of the nineteenth century this was not so noticeable, and in the more slowly-growing industrial

---

*Population growth in Wales (in thousands)

	1801	1851	1911
Wales and Monmouth	577	1,163	2,027
Glamorgan and Monmouthshire	111	389	1,517

county of Carmarthen, the Welsh language retained some foot-hold. But in the second half of the nineteenth century, when the coal-fields entered on their period of headlong expansion, Wales was utterly transformed; or rather, divided into two culturally (but not linguistically) equally Welsh sectors, which had in-creasingly little in common with one another except the fact of not being English. Difficulties of communication between them – the point within easiest reach of all parts of Wales is the English town of Shrewsbury – made this division even more noticeable.

Wales had hardly any share in the characteristic industries of the first phase of industrialization, and especially textiles. Her importance lay entirely in the heavy industries, which did not fully come into their own until the second half of the nineteenth century: at first iron (and the less important lead and copper), later and above all, coal. Iron dominated the first part of the century, and for industrial Britain and the industrial world Wales meant primarily the great forges and foundries of Dowlais and Cyfartha, and their masters the (originally English) Crawshays and Guests. Coal, and with the rise of the steamship and British maritime supremacy, above all the exportable 'steam coal', utterly dominated the great Welsh boom of 1860–1914. The heavy industries with their fiery glow, their slagheaps, and winding gear, their long rows of bare slate-roofed cottages crawling in parallel rows up the sides of denuded valleys, produced the typical nightmare landscape in which most of the Welsh lived their lives between pit and chapel. Iron rose, fluctuated, and after the mid-century stagnated. Coal fluctuated, but its rise was so extraordinary as to obscure the fragility of a region based on a single product and a single occupation. Not until after the First World War did it reveal itself, and thereafter South Wales lay derelict for a generation, while those of its inhabitants who did not emigrate – and the three counties lost population absolutely after 1921 – waited and rotted between their slagheaps. The years after the Second World War brought a diversification of the local economy and prosperity, but no Welshman is ever likely to forget the years between the wars.

Isolated by geography, by culture, and in the valley villages which remained the characteristic location of industry there, Welsh life remained relatively untouched by the larger currents of Britain until the end of the nineteenth century, though linked to them through Liberalism and nonconformity. Even that national form of working-class life, association football, stopped short of the valleys, which preferred the alternative and more muscular pursuit of Rugby football. Welsh culture went its own way, increasingly formalized in the local and national *eisteddfodau* (festivals of competitive singing, poetry, and so forth) with their – largely invented – national rituals of pseudo-Druidism. Even the Welsh labour movement, essentially the miners' movement, had little contact with the rest of the nation, until the miners' strike of 1898. The national labour revival of 1889 began to bring Wales into Britain – partly through the nationalizing influence of the socialists who formed the core of its leaders. Between then and 1914 the two countries drew more closely together on the basis of the common militancy of their left wings, and of the growing importance of the anti-conservative fringe nationalities in the British Liberal Party after its split in 1886. The political rise and triumph of the Welsh solicitor Lloyd George symbolized one aspect of this convergence; the election of the socialist leader Keir Hardie for a Welsh constituency, the other.

The inter-war catastrophe continued this process, which was accelerated by the development of national mass media such as the press, radio and the cinema, and even more after the Second World War by the prosperity which brought standardized consumer goods and television. The collapse of Liberalism transferred the loyalty of the bulk of Welshmen to Labour (with a marked dash of the extreme left – revolutionary syndicalist and communist – which provided the militant leaders of the miners). Depression and education spread Welshmen throughout the country as never before: the Welsh teacher, civil servant, politician and trade unionist replaced the Welsh dairyman or nonconformist minister as the characteristic representative of his nation in England. Conversely, tourism and holidays brought Englishmen in hitherto unaccustomed quantities into the heart of Welsh Wales. What is more, after the Second World War the economic differences between England, a varied economy, and Wales, a mining annexe of it, diminished. Nor were these convergences offset by the increasing cultural and administrative autonomy of Wales, which Welsh political pressure brought in the twentieth century.

*

The case of Scotland, though in some respects comparable to Wales, is much more complex. It was united to England in 1707 as an established society with an entire class structure and system of its own, and a functioning state with an ancient history, and an entirely independent institutional framework – notably in law, local administration, education and religion – which it retained under the union. Unlike Wales, which developed a dualism through partial industrialization, it had always been a dual society, composed of the – speaking very roughly – feudal Lowlands and the tribal Highlands, which covered the greater part of its territory, though only a small part (in 1801 about one seventh) of its population. Moreover, unlike Wales, the Scots Lowlands were a separate and dynamic economy, though one which deliberately sought its opportunities – and found them – in closer association with the vast markets of England, and rapidly converged with the English economy, of which it was to form a particularly dynamic sector.

Compared with England, all Scotland was economically backward, and above all poor. In 1750 the prosperous Scotsman ate more simply, was housed worse, and possessed fewer household goods (except perhaps for the abundant home-produced linen) than Englishmen of more modest social standing, and rich Scotsmen – at least by southern standards – hardly existed outside the small ranks of the landed aristocracy, though trade and industry were soon to produce them. 'Dearth', the periodic food shortages and near-famines which scourged underdeveloped countries before the age of industrialization, had long disappeared from England. In the mid eighteenth century it remained a reality, or the most recent of memories even in the Lowlands. In economic terms, Scotland lacked capital, which meant that it had to devise a much more efficient means of mobilizing and distributing capital than England, not to mention a much more intense spirit of saving (which is still reflected in the familiar, and unjust, jokes about Scots avarice). In fact, the Scots banking system was superior to the British and the country pioneered the joint-stock bank and the popular investment trust. Again, the thinly populated country lacked labour, and constantly tended to lose some of what it had to the higher-paying outside world. Yet its poverty and backwardness ensured that this labour shortage (which was eventually remedied by a mass immigration relatively much greater than that into England, mainly from Ireland) did not produce unduly high wages. Scotland therefore retained the advantages of a low-cost producer. Thirdly, Scotland was too small and too poor to provide much of a domestic market. Its economic growth had to depend on the exploitation of the much greater English market, and even more on the world market to which it had access through its English connexion. Scots industry therefore developed essentially as a low-cost producer of export goods, and this gave it its unusual buoyancy in the nineteenth and early twentieth century: and, conversely, led to its collapse between the wars.

However, though all parts of eighteenth-century Scotland were poor, not all were economically progressing. The Highlands, and to a lesser extent the agrarian peninsula of Galloway in the extreme south-west, were moving into a state of permanent social and economic crisis, similar to that of Ireland, even to the parallel catastrophes of famine and mass emigration. In fact, in Scotland two polar opposites in social and economic life coexisted: a society which adopted and utilized industrial capitalism with unusual readiness and success, and one to which it was not merely disagreeable but incomprehensible. The foundation of Highland society was the tribe (clan) of subsistence peasants or pastoralists settled in an ancestral area under the chieftain of their kin, whom the old Scottish kingdom had (wrongly) attempted to assimilate to a feudal noble, and English eighteenth-century society (even more wrongly) to an aristocratic landowner. This assimilation gave the chiefs the legal – but by clan standards immoral – right to do what they wanted with their 'property', and entangled them in the expensive status-competition of British aristocratic life, for which they had neither the resources nor the financial sense. They could raise their income only by destroying their society. From the point of view of the clansmen the chief was not a landlord, but the head of their tribe to whom they owed loyalty in peace and war and who in turn owed them largesse and support. Conversely the social standing of the chief in Highland society depended not on the number of his acres of moorland and forest, but on that of the armed men he could raise. The chiefs were therefore in a double dilemma. As 'old' chiefs their interest lay in multiplying primitive subsistence peasants on increasingly congested territory; as 'new' noble landlords, in exploiting their estates by modern methods, which almost certainly meant either exchanging human tenants for livestock (which requires little labour), or the sale of their land, or both. In fact they did all these things successively, first multiplying an increasingly pauperized tenantry, and later forcing it into mass emigration.

Remoteness, isolation, and, until after the rebellion of 1745, the virtual autonomy of the Highlands and Islands kept the process under some control. The rapid industrialization of both England and the Lowlands faced this archaic economy with the brutal choice between modernization and ruin. It chose ruin. A very few of its chiefs, notably the Campbells, Dukes of Argyll, whose family policy had long been one of systematic alliance with the progressive Lowlands, attempted to combine modernization with some concern for clan society. Most of them merely raised their incomes as best they could, exchanging the barbarous simplicities of their hills for the more sophisticated and expensive pleasures of the urban aristocratic life. In 1774 Breadalbane rented at £4,900, in 1815 at £23,000. As usual, the boom years of the late eighteenth century and the Napoleonic Wars postponed the catastrophe. During this period the remoter coasts and islands also found a short-lived economic resource in the manufacture of kelp (an alkaline ash) from seaweed, for which there was an industrial demand. After the wars the times of horror began. Greedy or bankrupt landlords began to 'clear' their uncomprehendingly loyal tribesmen from the land, scattering them as emigrants throughout the world from the slums of Glasgow to the forests of Canada. Sheep drove men from the hills, and crowded a growing population, increasingly dependent on potatoes for their subsistence, further into pauperized congestion. The failure of the potato crop in the middle forties produced a miniature version of the Irish tragedy of the same period: famine and a mass emigration which led to progressive, and until the present unbroken, depopulation. The Highlands became what they have ever since remained, a beautiful desert. In 1960 an area rather larger than the Netherlands was inhabited by a population about the same as that of the city of Portsmouth.

The Lowlands not merely adapted themselves to economic development, they welcomed it and led it. In the mid eighteenth century the first 'improving' Scots lairds began to import English agricultural experts, tools and know-how to improve Scots farming. By the beginning of the nineteenth century progressive agriculture was almost a Scots speciality. Northern writers (and they monopolized the literature of agricultural improvement) blamed the English for their slowness in mechanization, and Jane Austen's southern landowners debated whether it would be wise to hire one of the well-known and briskly efficient Scots farm-managers. Scots economists, ever since the great Adam Smith (1723–90), dominated the most characteristic science of the era of industrialization. Scots philosophers were the target of the English populist Radical's abuse and the English conservative's irony. Scotsmen played a disproportionately large part in the history of invention and technical innovation: James Watt of the steam-engine, Mushet and Neilson in the iron industry, Telford and Loudon Macadam in transport, Nasmyth and Fairbairn in engineering. The higher levels of English business and government were not to be filled with the proverbially successful Scotsmen until the late nineteenth and twentieth centuries, but overseas enterprise, material and spiritual, was already a very Caledonian affair before 1850: Jardine Matheson pioneered and dominated the Far Eastern trade, Moffatt and Livingstone the missions to darkest Africa.

How much of this extraordinary readiness of the Lowland

Scots for industrial society was due to their Calvinism, or perhaps more exactly to the democratic and almost universal educational system it created, is a complex question. It is part of the even larger and perennially fascinating and important problem of the relations between Protestantism and capitalism, or more generally between ideology and economy, which have been much discussed since Karl Marx and Max Weber. We cannot plunge into it here, but it must be difficult to deny that the remarkable record of Scotsmen in the nineteenth century– which was by no means confined to success as businessmen or technologists – had some connexion with the institutional system the country had acquired in the Revolution of 1559, which was made under the banner of Calvin and John Knox. It had clearly *not* been a 'middle-class revolution', however that may be defined, and what was to become the Scots entrepreneurial and middle class in the eighteenth and nineteenth centuries tended to soften its theological zeal considerably, leaving the undiluted liquor of Geneva to be drunk in the more backward regions and by the less propertied strata. Moreover, the rise of a social hierarchy independent of the old landlords and lairds undoubtedly had something to do with the Great Disruption of the Kirk in 1843; very few landlords joined the new Free Church, whose links (at least in the Lowlands) were with a Liberalism which was acutely critical of the landed gentry. Furthermore, the characteristic ideology of industrial capitalism (and also of those of its critics who accepted industrialism)* was the deist or agnostic rationalism which the world imbibed from the great Edinburgh and Glasgow professors of the eighteenth-century 'Scottish Renaissance': David Hume, Adam Smith, Ferguson, Kames and Millar.

However, Scotland certainly derived three things from its Calvinist revolution, which were of undoubted value in the industrial society. The first was its remarkably democratic educational system, which allowed the country to draw on a very wide reservoir of ability, which opened the road to talent far wider than England, and (aided perhaps by the intellectualism

---

*Professor J. Harrison has shown that Robert Owen's thinking owed much to the Scots philosophy he absorbed during his period at New Lanark.

of Calvinist disputation) emphasized systematic thinking. The shepherd boy who became a great engineer (Thomas Telford, 1757–1834), though not as common even in Scotland as the myth has it, was less uncommon than in England. The second was the absence of an English Poor Law; for until 1845 the relief of the poor remained (via the Kirk) in the hands of the organized local community, and it may be argued that this contributed to preserving rural and small-town Scotland – eighty-seven per cent of the population in 1801 and eighty per cent even in the 1830s* – from the demoralization of so much of England. With the growth of cities and industry this system broke down, and the Scots working class was not merely (as it had always been) much poorer than the English, but also, in the vast stony tenements of its towns, filthily and shockingly poor. Thirdly, it is possible that the Calvinist ideal of perfection through labour contributed to that remarkable technical competence of the Lowland Scots which was to make Clydeside the great centre of shipbuilding and to fill the steamers of the world with Scots engineers. For Scotland is certainly one of the rare backward economies which caught up with the advanced ones not merely in industry, but in widely diffused and top-quality industrial *skills*.

How much of these effects were due to Calvinism, how much to the backwardness of Scots society which saved it from some of the inequalities and inefficiencies of more advanced ones, how much to a combination of both, must remain unanswerable. But the results are not in dispute. Few if any areas of the world have contributed proportionately more to industrialism than Scotland.

*

A poor but developing country acquiring economic impetus through the foreign markets opened to it by union with England and exploiting its advantages: such, in brief, is the economic history of modern Scotland. It gave the Scots economy dynamism, but also great instability; except in agriculture. Here the poverty of the soil and the rawness of the climate prevented

* Namely the Scots who did not live in Glasgow, Edinburgh, Dundee and Aberdeen.

the Scots farmer from the excesses of specialization on grain crops to which the English farmer periodically fell victim, as after the Napoleonic Wars and after the 1870s. Mixed farming with some emphasis on livestock was almost everywhere his best policy, and he therefore benefited virtually without interruption from the rocketing demands of the English cities for food, which the railways enabled them to supply. Indeed, during periods of English agricultural depression, as after 1873 and between the wars, Scotsmen tended to come south to take over, and make pay, English farms which the natives had abandoned.

Scots industry and trade, on the other hand, followed a more dangerous course. Its history is that of successive concentration on particular products or markets, successive bouts of glory followed by collapse, which the country surmounted only because, until after the First World War, some new and wider field always appeared ready for conquest by Scots. The tobacco trade, which made the fortunes of eighteenth-century Glasgow, was the first of these boom activities. It collapsed with the American War of Independence and, though it revived sometime later, never again occupied its old importance in the Scots economy. Cotton – the pioneer of industrialization as in England – came next. It developed round Glasgow, the great centre of the export and re-export trade and Scotland's commercial link with the wider world, and on the foundation of the skills and experience of the linen industry, the country's basic textile. Highly concentrated on fine quality goods, it could not, after the Napoleonic Wars, sustain the competition of cheaper goods in the overseas markets of South America which Britain had hitherto monopolized, and unlike Lancashire, it was in no position to expand the exports of coarser goods to the newly opened markets of the East. The industry stagnated and eventually almost disappeared.

Fortunately from the 1830s and 1840s the country discovered an alternative base for its industries: iron and coal. (The two were closely linked, for the Scots coal industry depended on the heavily coal-using iron producers.) In 1830 Scotland had accounted for five per cent of British iron output, but by 1855 for a quarter. This industry also grew up overwhelmingly on exports, about two thirds of its output being loaded on ships. Indeed, between 1848 and 1854 ninety per cent of the pig-iron exported from Great Britain came from Scotland. (Thereafter the North of England began to compete.) It is true that what the Scots (and the British) were doing in those golden mid-Victorian years was largely to build the future industrial potential of Britain's foreign competitors, but when the Scots iron industry went into a relative decline in consequence, yet another new field of expansion opened: shipbuilding and the related industries of steelmaking and marine engineering. From 1870 to the end of prosperity after the First World War these were the main foundations of the Scots economy. In the record year of 1913 almost a million tons of shipping were built in the United Kingdom: 756,976 tons were launched on the Clyde.

The point has been made that, while these developments opened up plenty of opportunities for Scotsmen (and there were times when morose English observers saw the British Empire largely as a system of providing employment and profits for their northern neighbours), it did not do much for Scotland. This is true. Scots wage rates remained on the whole much below the English level throughout the nineteenth century. The mid-Victorian growth industries had a tradition of harshness and compulsion (until 1799 Scots miners were actually serfs), and recruited their labour consequently from the unorganized and helpless, and especially from Irish and Highland immigrants used neither to a decent income nor to urban and industrial life. Scots housing was and remains not only scandalously bad, but notably worse than English housing. Moreover, the squalor and dirt which came with industrial expansion, which was merely awful in the semi-rural mining settlements, became dangerous in the slightly superior but nevertheless appalling prison-cells of the vast and sombre tenement blocks which grew up in the raw smoky fog of Glasgow, where more than one out of every five Scotsmen lived by 1914. The traditional institutions of pre-industrial Scotland such as the educational system lost their effectiveness in the industrial society. They broke down in the 1840s, which saw the end of the old Scots poor-relief system and the Disruption of the Kirk. As in England, eventually they were replaced by the home-made and informal institutions of working-class life (of which the Scots passion for, and success at, football, is a symptom),* and the formal institutions of mass parties and movements, and the welfare arrangements of the state. But in the years from the 1830s to the 1880s there was little to fill the lives of Scotsmen except work and drink. Even labour organization remained notably feebler and less stable than in England. If the mid-Victorian years were a gloomy age in the social life of the English poor, they were a black one in Scotland.

With the end of the century the Scots, buttressed this time by basic industries which were essentially skilled, recovered their identity. For the first time the Scots labour movement not only took a serious hold on its working class, but established a sort of hegemony over the English. Keir Hardie became the leader of British socialism (and his Independent Labour Party had its firmest base on the Clyde), James Ramsay MacDonald became the first Labour Prime Minister† of this country, and Clydeside became, during the First World War, the synonym for revolutionary agitation, and helped to give the post-1918 Labour Party a slant to the left and the Communist Party a solid core of leaders. The collapse of Scots industry between the wars halted this development, and turned a derelict country in upon itself. This is perhaps most visible in the fringe phenomena of a Scottish nationalist culture, which sought to create a literature in the artificially archaic idiom of 'Lallans', inaccessible to most outsiders, and indeed to most Scotsmen. The inter-war slump was indeed a traumatic experience for the

---

*The function of football teams was to organize the (male) working-class community, normally round two permanently rival, local poles: most industrial cities developed *two* leading and competing teams. In Scotland (as in Liverpool) this took the special form of teams associated specifically with the Irish (Catholic) immigrants and the native Scots (Protestants): Glasgow Celtic and Rangers, Edinburgh Hibernians and Hearts of Midlothian.

†From the 1890s on Scots noblemen and gentlemen also broke the monopoly of English Prime Ministers, and even a Glasgow iron merchant, Bonar Law, became Prime Minister of Britain in 1922, helped by the activities of the expatriate Scot Max Aitken, Lord Beaverbrook.

country. For the first time since the eighteenth century it ceased to be the cutting edge of a world industrial economy. The excitement of dynamic expansion had obscured the absence of independence, and, more important, the erosion and collapse of its native institutions, and notably of its educational system and religion. Once again Scotland searched for itself; and in spite of the post-1945 revival (though this was less marked than in Wales) the doubts and uncertainties continued.

As will be clear by now, neither Wales nor Scotland, though undoubtedly nations with strong though complex national feelings, had by the 1960s developed political nationalism of the type familiar in most of the twentieth-century world. They had rather tended to express their national separateness and aspirations through the radical and labour movements and parties of the United Kingdom, whose character was certainly affected and partly transformed by them. The independent nationalist parties which developed in both countries during the inter-war depression remained marginal to their politics. However, from the middle 1960s disillusion with the Labour governments of that decade led for the first time to a massive migration of voters from Labour to Scottish and Welsh nationalism. Whether or not this was to prove permanent, the historic significance of this development is not open to much doubt.

*

Finally, the Irish in Britain. Expelled by poverty and famine from their island, the Irish flocked into a Britain by which they had been conquered, and to which they had been united in 1801 against their wishes, not because they liked it, but because it was the nearest place to go that was not Ireland. They came first as seasonal harvest labourers, as waterside workers in port towns, as the miscellaneous poor. They came later for any job that was going, and, since they had no skills which had much bearing on industrial or urban life except perhaps digging, for such jobs as required strong backs and the willingness and ability to work themselves to the limit for intermittent packets of effort. There were many such, for industrial society needs not only routine regularities of labour, but also impetuous and dashing labour.

They became the dockers and coal-heavers, the navvies and construction gangs, the iron and steelworkers, the miners, and when the English and Scots did not want the jobs, or could no longer live on the wage, those who did the unwanted work – the handloom weavers or unskilled labourers. They became, more than any other people, the soldiers of the Queen (for it is a characteristic of empires that they turn their victims into their defenders), while their sisters became the servants, nurses and prostitutes of the big cities. Their wages were lower than anyone else's, they lived in the worst slums, and the English and Scots despised them as semi-barbarians, distrusted them as Catholics and hated them as undercutters of their wages.

Apart from their language (if they happened no longer to be Irish-speaking), they brought nothing with them which would have enabled them to make more sense of nineteenth-century England or Scotland than of China. They came as members of a pauperized, degraded peasantry whose own native society had been crushed by some centuries of English oppression into fragments of old custom, mutual aid and kinship solidarity, held together by a generically Irish 'way of life' (wakes, songs, and so on), by a hatred of England and by a Catholic priesthood of peasants' sons and brothers. In the last third of the nineteenth century they also acquired additional cohesion through the rise of a national independence movement. The Scotland division of Liverpool – a city in which twenty-five per cent of the population in 1851 had been born in Ireland – actually elected an Irish nationalist MP for many years, though most of the immigrants voted for the Liberals as the party of Irish Home Rule and, after it was won, for Labour as the party of the class to which they almost all belonged.

Partly because they brought with them the habits of a peasantry on the verge of starvation and discouraged by the Irish landlord system from savings or investment, partly because they entered the occupations which least called for industrial routines, they were remarkably slow to adapt themselves to industrial society, though their appearance, knowledge of English and – after the initial period – their adoption of normal urban working-class clothing made them a great deal less 'visible' as strangers than later groups of immigrants such as the Jews, Cypriots, West Indians or Asians. They initially lived in Liverpool slums as in Munster cabins, and even generations later continued to provide a large part of the inhabitants of those decaying and socially disorganized quarters which so often develop on the periphery of the core of great cities. To the English and Scots, and especially their middle class, they were merely dirty and feckless, undesirable semi-aliens subject to some discrimination. Yet their contribution to nineteenth-century Britain was capital. They provided industry with its mobile vanguard, especially building and construction into which they have always flocked, and the heavy industries which needed their muscle, their dash and their readiness to work in huge spurts. They provided the British working class with a cutting edge of radicals and revolutionaries, with a body of men and women uncommitted by either tradition or economic success to society as it existed around them. It is no accident that an Irishman, Feargus O'Connor, was the nearest thing to a national leader of Chartism, and another, Bronterre O'Brien, its chief ideologist, that an Irishman wrote 'The Red Flag', the anthem of the British labour movement, and the best British working-class novel, *The Ragged-Trousered Philanthropists*.

Irish immigration reached its peak in the decades after the Great Famine of 1847, and thereafter declined, though the extent of the Irish minority is perhaps more accurately measured by the size of the Roman Catholic population in Britain – in Scotland it is still fifteen per cent – than by the census records of the Irish-born. However, with the ending of mass migration into the USA the movement into Britain revived, and in the past thirty years it has become by far the greatest receptacle for the Irish emigrant. In 1961 there were probably one million persons of Irish birth in Britain, the equivalent of twenty-five per cent of the population of Ireland or of one third of the population of the Irish Republic.* The flow has gone less to the traditional centres of Irish immigration, Clydeside and Mersey-side, and increasingly to the flourishing areas of middle and

* Two sevenths of the immigrants in 1951 came from Northern Ireland, which still forms part of the United Kingdom.

southern England and London. Building continues to employ most of them – almost one fifth – followed by the metal industries (thirteen per cent). Domestic service and similar occupations (nursing) occupy the bulk of the women. However, the relative backwardness of the Irish economy has increasingly also produced an emigration of professional people attracted by the greater opportunities of Britain. Twelve per cent of all British doctors are of Irish origin.

To say that this immigration has been assimilated would be misleading. However, it has increasingly become accepted, because invisible – at any rate compared to the much more obviously recognizable new migrants of the 1950s. The political separation of Ireland from Britain in 1921 had also eliminated one major reason why Englishmen and Scotsmen should be aware of Ireland and the Irish. Little by little the tensions between the communities have become less. When in 1964 the Labour Party recorded its largest national gain in and around Liverpool, one reason was that large numbers of non-Irish and non-Catholic workers in that city had at last become ready to vote for a party which had in the past been largely identified with the local Irish community.

NOTE

1. See the relevant works in Further Reading 3 and 4 and John Jackson, *The Irish in Britain* (1961), and on coloured immigration R. Glass, *Newcomers* (1960). A. H. Dodd, *The Industrial Revolution in North Wales* (1953), A. H. John, *The Industrial Development of South Wales* (1950), are useful special studies. Cecil Woodham Smith, *The Great Hunger* (1962), is essential background reading about the Irish in Britain and anywhere else.

CONCLUSION

A HISTORY which goes up to the present, or as near to it as makes no matter, cannot conclude, for the date when it finishes need represent nothing but the date when its writer completed his manuscript. Possibly it represents more, though in economic and social history important turning-points are not so easily dated as in, say, the history of politics or military operations. But even if we suppose that the early 1960s will be recognized in future as the end of a phase in British development, it may be too early to recognize this now, or if we recognize it, to assess the nature of the turning-point. It is indeed possible that we are drawing to the close of an era, or are at the beginning of another. For the past century and a half – some would say for much longer – economic life in the 'advanced' parts of the world has tended to follow a curious, half-century-long rhythm, which is best known as the 'Kondratiev Long Waves'. Their significance is a subject of debate and speculation; though, of late, not of very intensive debate. They appear to manifest themselves most obviously as an alternation of roughly twenty-five years of inflation and an atmosphere of business confidence, followed by a similar period of price fluctuation or deflation and an atmosphere of business malaise and social tension. Readers of this book may have noted this alteration in passing; the 'upswing' from the 1780s to the end of the Napoleonic Wars, followed by the troubles of the period from then to the 1840s; the upswing of the 'golden years' of the Victorians, followed by the 'Great Depression' of 1873–96;* the upswing of the Edwardian 'Indian summer' and the First World War, followed by the inter-war depression. Since, say, 1940, we have been very obviously in an upswing. If there are Kondratiev periodicities, whatever their nature, we might very well expect this era to end very soon, and

---

*For various reasons this phase of the 'long waves' has attracted more discussion among economic historians than any other.

the 1970s to have different and probably less pleasing characteristics. But we do not know yet.

It is of course easy to recognize the general shape of British economic history during the period with which this book has dealt. The history of the world from the late fifteenth to the mid twentieth century is that of the political and economic rise and decline of its domination by one or other of a group of economies based in Western Europe or on European settlers. At present the decline in this political and military dominance is more dramatically evident than that in its economic power, for the vast bulk of world industrial output is still to be found in the combined area of Western Europe, and the USA. Nevertheless, the emergence as major industrial powers of Japan, the USSR and perhaps soon China demonstrates that even in this respect the change has been fundamental. Within this general development, the history of Britain is that of the first phase of world industrialization – the Industrial Revolution, the construction of a single liberal world economy, and the final penetration and conquest of the undeveloped or non-capitalist world by capitalism. Its triumph was the triumph of the pioneer of this phase of history, its decline the decline of an entire world economic system.

If this were all, then we ought not perhaps to speak of Britain's decline, for part of it would be simply the reflection of a general and global change, and part the mere – almost tautologous – assertion that in a fully industrialized world the share of what was once the unique pioneer industrial economy must decline. If we nevertheless speak of such a British decline, it is because of the comparative inability of this country to adapt itself to such a situation. Ideally it might well have settled down as a flourishing economy of the second class – smaller than the super-powers of the twentieth century, but nevertheless (together with such countries as Western Germany, France or Japan) immensely more powerful economically than the third-rank states (for example the Scandinavians or the Swiss). Such adaptations are not impossible. France, for instance, which showed many signs of an analogous inadaptability in the nineteenth century, appeared to turn over a new leaf with remarkable success after the Second World War, and Germany showed a striking capacity for not only surviving, but turning to excellent account, the political and economic catastrophes of the present century.

At the time of writing Britain did not yet seem to have adapted itself with equal success. The nostalgia for its past – for the kind of world in which London was the commercial and financial centre of the world and the sun never set upon the British Empire, the kind of world in which sterling was even more obviously king than Edward or George – had not yet been overcome. Until it had, Britain must still be analysed in terms of decline, and in at least one aspect of British behaviour this was still patent: migration. For the current of migration nowadays normally tends to run from the backward to the advanced, from the static to the dynamic, and until the early 1960s British emigration – generally of the more skilled, the technicians and professionals, seeking for better opportunities than they believed available at home – still outweighed, on balance, the immigration of skilled and unskilled labour and technicians from under-developed countries, mainly in the former Empire. This emigration showed no sign of slackening, though the inflow was rapidly overhauling it until political restrictions were imposed upon it.

It is possible that the historians of the future, with the wisdom of hindsight, will nevertheless discover that the decisive steps towards this adaptation were already being taken, or had been taken. We, who have not the advantage of hindsight, cannot be sure.

In these circumstances the historian can only conclude by a few brief comparisons, abstaining from predictions. Britain in the early 1960s was a country of some fifty-three million inhabitants, or of the same order of magnitude as France (forty-eight million), West Germany (fifty-five million) and Italy (some fifty million), and of about half the population of Japan (ninety-six million), a quarter of that of the USA and the USSR, to mention only unquestioned industrial powers. Its share of world industrial production in 1961 was much below that of the USA and USSR, but still about as large as that of Western Germany and considerably larger than France, Italy and Japan, its share of world trade (roughly eight per cent of exports, nine per cent of imports in 1960) rather more than half what it had been in 1913, but it was no longer the greatest exporter, even in Europe. In 1963 it produced less cotton yarn than six other countries, less iron than five others, less steel than four others, less cement than seven others, less sulphuric acid than four others, but more electricity and coal than any other purely European state. In 1960 it was the third largest producer of motor-vehicles, the fifth largest of radio and television sets, and still the second largest shipbuilder and the possessor of the second largest merchant fleet. In other words, Britain was probably still just the third largest industrial economy, but a long way behind the two world leaders, and not itself a leader in any significant branch of production.

In terms of the actual human use of its wealth and productive power, the British people enjoyed the advantages of the most advanced economies: better health, a higher standard of living and better education. Few peoples were better fed or housed.* Britons did not own more durable consumer goods per head than other comparable countries in Europe, but they certainly belonged to that small and favoured number of peoples most of whom were well above the level of necessity and in the sphere of enjoyment. 'Poverty' existed, but it did not mean what it still meant over most of the world, namely hunger and rags. Thanks to a system of social security (different in detail from, but analogous to, those by now adopted very widely in Europe), Britain no longer even contained those patches of old-fashioned squalor and near-destitution which still so obviously disfigured the much wealthier USA. On the other hand the rise in the British standard of life after the Second World War was probably less rapid and less striking than in several other socialist and non-socialist European countries.† The number of cars in Britain

---

*That is over 3,000 calories per day per person, a level achieved – in 1960–1 – in only Austria, Denmark, Finland, Ireland, the Netherlands, Canada, the USA, Australia and New Zealand. The average British dwelling had more rooms than any other in Europe except in Switzerland and Luxemburg.

†The median rate at which real wages increased in twenty countries between 1950 and 1960 in manufacturing industry was 2·7 per cent per

multiplied about three times over between 1950 and 1960, but in Sweden it increased over six times, in France and the Netherlands about five times, in West Germany, Italy and Austria about ten times. In other words, Britain's progress was not impressive, even when judged against several countries which also ended the Second World War with a relatively high standard of living.

Such comparisons fail to bring out the peculiarities of a country, and Britain had several. It remained, for instance, much the most urbanized, industrialized and 'proletarianized' state in Europe.* The absence of a peasantry and a large class of small shopkeepers or artisans was perhaps the most lasting social heritage of Britain's early start and ruthless plunge into industrial capitalism. Its relatively simple two-class system, and the unusually important role of the industrial working class in politics, was another. Of all the major industrial states in nonsocialist Europe, Britain in the 1950s was the only one in which an old-fashioned proletarian socialist party (the Labour Party) stood a reasonable chance of winning a general election and forming a government *alone*, and in fact did so in 1964. Everywhere else (except in the special and untypical case of the three Scandinavian states) socialist working-class parties, either singly or, where strong Communist parties existed, in combination, seemed doomed to almost permanent opposition as minorities or to equally permanent coalition. A third peculiarity inherited to

---

annum. In Britain it was just about average, in Czechoslovakia, West Germany, France, Japan, the Netherlands, Poland, Sweden and Bulgaria it was over four per cent.

*Labour force by employment status and in agriculture (per cent) 1960

	In agriculture, forestry, fishing	Paid employees	Employers and self-employed	Unpaid family workers
Non-socialist Europe	20·9	75·3	16·4	8·3
France	20·0	72·8	18·7	8·5
West Germany	14·2	77·4	12·6	10·0
Italy	35·2	64·5	23·2	12·3
Belgium	7·4	78·1	17·0	4·9
Sweden	13·7	83·9	13·3	2·8
Britain	4·3	92·8	7·0	0·2

some extent from Britain's early industrial start, though also from its political past, was the comparative unimportance of regionalism. On the continent federalism, or pressure in favour of it, were common; regional parties and pressure-groups influential. The travelling Englishman could go all the way from Ostend to Sicily without ever leaving countries in which this was so. Yet in Britain not even the existence of the Welsh and the Scots posed a significant problem of the kind, for as we have seen both had been – with marginal exceptions – economically so integrated into a single all-British economy as to deprive such demands of mass support, though not always of mass sympathy. Britain was a country in which the middle classes had learned to speak a single, readily identifiable idiom and (with the exception of Scotland) no dialect; by no means a very common situation. It was a country in which a single national press circulated throughout the length of the country; in which (in spite of efforts to the contrary) cultural life was unusually concentrated in a single giant capital.

Nevertheless, these and other traditional differences tended to grow less. The mid-twentieth-century phase of Western industrial capitalism increasingly provided a pattern – perhaps above all a visual pattern – which absorbed national differences. From the airports in which men disembarked, uncertain, but for the language of the notice and the climate, in which continent they found themselves, to the car-filled motor-roads, the rapidly multiplying geometrical blocks of office buildings and public housing, the public lights and advertisements, the visual junk of modern civilization such as pylons, filling-stations or traffic signs, cities and the lines of communication between them grew rapidly more alike. Perhaps not more than they had done in the nineteenth century, for nothing was more standardized than the nineteenth-century industrial quarter, if it was not the late-nineteenth-century middle-class district. Nevertheless, by 1960 the standardized parts of Britain, and of other countries, covered a much larger area, or at all events a much larger part of the population, than ever before. This rapid process of assimilation became particularly visible in Britain in the later 1950s, when a vast wave of building and rebuilding transformed cities, sometimes out of all recognition. Communication, and especially mass travel, and, what is not quite the same, the mass willingness to travel, further blurred the edges between formerly distinct countries. One of the curious phenomena of Britain after 1945 was that, as it ceased to be the ruler of a vast multi-national empire, it became far more visibly, and actually, cosmopolitan than ever before, both because immigration now came from a variety of countries, mainly within the former Empire, and because for the first time there was mass tourism.

Britain was becoming more like other Western industrial countries, but at the same time its position among them, its impact on the world, was visibly diminishing. If we ask ourselves what impact the British economy and British society have made on the world outside, independent of the political power of Britain to shape the institutions of its colonies, we observe a curious change. The pioneer of industrialization gave the world, its machines, its ships, perhaps above all its railways – the Russians still call every station a 'Vauxhall' – its entrepreneurs and skilled technicians. The trader and banker of the world gave it mechanisms and institutions, such as Lloyds of London, which are familiar to every businessman. The greatest exporter and importer of the world gave to its dependent economies – which does not mean only its formal colonies – a miscellaneous legacy of material and commercial artefacts, so that the observer can tell, from the shape of mail-boxes or the names of Harrods or Mappin and Webb in Oporto or Buenos Aires, that the British influence once extended here, even without the Union Jack. British industry gave the world that most powerful cultural export, association football, the names of whose clubs still sometimes echo the names of the expatriate British works teams which pioneered it, far from Bolton or Leeds. And the power of industrial Britain, reinforcing the earlier power of commercial and aristocratic Britain, gave the world what has hitherto been its most lasting pattern of life for the masculine nobility: sport (whose international vocabulary is still largely English), and in particular horse-racing and 'Jockey Clubs', the basic style of formal and semi-formal male clothing, and the reputation of the expensive specialist craftsmen in London's West End who produced such articles.

Yet all this essentially belongs to the period before 1914, or even earlier. It was Britain as seen in the era of – and through the eyes of – Jules Verne, which impressed its image on the world, and it was the image of Phileas Fogg, not least in his capacity as an intrepid but adaptable tourist; for middle-class tourism and mountaineering – Thomas Cook and the Alpine Club – also reflected and radiated British influence. Little of this remains today. If anything, Britain is at the receiving end of the cultural and commercial interchange, in so far as it does not hold aloof from it. The most characteristic machines used by the non-expert are not British. The basic pattern of the mass-production motor car between the wars was American, supplemented since 1945 by the continental countries (except for the limited luxury and semi-luxury production of Rolls Royces and some sports models). The coffee machine, motor scooter and typewriter have been revitalized, like so many other pieces of contemporary everyday equipment, by post-war Italy; the radio and camera (once a German and US speciality), by the Japanese. The cinema, television and the arts of popular entertainment are still dominated, as they have been ever since the triumph of the mass market, by the USA,* and since 1945 even that late but powerful cultural export, the British detective story, has lost its hold, conquered by the American-patterned thriller. In more narrowly industrial terms, British industry has ceased to be superior to others, not merely in general, but in particular. With the possible – and temporary – exceptions of some electronic products and scientific instruments, there was in the 1950s no single British industry that was clearly superior to all its equivalents in the USA or on the continent of Europe.

Oddly enough, Britain's exceptionally proletarian character has resisted this retreat of the country's influence best. Few other countries ever tried to imitate the British political system, or its Conservative and Liberal parties, but with the decline of moderate social democracy in the world the British Labour

---

* Middle-class entertainment was dominated by the French and Austrian based operetta.

Party remained one of the rare and sometimes the only bastion of a reforming working-class movement with real claims to power, and its ideological influence therefore remained strong. The rebellious cultural works of the anti-conservative intellectuals of the 1950s, notably in the theatre, anticipated the world expansion of the deliberately plebeian and egalitarian popular music and clothing fashions of the early 1960s. But until then there was little else – and that also mainly in the field of intellectual and cultural achievement – to set against the general recession of British influence.

Britain in the early 1960s was a much more comfortable country to live in than ever before, a much more entertaining country, but also, from the historian's point of view, a much less important country. Contrary to the analysts, sometimes rather hysterical, who investigated the nature and crisis of Britain in these years, creating an unprecedented fashion for introspection and self-doubt, it was not a paralysed or sinking wreck. Its resources, both human and technical, and its potentialities were great. Only it was by no means certain how they could be utilized or realized effectively. Still, at a time when most people were better off than before, one might have expected them to be, perhaps regrettably, content. They were not. They were uneasy. Perhaps they were uneasy about the distance between reality and hope. Man does not live by gas central heating alone, even though the assumption of the advertisers, the most effective mass ideologists since the decline of the churches, seemed to be that he should. Hope and pride had grown dim. 'Few', writes A. J. P. Taylor, 'now sang "Land of Hope and Glory". Few even sang "England Arise".' And yet, if there was not much scope left for the first of these songs, there was still plenty left for the second.

DIAGRAMS

WRITERS in the field of economic and social history are torn between the rival demands of prose and numbers. It is not easy to include a sufficient selection of quantitative data in a text without making it unreadable. I have therefore added a number of diagrams in the form of an appendix. Some of these present information covering the entire period of this book, and which could not be readily fitted into any of the chronologically limited chapters, or which would not make their point adequately if divided between different chapters. Others illustrate particular points in greater detail than is possible in the text. Yet others present material which is undoubtedly relevant to the economic or social history of Britain in the period since 1750, but would have diverted the line of exposition and argument I have chosen. The notes at the end of each chapter draw attention to the diagrams which may be usefully consulted in conjunction with it. These diagrams are intended as visual aids. They cannot replace the statistical sources on which they are based, some of which are mentioned in the note on further reading (p. 364).

LIST OF DIAGRAMS

Diagrams

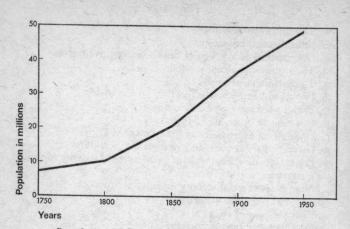

I. Population of Great Britain, 1750–1951 (in millions)

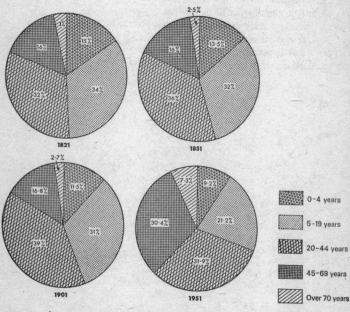

0-4 years

5-19 years

20-44 years

45-69 years

Over 70 years

2. Age-composition of the British population at various dates

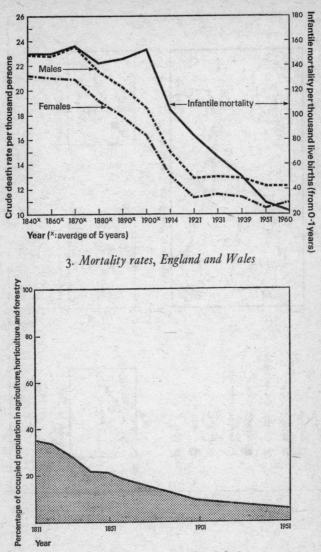

3. *Mortality rates, England and Wales*

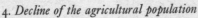

4. *Decline of the agricultural population*

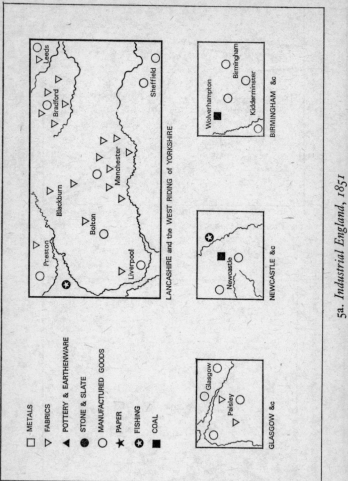

METALS □

FABRICS ▽

POTTERY & EARTHENWARE ▲

STONE & SLATE ⬤

MANUFACTURED GOODS ○

PAPER ★

FISHING ✪

COAL ■

LANCASHIRE and the WEST RIDING of YORKSHIRE

Leeds
Bradford
Preston
Blackburn
Bolton
Manchester
Liverpool
Sheffield

BIRMINGHAM &c

Wolverhampton
Birmingham
Kidderminster

NEWCASTLE &c

Newcastle

GLASGOW &c

Glasgow
Paisley

5a. *Industrial England, 1851*

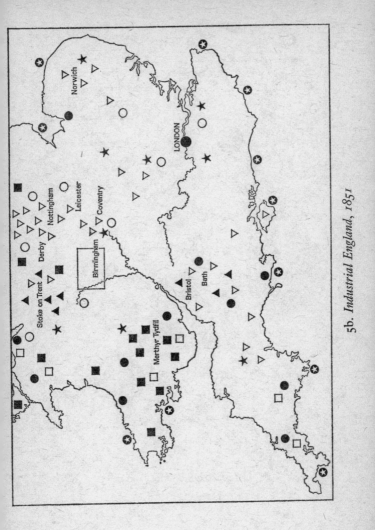

5b. Industrial England, 1851

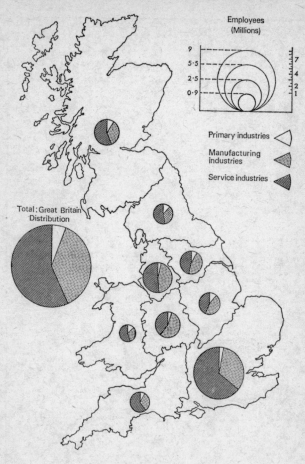

Employees
(Millions)

Primary industries

Manufacturing
industries

Service industries

Total: Great Britain
Distribution

6. *Industrial Britain, 1963*

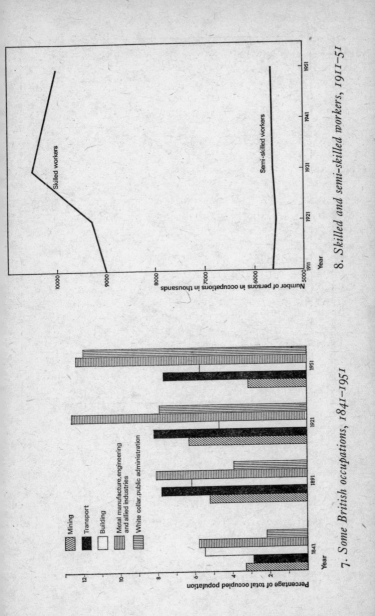

8. *Skilled and semi-skilled workers, 1911–51*

7. *Some British occupations, 1841–1951*

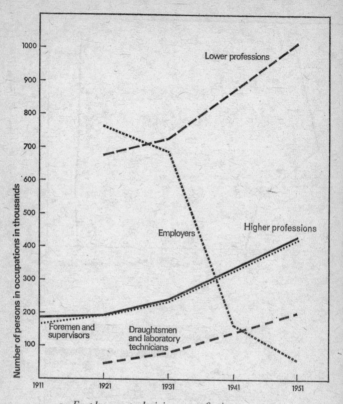

9. *Employers, technicians, professions, 1911–51*

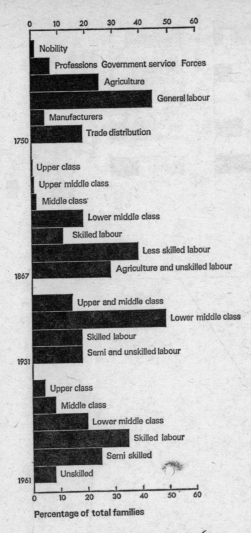

10. *Class structure, 1750–1961.*
(Sources: *1750, Joseph Massie; 1867, Dudley Baxter;*
1931, 1961, D. C. Marsh)

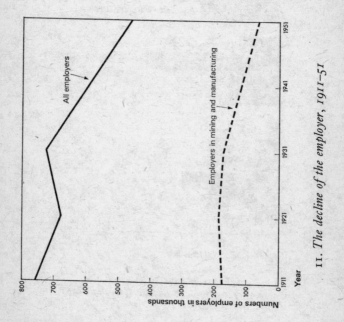

11. *The decline of the employer, 1911–51*

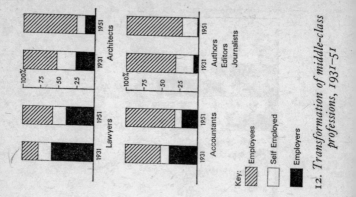

12. *Transformation of middle-class professions, 1931–51*

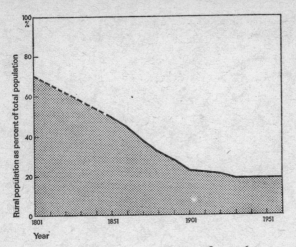

13. *Urban and rural population, 1801–1961*

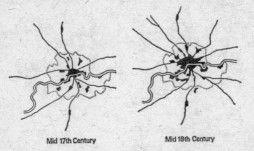

Mid 17th Century

Mid 18th Century

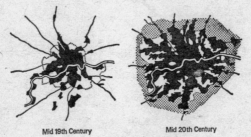

Mid 19th Century

Mid 20th Century

14. *Growth of London*

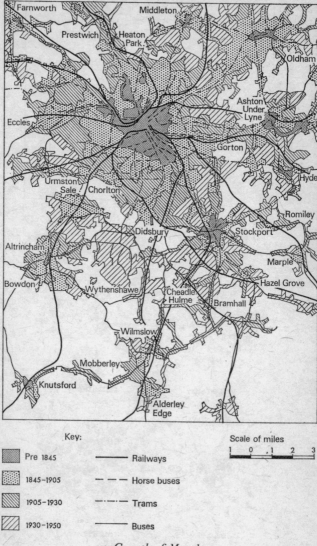

Key:

▨ Pre 1845	—— Railways
⬚ 1845–1905	– – – Horse buses
▧ 1905–1930	–·–·– Trams
▨ 1930–1950	—— Buses

Scale of miles
1 0 1 2 3

15. *Growth of Manchester*

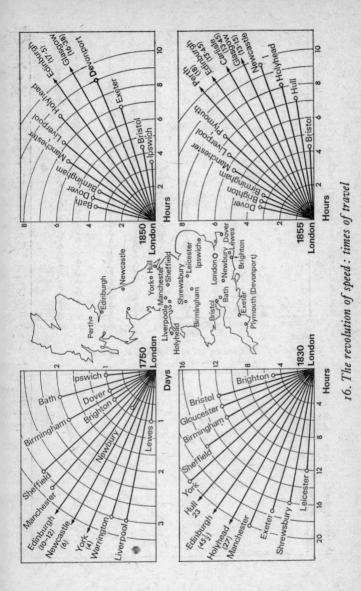

16. *The revolution of speed: times of travel*

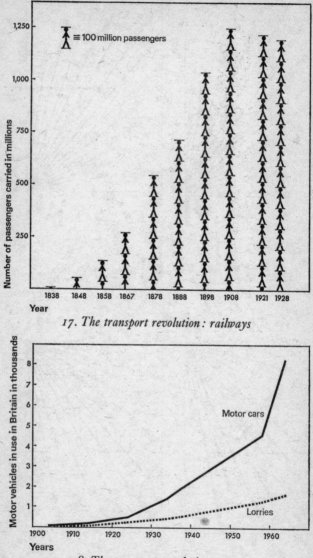

17. *The transport revolution: railways*

18. *The transport revolution: cars*

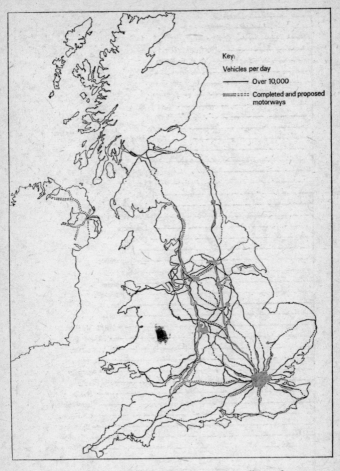

19. The transport revolution: road traffic, 1960

Percent of men signing marriage register with mark

20. *Communication: illiteracy in England, 1840*

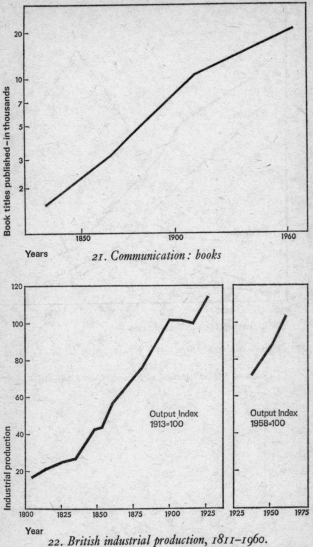

21. *Communication: books*

22. *British industrial production, 1811–1960.*
(Sources: *1811–1937, W. Hoffmann; 1938–60,
London and Cambridge Economic Service*)

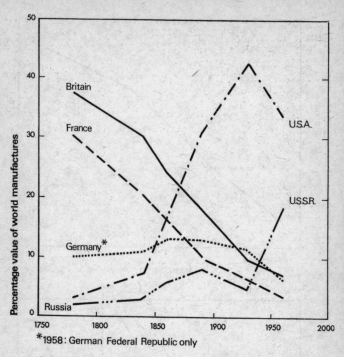

*1958: German Federal Republic only

23. *British industrial output as a percentage of the world total,
1780–1958.*
(Sources: *Mulhall, League of Nations, United Nations*)

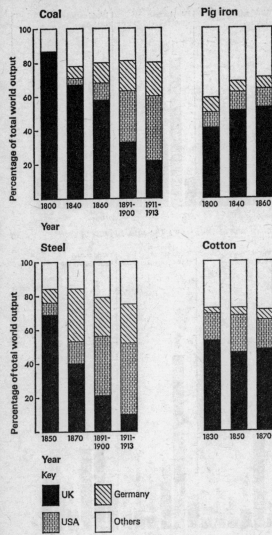

24. *Britain in world industry: the nineteenth century*

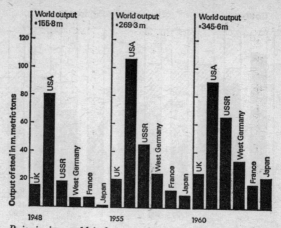

25a. Britain in world industry : the mid twentieth century. Steel

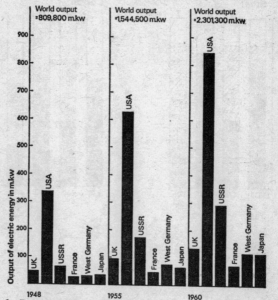

25b. Britain in world industry : the mid twentieth century. Electric power

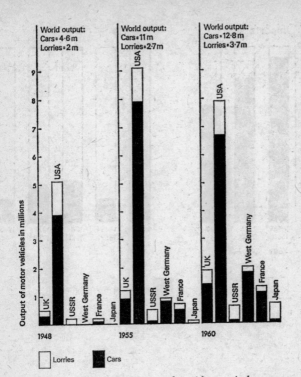

World output:
Cars = 4·6 m
Lorries = 2 m

World output:
Cars = 11 m
Lorries = 2·7 m

World output:
Cars = 12·8 m
Lorries = 3·7 m

Output of motor vehicles in millions

USA

UK | USSR | West Germany | France | Japan

1948

USA

UK | USSR | West Germany | France | Japan

1955

USA

UK | USSR | West Germany | France | Japan

1960

☐ Lorries ■ Cars

*25c. Britain in world industry: the mid twentieth century.
Motor vehicles*

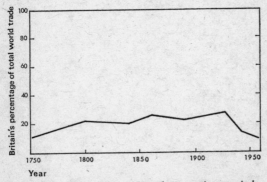

Britain's percentage of total world trade

Year

26. British share of world trade at various periods

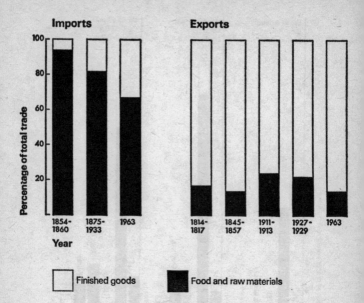

27. *British trade, by commodity groups, 1814–1963*

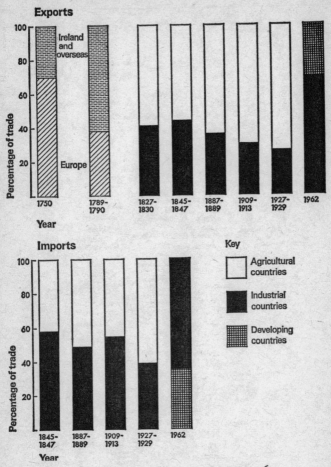

28. *The British trading pattern, 1750–1962*

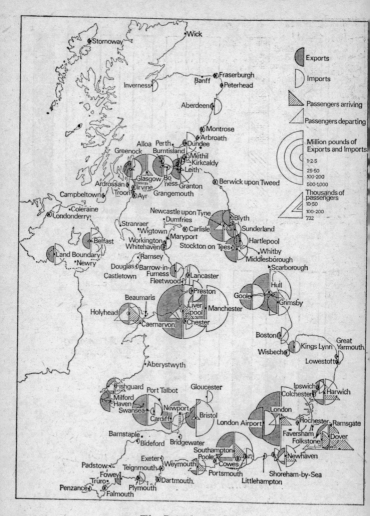

29. *The British ports in 1960*

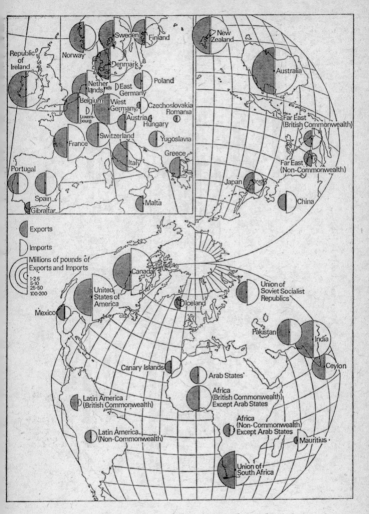

30. *The pattern of overseas trade, 1960*

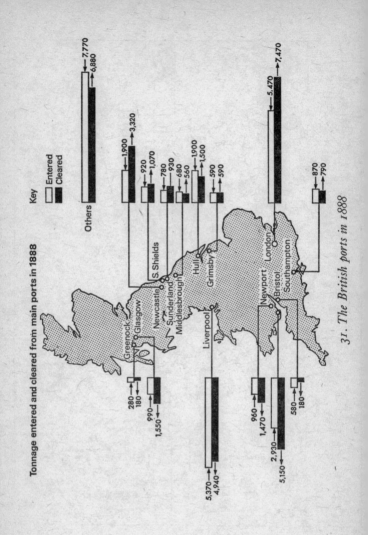

Tonnage entered and cleared from main ports in 1888

Key

□ Entered
■ Cleared

Others 7,770 / 6,880

Greenock 280 / 180
Glasgow 990 / 1,550
Newcastle 1,900 / 3,320
S. Shields 920 / 1,070
Sunderland 780 / 930
Middlesbrough 680 / 560
Hull 1,900 / 1,500
Grimsby 590 / 590
Liverpool 5,370 / 4,940
Newport 960 / 1,470
Bristol 580 / 180
London 5,470 / 7,470
Southampton 2,930 / 5,150
870 / 790

31. The British ports in 1888

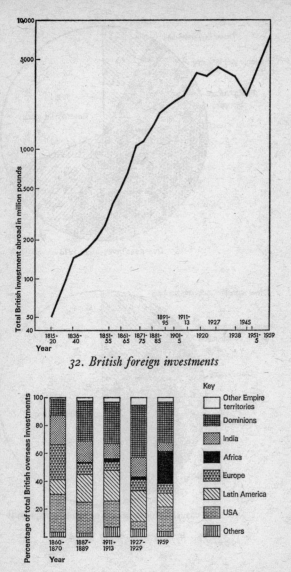

32. *British foreign investments*

33. *Geographical distribution of British foreign investments*

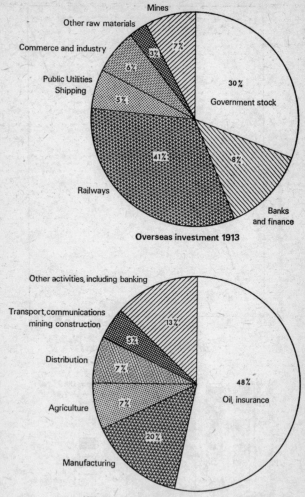

Mines

Other raw materials

Commerce and industry

Public Utilities
Shipping

30 %
Government stock

3%

7%

6%

5%

41%

8%

Railways

Banks
and finance

Overseas investment 1913

Other activities, including banking

Transport, communications
mining construction

Distribution

Agriculture

13 %

5%

7%

7%

20%

48%
Oil, insurance

Manufacturing

UK direct investment abroad by industry 1958–1961

34. The British investment portfolio

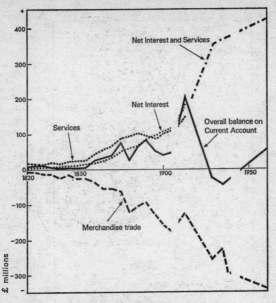

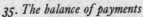

35. *The balance of payments*

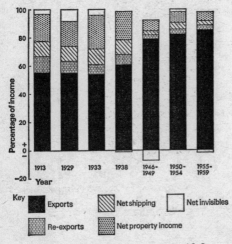

36. *How British imports were paid for*

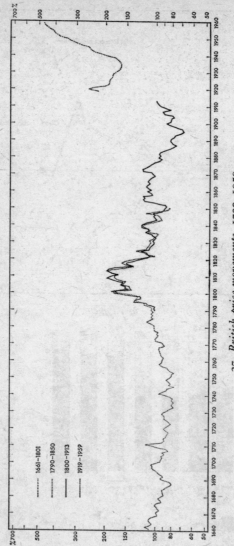

37. *British price movements, 1700–1959*

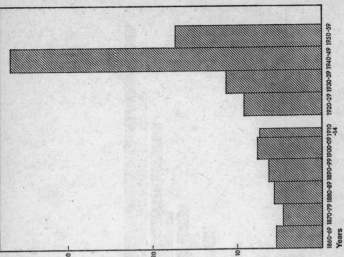

38. Government expenditure, 1792–1955

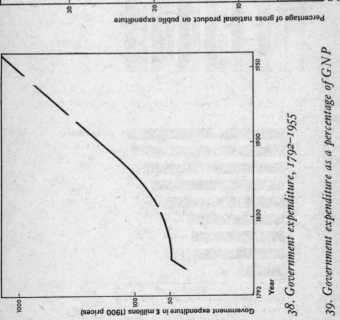

39. Government expenditure as a percentage of GNP

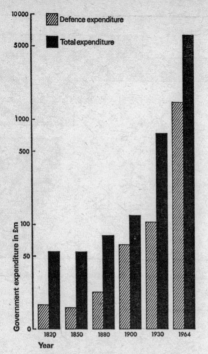

40. *Defence as a share of total government expenditure*

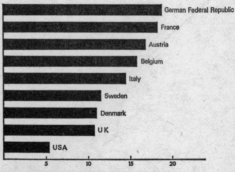

41. *Percentage of national income spent on social security in various countries, 1950s*

1900	1910	1925	1935	1955
Poor relief 8·4	Poor 12·4	Poor relief 31·4	Poor relief 34·3	National assistance 114·4
	Old age pensions 8·5	Pensions 94·8	Pensions 98·0	Pensions 94·1
	Housing 0·6	Housing 18·1	Housing 42·3	Housing 83·5
		Unemployment 16·9	Unemployment 73·9	National insurance 493·2
		Health insurance etc 21·1	Health insurance etc 25·7	National health service 445·5
				Family allowances 94·1
Total in millions of pounds 8·4	21·5	182·3	274·2	1324·8

42. *Main items of social security expenditure, 1900–55*

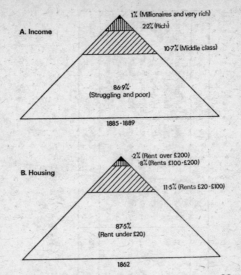

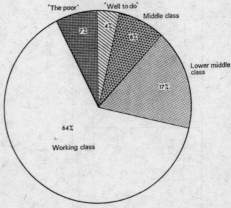

43. *Rich and poor: the Victorians. A: income, 1885–99;*
B: housing, 1862

44. *Rich and poor in 1955. (Source: Social Class 1955,*
Hulton Survey)

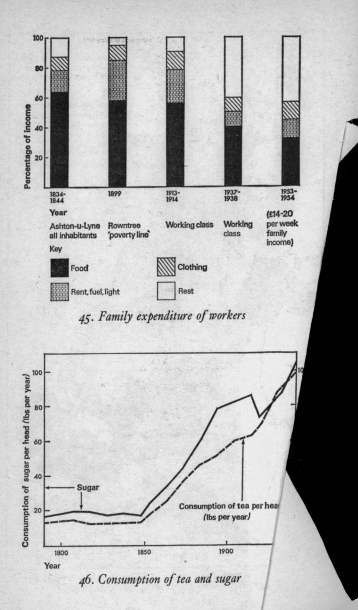

45. *Family expenditure of workers*

Key

- ■ Food
- ▨ Clothing
- ▦ Rent, fuel, light
- ☐ Rest

46. *Consumption of tea and sugar*

Areas in which more than
35% of personal incomes
were below £500 in 1959-60

Areas in which more than
15% of personal incomes
were over £1000 in 1959-60

Area with an excess of
both high and low incomes

Miles
0   30   60   90   120

0   30 60 90 120
Kilometres

High- and low-income areas, 1959-60

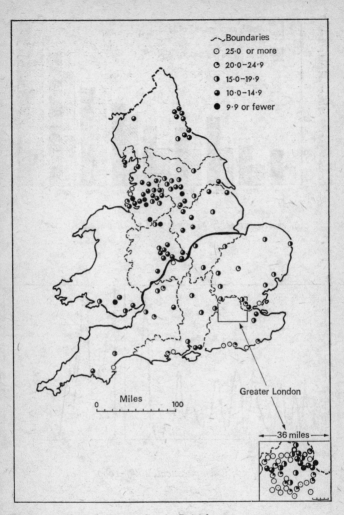

48. *Infant mortality in British towns, 1955–7*

49. *Average weekly earnings and retail prices, 1900–58*

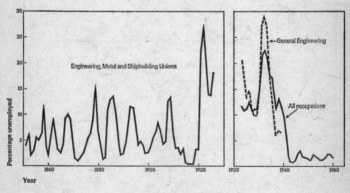

50. *Unemployment, 1860–1960*

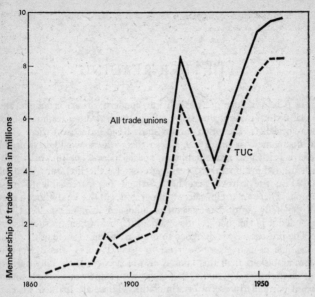

51. *Trade Union membership, 1860–1960*

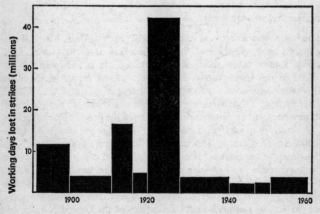

52. *Working days lost in strikes, 1890–1960*

FURTHER READING

THE patchy nature of research into modern British economic and social history make it unusually difficult to draw up a reading list for non-specialists. For often (as for most basic industries) there is no adequate modern history at all, so that readers would have to be referred either to monographs on special periods or to works published anything up to 120 years ago, or else the literature is to be found in the learned periodicals, which are inaccessible to most people. There are useful select bibliographies of this kind, though they are generally out of date as soon as published, as mine would be, if I included it in this book. Titles marked (B) below contain such lists.

The present note is designed to draw attention to some of the most accessible or convenient sources, to general works whose scope is more ambitious than this book's, or which cover fairly long periods within the general period 1750–1960, and to some works which I have found particularly useful or stimulating. These are marked with an asterisk. I have also now and then warned readers against some work which the layman may still regard as adequate.

1. Sources, mainly statistical

The basic figures are most easily available in *(B) B. R. Mitchell and Phyllis Deane, *Abstract of British Historical Statistics* (1962), from which I have taken most of my statistics. It is indispensable for reference and bibliography. For those who can get it, M. Mulhall, *Dictionary of Statistics* (1892 edn), is almost as useful. D. C. Marsh, *The Changing Social Structure of England and Wales 1871–1951* (1958) summarizes and explains the occupations of the people. Mark Abrams, *The Condition of the British People 1911–1945* (1946), and A. M. Carr-Saunders, D. Caradog Jones and C. A. Moser, *A Survey of Social Conditions in England and Wales* (1958), contain much material on the twentieth century. For current conditions, the annual *Britain, An Official Handbook* (Central Office of Information) and the *Annual Abstract of Statistics* may be consulted. For comparative purposes, see the annual and periodical publications of the United Nations and their special agencies (ILO, FAO, etc.).

Further Reading

Ford's, *A Breviate of Parliamentary Papers 1900–1916* (1957) and *A Breviate of Parliamentary Papers 1917–1939* (1951) are guides to the most important earlier source of social and economic information. G. D. H. Cole, *The Post-War Condition of Britain* (1956), gives a good list of mainly official sources up to that date.

There is no good atlas of economic history, but the *Oxford Atlas* (1963) gives a lot of economic and social information. (B) K. Hudson, *Industrial Archaeology* (1963), may introduce the material relics, but N. L. B. Pevsner, *The Buildings of England* (Penguin Books, to be completed), is invaluable; each volume covers a county or part of one. *F. D. Klingender, *Art and the Industrial Revolution* (1968), is a guide to the iconography, and *S. Giedion, *Mechanisation Takes Command* (1948), not only contains a wealth of illustrations but is the nearest thing to a history of mass-production. The iconography of social history is very poor. C. Singer *et al.*, *A History of Technology* (Vols. IV, V, 1958), is the standard work and rather indigestible. W. G. Hoskins, *The Making of the English Landscape* (1958), teaches historians to walk and see as well as read.

2. General British History

G. D. H. Cole and R. W. Postgate, *The Common People* (1956 edn), covers the period since 1745 with special attention to the conditions and movements of the working classes. Three volumes in the Pelican History of England (J. H. Plumb on the eighteenth, D. Thomson on the nineteenth and twentiety centuries) fall within the chronological limits of the present book. Shorter periods are covered by *Asa Briggs, *The Age of Improvement 1780–1867* (1959), R. C. K. Ensor, *England 1870–1914* (1936), older and rather more conservative, *(B) C. L. Mowat, *Britain between the Wars* (1955), and A. J. P. Taylor, *English History 1914–1945* (1965). E. Halévy, *History of the English People in the 19th Century*, remains valuable, especially Vol. I (England in 1815) and Vol. V (Imperialism and the Rise of Labour). Unfortunately this work does not deal with the period 1840–95.

3. General British Economic History

Every serious student must consult the files of the *Economic History Review*, in which the bulk of new research appears. Other periodicals likely to contain relevant articles are the (US) *Journal of Economic History*, specialized journals like the *Agricultural History Review* and the *Bulletin of the Society for the Study of Labour History* or *Population*

Studies and the *Amateur Historian*. The economic and sociological periodicals should also be referred to. The back files of the *Journal of the Royal Statistical Society* deserve a special mention. Valuable selections of periodical articles are *E. Carus-Wilson ed., *Essays in Economic History* (3 vols., 1954–62), W. E. Minchinton ed., *Essays in Agrarian History* (2 vols., 1968), and *D. V. Glass and D. E. C. Eversley ed., *Population and History* (1965). In 1968 the Economic History Society began to publish a most useful series of short pamphlets, *(B) *Studies in Economic History*, several of which deal or will deal with topics briefly considered or neglected in this book.

A single volume for the period since 1750 is W. H. B. Court, *A Concise Economic History of England since 1750* (1954). Shorter periods are dealt with in (B) C. Wilson, *England's Apprenticeship 1603–1763* (1965), T. S. Ashton, *The Eighteenth Century* (1955), (B) S. G. Checkland, *The Rise of Industrial Society in England 1815–1885*, with a useful bibliography, *W. Ashworth, *An Economic History of England 1870–1939* (1960), and *S. Pollard, *The Development of the British Economy 1914–1950*, which is encyclopedic. *J. H. Clapham, *An Economic History of Modern Britain* (3 vols., 1926–38), is essential for reference, but few will be able or want to read it through. It covers the period 1830–1914. Two volumes in the Home University Library, T. S. Ashton, *The Industrial Revolution*, and J. D. Chambers, *Workshop of the World*, are brief, but have been made obsolete by *D. S. Landes' remarkable *The Unbound Prometheus* (1969), a history of industrialization in Western Europe. Phyllis Deane, *The First Industrial Revolution* (1965), and W. H. B. Court, *British Economic History 1870–1914* (1965) – the latter a combination of documents and commentary – are recent works on the two periods which have been most hotly debated. P. Deane and W. A. Cole, *British Economic Growth 1688–1959* (1962), is a valuable – perhaps a premature – attempt at synthesis, but not very suitable for beginners.

*R. H. Campbell, *Scotland since 1707* (1965), has no Welsh equivalent, but there is Brinley Thomas, *The Welsh Economy* (1962), whose interest is partly historical.

4. Social History

This is in its infancy. There is as yet no general textbook for Britain, but P. N. Stearns, *European Society in Upheaval: Social History since 1800* (1967), has attempted a synthesis in order to help students of what is a rapidly expanding subject. It is probably too early for one, and the book has limited value. G. M. Trevelyan's *Social*

Further Reading

History of England (1944) is no longer acceptable, if it ever was. Several of the works under 2 and 3 above deal with relevant aspects. A few important or stimulating works must take the place of a list of textbooks. *E. P. Thompson, *The Making of the English Working Class* (1968 edn) – 1780–1830 – will be a classic; *F. M. L. Thompson, *English Landed Society in the Nineteenth Century* (1963), covers nobility and gentry rather than the lesser courntrymen, and perhaps a shade indulgently. G. D. H. Cole, *Studies in Class Structure* (1955), attempts quantitative estimates, and W. L. Guttsmann, *The British Political Elite, 1832–1935* (1965 edn), contains a mass of information. For the social aspects of industrialization, Neil Smelser, *Social Change in the Industrial Revolution* (1959), is useful though it hides behind thickets of jargon, and so is (B) Asa Briggs, *Victorian Cities* (1963). J. Burnett, *Plenty and Want* (1965), is an up-to-date history of food consumption but does not supersede that magnificent monument of scholarship and humanity *R. N. Salaman, *The History and Social Influence of the Potato* (1949). Peter Laslett, *The World We Have Lost* (1965), is a controversial essay on pre-industrial society, but perhaps readers are on safer ground with E. A. Wrigley ed., *An Introduction to English Historical Demography* (1965), which presents a subject of very direct relevance to social history.

For Scotland and Wales there are a few stimulating studies on special subjects: *L. J. Saunders' ill-named *Scottish Democracy 1815–1840* (1950), David Williams, *The Rebecca Riots* (1955), and E. D. Lewis, *The Rhondda Valleys* (1959).

Fortunately there are some splendid primary sources in social history. *F. Engels, *The Condition of the Working Class in 1844*, T. H. S. Escott, *England, Its People, Polity and Pursuits* (1879), and J. B. Priestley, *English Journey* (1934), provide cross-sections at various periods. *M. K. Ashby, *The Life of Joseph Ashby of Tysoe* (1961), gives voice to the voiceless – the rural poor. Henry Mayhew's *London Labour and the London Poor*, now again reprinted, does the same for the mid-nineteenth-century Cockney. There is some marvellous fiction, notably *John Galt, *Annals of the Parish* (Scotland, 1760–1820), Charles Dickens' *Hard Times* – spiritual rather than documentary truth – George and Weedon Grossmith, *Diary of a Nobody*, for the lower middle class, *R. Tressell, *The Ragged-Trousered Philanthropists*, for the working class. After 1914 there are too many novels for even a selective list, but A. J. P. Taylor op. cit. (Further Reading 2), contains one.

INDEX

Aberdeen, 305 n

acoustics, 173

advanced world, 35, 48, 51, 52, 115, 131, 136, 137, 138, 139, 276, 316

advertising, 220, 284 n, 292

affluence, 126, 164, 166–7, 213, 274, 278, 292

Africa, 52, 53, 57, 131, 150, 191, 199, 303

agriculture, 21, 28, 45, 97, 98, 99, 106, 115, 128, 128–9, 130, 142, 142–3, 143 n, 158, 167, ch. 10 *passim*, 214, 228, 242, 243, 287 n, 295, 297, 299, 301, 302, 303, 305, 317 n; increase in productivity, 98; efficiency, 99; marketing schemes, 242

Ahmedabad, 48

aircraft industry, 219, 223, 242, 246, 254, 269

Albion Steam Mills, 46

alcohol, 46, 124, 145, 220, 254, 286 n

Alpine Club, 320

Amalgamated Engineering Union, (1921), 250, 268, 290

American Civil War (1861–5), 68 n, 136, 140, 179

American Independence, War of (1776–83), 49 n, 53, 179, 306

American Revolution, 47

Americas, the, 35, 53

Amsterdam, 52

'Andy Capp', 283

Anglo-Persian Oil Company (1914), 241

aniline dye, 173

Appalachians, 254

Argentina, 20, 136, 147, 148, 148 n, 150, 191

Argyll, Dukes of, 302

aristocracy, 16, 26, 31, 32, 80, 83, 97, 107, 120, 125, 132, 144, 166, 168, 183, 185, 185 n, 186, 201, 202, 229, 234, 265, 275, 276, 281, 300, 301–2

Arkwright, Richard (1732–92), 59

armaments, 175, 190, 222, 233, 234, 239, 289, 289 n

Armstrong, 190 n; merger, 249

artisans, skilled, 20, 90, 91, 181, 186

Ashworth, Henry, 83

Asia, 147, 191, 311

Asquith, H. H., 228

Associated Electrical Industries (AEI), 249

atomic, 111

Attwood, Thomas, 235

Austen, Jane, 120 n, 303

Australia, 20, 136, 148, 191, 285 n, 316 n

Austria, 137, 247, 316 n, 317, 320 n

Austrian Succession, War of (1739–48), 49 n, 54

automatic lathe, invention of (*c.* 1870), 176

automation, 67–8, 174, 181

Babbage, Charles, 122

Baldwin, Stanley, 203

Balfour, A. J., 203

Balkans, the 113

Baltic, the, 51, 141

banks, 75, 82, 135, 156, 168, 191, 210, 212, 215, 235, 247, 249, 261, 301; 'Big Five', 215; Bank Holidays, 154; Bank Rate, 212, 236, 237

Bank Charter Act (1844), 236